RELAND
THE TASTE &
THE COUNTRY

IRELAND

THE TASTE &
THE COUNTRY

MIKE BUNN

GILL AND MACMILLAN

To Betty – and to Ireland, for being herself.

Published in Ireland by Gill and Macmillan Ltd
Goldenbridge, Dublin 8
with associated companies in
Auckland, Delhi, Gaborone, Hamburg, Harare, Hong Kong,
Johannesburg, Kuala Lumpur, Lagos, London, Manzini, Melbourne,
Mexico City, Nairobi, New York, Singapore, Tokyo

Published in Great Britain in 1991
by Anaya Publishers Ltd, 49 Neal Street, London, WC2H 9PJ

Text and photographs copyright © Mike Bunn 1991
Copyright © recipes, directory and maps Anaya Publishers Ltd 1991
ISBN 0 7171 1880 0

Art director Jane Forster
Editors Esther Jagger, Sue Fleming, Sue Wason
Maps Sarah Willis
Production Charles James and Jenny May

Picture captions: PAGE 1 Seafood from County Galway. PAGE 5 A
cafe in Thomastown, County Kilkenny, a place well known for
its shopfronts. JACKET FRONT FLAP Autumn fruits from the
Roscommon hedgerows. BACK FLAP Portrait of the author by
Hugh Reid. FRONT COVER Roast pheasant from Mount Juliet,
oysters from Galway and freshly baked bread from the bakery at
Schull, County Cork all set against a background of Lough
Arrow, County Sligo

Typeset in Great Britain by Tradespools Ltd, Frome, Somerset

Colour reproduction by Columbia Offset, Singapore
Printed in Hong Kong

BERNARD KAVANAGH BED & BREAKFAS

CAFÉ

CONTENTS

WHERE GRASSES GROW & WATERS FLOW IN A FREE & EASY WAY

IT'S HOME SWEET HOME WHERE'ER I ROAM THROUGH LANDS & WATERS WIDE

AND BRIGHT IN THE SUN SHONE THE EMERALD PLAIN

FOREWORD

Wherever they may in the distance go, the world of this land is never forgotten by its born. And as Ireland emerges an oasis on the western tip of Europe and despite the ancient feud and one of the most astonishingly prolonged incompatibility of peoples this planet has ever known, the most of this scholarly saintly isle still is and remains compared to the rest of the globe, a relatively peaceful place. And as emerald green as it always was. No doubt there might be occasionally a deserved fist delivered in the gob, but for the most part decency and dignity are to be discovered everywhere. Indeed, if these two warring tribes had to choose their favourite people on this earth they would, a little shamefacedly, perhaps, choose each other.

Therefore we will forgive you your foregone conclusions. And wherever you are now don't listen to anyone telling you that this isn't the greatest place going yet to stay in or to get to for a complete pleasant change. To wake up to one of its pale cool dawns. The gulls squawking over the rooftops of its coastal towns and cities and the birds chirping across the countryside. And where the worst that can happen to you has often already happened before you've gone two inches and there is nothing further to worry about in any of the joyful undisturbed miles ahead. For inevitability is an Irishman's credo. And he'll tell you, you won't change fate by rushing into it. Best to wait, leisurely, for it to overtake you – preferably with your and his elbows propped on a bar.

Now having said that, I can say this. There is no doubt that the sun is shy in Irish skies. And the inclement often continual. But the nature of the weather can be the least of your concerns. And I'll tell you why. Ireland is a place where dreaming takes on a reality so real that it's all you'll ever need for entertainment. It would keep you indoors with a drink and in the company of other dreamers. And you'd be like your small Irish farmer. Standing nearby. In the middle of his making hay, it's rained. You'd see indifference written all over your man's face. And know that he's said to himself, well then that's that, let God have his way. And it's only for the sake of letting the neighbours know he is not to be trifled with, that your man when the first drops of rain fell, ran back and forth over fields

shaking his fist against the sky and gesticulating his legs in his dance of rage.

But it's not only for the matter of a calm spirit, Ireland is grand for other reasons, too. Culture, ancient and modern, is all over the place. There are living and breathing examples of authors, painters, composers and poets, plus the odd sculptor lurking up the end of every main street and down many a country boreen. Each and every one of them in action, with instruments, poems and pictures at the ready to entertain you. Even the architects are in on the act. And some getting very exotic. New buildings good to look at are sneaking up here and there. Many of the old ones, even better to look at, are being cherished and have a citizenry and a Georgian Society fighting to keep them preserved and protected.

Now outwardly as things change, inwardly the Irishman remains the same. And in some ways this contradicting conundrum prepares you best for coming as a traveller to this isle. For what goes on here now seems to turn on its head nearly all that has preceded in the centuries. James Joyce, above all, has won his victory. He's now seen to be there in Dublin, standing life-sized in bronze surveying his city. This same man once accused of having the filthiest mind this century. But along with Joyce's words the Irish mind too has been unchained and is alive with a lustiness expressed in the very latest American vernacular. Poets are no longer rude but polite. They will for a modest fee read you their poems. Or a verse out of the literary past. Nor would he be churlish if you handed him one of your own sonnets to read. Except he might have to charge you a higher fee. So take it that this darling land has at last thrown off its ancient repressive coverings. And its grey veil of rain has drawn back to reveal a brand-new Ireland awake.

So, sitting pretty in its natural glory, the world can now come and take more than a peek at the most newly glamorous place in God's kingdom. And do so in a trice. Whirring helicopters and stiff-winged motor birds take off and land. Television signals criss-cross the sky and advertise the wonders of the outside world. But the natives, too, have originated their own brand of excellence of which to boast. And it is not only confined to great cheeses, crustaceans, beef, fish and lamb in which they triumph but also the soda bread, barmbrack and spice buns that melt in your mouth. Instead of your bumpy, lumpy damp mattresses sloping in the middle, hotels now provide magic slumbering where all earthly comfort is guaranteed. Plus now there is the softest of toilet tissue on tap, when once you'd find yourself crouching, mournful, in wind and rain, searching around, anxious, for a leaf of shrubbery to use.

But there is more. Even when left in his ignorance, the Irishman was always ahead of the whole world. And has held up his hand to object to the poisonous residues which grant nations their badges of progress. He has saved his cattle, horses and sheep to live for another and better day. He no longer lets the slates fall from the big houses that he did not burn. Nor with their roofs still on does he any longer send his cattle in to shelter and to manure on the parquet. Now he proudly installs himself. And beneath the Georgian glory of the plasterwork he may even knock back a glass or two of champagne. For every Irishman is a king. And lucky there is no empty throne available, for by God if there were, there would be a lethal stampede. Nor would there be any scarcity of Irish queens, either, in on the rush and getting in the way.

With the fair-minded nature of the populace, the Irish are, in general, a nice helpful bunch and they often don't mean to do the awful things they sometimes do. It is only that Ireland with its few mountains is a great place for making them out of its molehills. But now, as big things happen all over Europe, they wait patiently to take advantage of the best of them and as a small nation are doing more things right than you would dare believe. No need any longer to remind you of the fact that soda water and the electrical battery were first invented here. Or that here, too, took place the oft-mentioned first performance of Handel's *Messiah*. And although there are still heaps and loads of blarney and boasting to be heard coming around the corner of every snug of every pub, the Irish have at last achieved the heights in many and better walks of life, rearing up original as they always were. And under where glorious chandeliers still hang, instead of the forelock-

pulling, they do be welcoming you to enjoy their carrots served like caviar. Or the leeks or lobster, which come finger-tip fresh from garden and sea.

And now you're wondering why would Ireland in the excellence of its food be any different than any other place. Well, for a start, it has some of the deepest, loamiest fertile soil in the world. And upon it does be falling gently year-round waters brought upon a moist mild wind from the Atlantic. And already nibbling upon this cornucopia, and leaping and bursting from cover, are your rabbits, pheasant, quail and snipe. And dying to be cooked. There be even Frenchmen and Germans who have come here and set about taking advantage of the great milk and cream to produce cheeses rivalling any on earth. And if you stood yourself in an Irish meadow you'd soon know why you were licking your chops at the sight of the chubby lambs and bullocks grazing. For, sniffing their way through the fields, they nurture themselves on grasses and herbs growing since Methuselah's time.

Now with the weather always suitable to do so, what would you be drinking. Well, there would be, if you know the right people, and that's nearly anybody, there would be poteen, the local firewater, to put you sooner than otherwise on your back. But best for your health would be to stay with stout, this dark beer which foams so creamily at the top of your glass. And now if you're wondering where would you especially go for these indubitable refreshments, for a start try Longueville House, Mallow or Rosleague Manor, Letterfrack, the country house hotels, homey and welcoming in their idyllic settings and wherein you dine by candlelight. Or for a fine pint of stout you could head to the pubs the Yukon or Canton Casey's in Mullingar. In the Yukon, as well as a library of best drink you can interest yourself in a library of American car licence plates. And in the metropolis of Dublin, there are still pubs with their traditions upheld. Try Ryan's of Parkgate Street, along the Liffey and just outside the gates of Phoenix Park. Here you'll find snugs. These are private, confessional little places for private people with private thoughts to express, and here in Ryan's they are especially reserved for nice deserving folk.

But if you're still footloose in Dublin, there remain other places of liquid invigoration not disembowelled for the sake of aggiornamento, as the Italians say. These are the sacred public houses of Mulligan's in Poolbeg Street, the Stag's Head off Dame Street and Doheny and Nesbitt's just down the road from the Shelbourne Hotel. Nor miss the oldest of them all, the Brazen Head up along the quays.

In Ireland you'd be making a great mistake to seriously overlook any of the pubs you pass by. Within is always another world not seen before and not to be experienced again. Even if empty the ghosts will whisper in your ear. If looking for the living, there be actors and actresses lurking about Neary's in Chatham Street. For prancing and preening models and film moguls, you have only to sit to a fine pint in the Bailey whose present day's existence is owed to the painter and writer John Ryan, the first Dublin publican ever to pay due homage to Ireland's great writers. And the fact there isn't some acknowledgement to this man up somewhere on this pub's wall is a great lack I hope soon to be corrected. But be sure of one thing, each public house attracts its own character of clientele, and if the people in it are wrong, the pub will be wrong too. So sniff first in the door. Of course, you'll be immediately invited in to put things right.

And now for a second let's rush back into the past. Once there was a great restaurant, Jammet's. The passing of which has brought many a tear to many a Dubliner's eye. But it has remained an inspiration to the many who have come afterwards. And who will now soon become equally revered. Locks restaurant on the canal. The Unicorn, an unpretentious and pleasant place habited by the natives. The Chinese, too, are here and their cuisine can be found up some stairs in Anne Street. But then if you're ready for elegance and luxury, the Shelbourne Hotel is where most of your needs and wants are met at once, and there be no need to stir a further inch. But if you do stir, out in the Meath countryside is Dunderry Lodge which will satisfy all you'd wish for and find in the best restaurants of France.

Guide you now across these landscapes, seascapes and moonscapes galore. And let you know that any season in this land has its joys. From the summertime flowerings of the honeysuckle and bursts of whitethorn in the hedgerows, to the sweet scent of turf glowing in a midwinter fire. And in a world that hurries and hurts where it hurts most, what nation anywhere deserves to pleasantly thrive better. Or merits that you come where the green gladness is and where the glooms shall enfold you not. Where the purple clover blossom sweetens the air at your feet and thistles tall as trees come raging out of the ground. Where under the sky can you find a land that will so kindly kiss your face.

Or be a place
That has got
To be forgiven
For its faults.

J. P. Donleavy

THE TASTE & THE COUNTRY

My obsession with Ireland developed from a fishing trip in May 1968, my first visit to the country. Like quicksilver dashed over rich green velour, the rivers and lakes of the midland plain presented themselves unpolluted, running crystal-clear and full of fish prepared to rise to the occasion. Lough Sheelin was my chosen spot – then the serious trout fisherman's mecca. Its fish were always in pristine condition, of polished chrome, with small heads and large brown spots, and their average weight considerably higher than anywhere else in Europe.

My boatman on that trip was Felix Harten, a small man of seventy-five years who had as many grandchildren. Two of his sons, Frank and Brian, were superb boatmen, though Felix was not. He did, however, make excellent tea! In Ireland, pulling up on to an island or any shoreline for lunch is part of the angling tradition and constitutes the main ritual of the day. A few dry sticks are gathered and a fire lit. With the smell of wood smoke sweetening the air, a blackened kettle is filled with lake water and placed on the now raging fire. When boiling, a handful or more of tea is thrown in to 'stew' – the brew is said never to be strong enough 'until you could trot a mouse on it'.

Felix would pick a sprig of gorse and shove it down the spout of the kettle to act as a strainer. He would often suggest, if the day was hot, that we should have black mint tea: far more refreshing. Wild water mint was readily available, growing everywhere along the shoreline. It is in fact very refreshing, but the crafty old fox didn't mention the fact that more often than not the milk had gone off.

During these pleasant interludes and in the bars late into the night I used to hear fascinating stories about wild men of hunting and shooting, of fishing and fishermen, of greyhounds and lurchers, of horse fairs and horses, of cockfights that went on for days – most of which were lies. On my return to London, I started to pine for this very special place that I knew so little about – I had to have more. And in due course, I did . . .

What I consider to be my introduction to the taste of Ireland occurred through another fishing experience. Once upon a time I happened to be on the shores of Lough Arrow in County Sligo. I landed at Arrow Cottage, where Tommy Flynn ran 'Ireland's Largest Fleet' – some twenty-five or so wooden boats for hire to fishermen, in varying shades of fading green, most of them in considerable disrepair, pulled up on a grass verge and shingle beach in front of his cottage.

It was a warm, dull, mid-September day and he suggested I tried trailing large wet flies behind the boat – a local way to catch trout at that time of the year. I pushed out the driest-looking boat I could find and tucked my newly acquired companion, a German short-haired pointer named Pluto, into the bow. I rowed slowly and happily down the lake past McCormack's Point and on to Andresma Bay. Tommy was right; some one and a half miles later I had six beauties on the boards, and I was delighted with myself.

Then there was a sudden change in the weather. The gentle, north-east vesper of a breeze whipped up into a strong wind and started curling the waves. The threatening sky blackened and began to leak very badly. Without waterproofs, within minutes I was absolutely drenched. The lake was now running like a sea, and the three- to five-foot waves had transformed themselves into a stampede of white horses with a few Clydesdales amongst them. I was petrified, being used to the security of small ponds and lakes in England and quite unfamiliar with the vastness of the Irish loughs. As I rowed for home against the wind – try it some time – the dog was howling and shivering; he was as scared as I was. . . .

Suddenly, the warmth of familiarity. I sensed a welcome aroma wafting downwind: the unmistakable smell of bacon and cabbage, accompanied by an intermittent, eerie sound, like someone sawing at a fiddle. Eventually, exhausted, I made it back to land. Like the proverbial drowned rat I squelched my way to pay Tommy Flynn his ten-shilling hire fee.

In the evening gloom of the tiny cottage stood Tommy, crouched over the pot-bellied range, prodding a side of bacon and its companion cabbage into submission in a large pot beside another full of floury, parboiled potatoes. In the heat pulsating from the range the steam was beginning to rise from my clothes. With a twinkle of his eye Tommy stared at me, and then lowered himself deliberately into the comfort of his armchair to light another Woodbine. With the insistence of genuine countryfolk, he begged me to stay for dinner. 'It'll be another ten minutes or so. Meanwhile hand me down the fiddle and we'll have a tune.'

Drying out, at last something was making sense. I stretched to the shape of the fiddle, high in the darkness of the raftered ceiling, and passed it on to Tommy.

'I can't play that – it's not in tune.'

Why not? How so? A foolish feeling, I'll tell you – finding myself holding the end of a blackened, wizened hank of bacon that had been drying into the shape of a Stradivarius. Such was my introduction to the Taste of Ireland.

Of course, there's much more to modern Irish cuisine than bacon and cabbage. But it's good to see the old favourites, staples of many a humble cottage traditional menu in the past, now being served up – admittedly often in a more sophisticated form – in candlelit Georgian dining rooms. For the Irish have discovered, as the French did long ago, that these are the best dishes of all. Cassoulet is wonderful – but no more wonderful than a perfect Irish stew.

In a discourse on Irish radio some years ago between the acclaimed Irish actor Michael MacLiammoir and the famous Dublin restaurateur Louis Jammet, MacLiammoir praised French chefs and their ability to cook good food. He also praised the French nation as a whole for their ability to enjoy it, and wondered why the Irish had such an indifferent attitude. Jammet too was astounded at this Irish indifference to food – particularly as, in his opinion, Ireland produced the best natural ingredients anywhere in Europe.

Throughout the eighties, a new awareness of food steadily grew, nurtured by a group of dedicated enthusiasts – champions of the renaissance in Irish gastronomy and the new awareness of their very own virtually untapped sources of superb-quality ingredients throughout the country. Stimulated by this cornucopia of potential, restaurants and country houses

opened with great gusto everywhere – and are continuing to do so. Their chefs, demanding daily for their kitchens only the very best of what is available, encourage a group of soil-conscious gardeners who grow herbs, fruit and vegetables to come knocking on their doors. Fish dealers too are amazed at the new enthusiasm on the home market, and provide daily deliveries of the very best white fish, giant scallops, clams, sea urchins, whelks, langoustines, winkles, lobsters, crabs, crayfish, and cockles and mussels alive, alive o. Irish lamb, mountain or *pré-salé*, is the very best that money can buy.

For those with a sporting palate, there is more than enough here already. For the angler, there are prolific catches of trout and salmon in almost every stream or brook, or where the rivers rush to the sea. For the hunter, fair game is to be had in every copse or wood or where the mountains yawn under winter skies.

The French never thought it could be done, but now

PREVIOUS PAGES It took the pale, watery sunshine of midwinter only twenty minutes to lift a blanket of early morning fog and expose Hog Island, as seen from the Rock of Doon, Lough Key, County Roscommon.
ABOVE This 2$\frac{1}{2}$lb trout was caught 'on the dap' only minutes before being gutted for lunch on the shores of Cullen's Island, Lough Arrow, County Sligo. Simply delicious.

RIGHT Milleens, strong-flavoured and smelly, and made from unpasteurized cow's milk, is one of a number of new cheeses that have won international awards.
OPPOSITE The perfect marriage: sea-fresh oysters and a pint of Guinness at Moran's of the Weir in County Galway.

most of the new Irish farmhouse cheeses have the edge on their European competitors and are picking up awards annually. Norman and Veronica Steele, two of the industry's pioneers, credit the quality to the pastures on which the cattle or goats graze. Many other accidental success stories grew out of people throwing up their city jobs and seeking an alternative lifestyle. A smallholding, keeping its own free-range chickens, its herb garden, its herd of goats and a cow or two, was invariably set on affordable land, usually somewhat removed from the intensive mainstream commercial farms. Although not a lot of milk was produced from these few animals, after the family had been fed there was usually enough left over to make butter and cheese – the latter a tradition that had almost been forgotten in Ireland. Here, small grassy fields remained free of chemical fertilizers and pesticides, still retaining the herbs and wild grasses that give distinctive character to Irish farmhouse cheeses.

The dominance of the colour brown in the Irish landscape is reflected in the taste as well. Guinness, that wonderful beer that blackens the glass, is a national hero. When I was a lad and zookeepers trained sea lions to balance pints of Guinness on their noses, I was told by advertisers (as we all were) that it was Good for You: the Irish know it for a fact. The brewery at St James's Gate in the heart of old Dublin was founded in

1759 by Arthur Guinness I, at a rent of £45 per year for nine thousand years. It is still the largest brewery in Europe, and today Guinness is sold to no fewer than 120 countries. Seven million pints are drunk daily throughout the world – most of which are transfused, I am sure, in Ireland.

In the early years, Guinness brewed ale that was soon replaced by porter, a much heavier drink named after those whose preferred tipple it was: the porters at London's Covent Garden and Billingsgate markets. This town porter, as it was termed, infiltrated the Irish countryside on barges trading out of Dublin on the canals. Known as country porter, it usually arrived 'flat'. Local connoisseurs raised a head on it by mixing it with bread soda – ouch! To deal with the competition Guinness was later brewed even stronger, and this concoction was called extra stout.

Proper Guinness is a robust beer, served with a creamy head, and is made by roasting malted barley which is then mixed with hops and yeast and pure Dublin water. A pint of Guinness is tailor-made to complement its smaller, but stronger, honey-toned brother. The two of them side by side, with a smouldering briar of Mick McQuaid or a sweet Afton cigarette, have determined the hue and tone of the better Irish pubs. I am, of course, talking of Irish whiskey.

Whiskey, drink divine!
Why should drivelers bore us
With the praise of wine
While we've thee before us?
WHISKEY, DRINK DIVINE
Joseph O'Leary

Just to put the record straight, real whiskey is of the Irish type. Malted barley is fermented into pot ale – a pale grey, cloudy, fizzy liquid that's about 8 per cent proof. Traditionally, the worker is given his morning tot, and then the pot ale is run off and distilled three times. It is transferred to wooden casks and bonded for a minimum of seven years to develop its rich colouring and flavour. It is then graded and bottled. So why not ask for Irish whiskey in future? It is much better served as straight whiskey than as Irish coffee; and *far* better than the other one that wears a kilt.

There is also, of course, that other medicine that has no colour, and is not to be discovered or mentioned by name. Sssh! After sludging around in the muddy dampness of any midwinter country pursuit, it really is rewarding. Just a thimble-full of poteen is all that's needed to hot-wire the tongue and kick-start the human engine into life again.

If I was asked what is the definitive taste of Ireland, I would not hesitate to say 'Brown bread.' Quite ubiquitous, it is to be found in restaurants, hotels, country houses, cottages – in fact any dwelling throughout the island. Most of it is home-made, in varying weights and textures, and its flavour is complemented by creamy Irish butter, which has no peers.

If, as we approach the year 2000, most of the new breed of Irish chefs continue to practise their calling here, Irish cuisine will have exerted a deep and distinctive influence on the world of gastronomy. It is to be hoped that their clients will adopt the new standards and that the reaction will ripple far down the food chain. As the superlatives ascend in describing the quality and imagination of the new cooking, go out again and again to the backwaters, the cottage restaurants, the country houses, the small hotels and farms of Ireland to discover a rose in the stew.

ABOVE The label says 'Paddy', but the colourless drop gives the game away. A small, reviving tincture is taken after a thin morning's session on the snipe bog.
OPPOSITE The smell of fresh, old-fashioned bread coming from the wonderful little bakery at Schull in County Cork is out of this world. Baskets, pans, French sticks, white rolls, white scones, wholemeal, molasses, wheatmeal and brown soda bread are baked here, using the original bread tins and moulds. The only other similar oven in Ireland is in a Cistercian monastery.

BELOW Traditional ivy-clad postbox.
RIGHT Rocks piled up higgledy-piggledy to create field boundaries in the Burren, County Clare.

And while you are searching for these out-of-the-way places, up rutted farm tracks, across fast-flowing streams and nestling at the foot of heather-clad hillsides, feast your eye on your unspoilt surroundings. I cannot think of anywhere else in the world that has so many boreens and small roads per square mile, leading apparently nowhere, as there are in rural Ireland. This micromesh pattern is evidence of the former high population in the pre-Famine days, and more recently before the mass emigration in the fifties. Now they serve a different purpose, and have opened up a thousand opportunities – an element of surprise around every bend – for the modern traveller in Ireland.

Under a semi-permanent backdrop of grey skies the rugged coastline stands firm, taking all the torment and good hidings the Atlantic can exact. Over the years Ireland's landscape and people have had their fair share of hardship, but now it is coming right. Today's small, privileged population can sing Ireland's praises proudly to the world and show off their country's lusty, generous beauty as never before.

This is a very green and pleasant land, where grey stone walls mark the boundaries and ivy-clad ruins crumble gracefully. Her rich grassland and dense green foliage, ever-thirsty, suck passionately on Ireland's soil. Rain, and lots of it, has given rise to countless thousands of streams, rivers, loughs and waterways both inky and clear, pumping out the brown and

often dobby soil and desperately trying to keep Ireland afloat.

In winter, or in a very wet summer, the bilges break down and vast tracts of land, especially along the Shannon where the banks are boggy or compacted, become awash. These wetlands have always caused concern with some farmers, who would prefer the rivers to be drained. But that just turns tenth-rate farmland into third-rate farmland, only good for selling by the gallon; it still won't stop the rain falling on the hay. Arterial drainage schemes in Ireland have proved time and time again that they have done very little for the land, and nothing at all for the wildlife and fish stocks. Many rivers have been rendered useless in this way.

In winter these wetlands take on a very special majesty all of their own. The cream and amber rushes and dying reed grasses rustle in the wind. In the lowland bogs the carpets of pale green sponge-like mosses soak up some of the water. Lichens cover the now bare branches of the trees, hanging delicately ghost-like in the mist. There is the zig-zagging flight of surprised snipe, flighting mallard and wigeon, along with the whistling rush of teal. This country is a haven for wildfowl and game, and for the true conservationist of the wetlands, the sporting gun; here the leftovers of autumn meet the woodland floor and assume the woodcock's colour. This is the landscape of Peter Emerson, that great Victorian photographer who put

In May and June, when the winter and spring rains have stopped but the land is still soft and sticky and easy to handle, turf cutting is a traditional activity in the West of Ireland. After cutting it is dried before being taken back to the cottages and stored for use as fuel in the coming winter months. Here, on a grey day with ominous skies, turf lies stacked and drying overlooking the Inagh valley and Lough Inagh in County Galway.

the first stamp of creativity into the art of photography and much later became one of my heroes. To walk a lowland bog and sniff the acid earth's air in a flooded winter landscape is a mucky business – tread lightly, so as not to touch the ground. It is worth the effort, especially to witness the setting sun crown the crock of a low horizon with gold.

Winter in Ireland really refers to the time of year rather than to any extremes in weather conditions. Apart from rain and the odd frost pocket, Ireland does not have a real winter: the winter months are rather mild. But it does have the month of February, and thank God it is only four weeks long, for without a doubt this is the bleakest time of the Irish year. The

And suddenly the bare bogland with the hump-backed mountain behind, the little white houses and the dark fortifications of turf that made it seem like the flame-blackened ruin of some might city, all was lit up in their minds.
IN THE TRAIN
Frank O'Connor
(Michael O'Donovan)

land is now at its wettest and the trees at their barest. Lakes and rivers are too high to fish, the shooting season is over and the fields far too sticky and heavy for hunting. Even on a relatively bright day the sun has a watery quality about it and the air feels thin.

Life in the country really starts on or after St Patrick's Day – 17 March. When the festivities are over and the shamrock that drooped from the buttonholes has finally wilted, we can begin. The countryside now sees its first flush of true colour, the daffodil. The water levels begin to drop and, after the winds have abated, the land begins to warm up, giving way to the budding foliage and the primroses that carpet the ditches with creamy-yellow and softest green.

BELOW Blackthorn powdering the face of the spring hedgerows. The first of the white blossoms, later it gives way to its fruit, the sloe. The stout wood is used in Ireland for driving cattle and chasing away goblins.

RIGHT In mid-May the whole countryside is enshrouded in dust covers of whitethorn or haw. County Roscommon is particularly beautiful at this season, which is also the time for mayfly fishing. In autumn these same bushes are laden with red berries, ripe pickings for birds and winemakers.

Green bursts out from every plant; leafy is the shoot of the green oakwood. Summer has come, winter gone, twisted hollies hurt the stag.
Anon, tenth century

Suddenly April is here and the birds are singing and the grass is growing. The air is heavy with a wonderful smell. Not the familiar nosegay of turf smoke clinging heavily to an autumn or spring day, nor yet the ever-present smell of silage. No, it is the wonderful fragrance of greenery growing, in the warmth of a damp, late April day.

Soon the hedgerows begin to fill out and the first of the blossoms begin to show. In Ireland the hedgerows are long ribbons of great beauty, a sad reminder for many visitors of how their own countrysides looked before modern farming techniques led to the creation of vast arable plains and the demise of the little confining hedges. Here, with flowers in profusion, not only are they a good source of nectar for the bees but they delight the human eye and nose too. Later, their fruits and nuts and berries provide a plentiful food supply for small hedgebank creatures and wintering birds.

Throughout the spring and early summer the Irish countryside is a bridal bouquet of white blossom. The first to show is the blackthorn or sloe, followed by the whitethorn or haw, then the elder and finally the bramble or blackberry. When the whitethorn is in full bloom, from the middle of May, you can see nature at its best. The whole countryside seems to be draped in enormous white dustsheets, as though everyone had packed up and gone away. Indeed some have, for it is mayfly time.

Dapping the natural mayfly from a drifting boat, along a shoreline or across a point of an island on one of the great Irish loughs, is a national pastime.

Had I the space I could write a whole chapter on the economic importance of this one insect, *Ephemera danica*, which has brought so much money and so many anglers into Ireland over the past years. Alas, the mayfly's future is at risk. On Lough Sheelin, for instance, once unquestionably the finest trout lake in Europe, the mayfly are no more. Thousands of gallons of slurry from the intensive pig farming enterprises around its shores have ended up in it, enriching the water and taking out a lot of the oxygen; as a result the algae die and silt up the lake bed, preventing the life cycle of the mayfly from continuing.

LEFT Fruits of the autumn hedgerows on the Roscommon–Sligo borders – from the top, anti-clockwise: sloes, blackberries, rosehips, elderberries and whitebeam, garnished with late-flowering heather and richly tinted elder foliage.

OPPOSITE A morning's catch of six brown trout, each weighing between $1^3/_4$ and $2^1/_2$lb, caught 'on the dap' and with artificial flies. The live green drake mayflies used for dapping are collected from the underside of the leaves of shoreline trees and kept alive in these little wooden boxes.

ABOVE Greyhounds, like horses, are many an Irishman's passion. Tony Murphy, breeder of racing greyhounds from Monasterevin in County Kildare, rests on a cleared peat bog with two of his pups, which we named there and then Peat and Moss. The flat land of Kildare is ideally suited to training these animals.
OVERLEAF This collection of old fishing records, salmon flies and tackle offers clues to some of the history of Newport House in County Mayo. The Newport River and nearby Lough Beltra have provided superb salmon fishing to guests for many years. The wonderful old wicker baskets are still used as picnic hampers.

One could not possibly write a book of this nature without including something of the people themselves. Their friendliness is legendary and their story-telling stands before them.

The Irish, living like Latins in a cold climate, are a young, fun-loving, somewhat carefree people, having cast aside vanity a long time ago and with no time for unnecessary false trimmings. But the men do have an obsession about strength and about their local heroes. Since the time when giants were said to stalk the land there have been stories in which it seems men have hands like shovels and necks like bullocks and are mighty to the world.

Not long ago I was shown a granite block weighing some six and a half hundredweight that had been put down as a cornerstone in a cottage in Bellass, County Mayo, by one 'Horse Durkan', who had carried it for some distance on his back using only two leather straps. A 'local historian' standing by butted in to tell me: '*I've* seen a man carry heavier.'. . .

28

A few years ago, a crate containing components for a combustion engine had been deposited on the west platform at Foxford station, to be collected on the east platform by a dray and two shires waiting there. How was the crate to be transferred to the east platform (it weighed seven and a half hundredweight)? Aloysius Roche, 'the man from the other side of Cullen', with shoulders as wide as a ball alley, was called for. All five feet eleven of him stepped down into the well between the two platforms and on one shoulder carried the load across – just short of twenty feet. I forgot to ask my informant what height Aloysius Roche was when he reached the other side.

However, according to folklore there is one man who might have been stronger. He was known as 'The Giant Lundy' – six feet seven tall and the finest man ever to cross the bridge at Foxford. Along with a group of other men he set off on foot for England from Belmullet in County Mayo to get casual work at harvest time, cutting corn. They slept rough, preferring to keep their little bit of cash for the various hostelries on the way. One night one of the men fell asleep near the fire, too drunk to notice that his foot was in the ashes. When he awoke he found he was badly burnt and could not walk. The Giant Lundy carried his lame workmate, all fifteen stone of him, on his back from the flatlands of Roscommon to the port of Drogheda, where they got the boat across the herring pond, and then on to Peterborough in East Anglia. That's a distance of 287 miles.

These stories and others can be heard at the salmon fishing hut in Bellass, County Mayo, told by my good friend and *raconteur extraordinaire*, Red John Colman – whether you want to go fishing or not. Over the years I have met Red John and Rakish Paddy, along with many of their friends. I have continued to enjoy listening to their tall stories and have learnt to tell a few myself – and why wouldn't I?

Neither must one forget the farmer's friend and workhorse of the bog, that little grey tractor – the Ferguson Twenty – that for nearly fifty years has guided them on automatic pilot on many an occasion back safely from an evening session at the pub and with God's speed to Mass on Sunday.

This, then, is a book on the taste and place of Ireland – or perhaps we can weave the two together, for they are really inextricable, and call it the flavour of Ireland. Although it takes the reader on a tour of the country it is not a guidebook – there are plenty of excellent books of this kind already in existence, and no traveller to Ireland will fail to arm himself with at least one. Nor is it an exhaustive account of the country house hotels or restaurants or producers of fine food in Ireland – that would of necessity end up as no more than a consumer guide, with stars and symbols and only a few brief words on each place, but without any of the flavour of the place and the food.

No, this is essentially a personal tour of Ireland and its gastronomic delights, paying due respect from time to time to my favourite sport of fishing. And why not? After all, fishing forms an important part of the Irish economy, both as an industry and from the viewpoint of tourism, and indeed where would those exquisite country house menus be without their locally caught trout and salmon, their salty fresh oysters and lobsters from the coast?

So you will find here no mention of the Blarney Stone or the Book of Kells – but you will find any number of personal recommendations about where to get the best conversation and the headiest pint of Guinness, and where to find the most genial hospitality in a Georgian family home. History is referred to only in passing – but again, any good guidebook will tell you that Ireland was once ruled by warring provincial chieftains and High Kings, and that wandering monks, and Norman and Viking invaders, all left their mark on the place long before there was any English connection. Legend and folklore will be all about you – indeed, you may be better served by listening to yarns spun in the snug of some tucked-away pub than in reading mere words on a printed page. At such moments you can feel the spirit of place that is Ireland – as you can alone in a rowing boat on a vast lough, at the bottom of a glass of Guinness, or in a dish of seafood laden with the tangy scent of salt water and seaweed, the product of a caring, knowing kitchen whose star performers know they have been blessed with a marvellous gift and are happy to share it with you.

29

_T_HE LOUGH
& _THE MOUNTAINS_
THE RUINS
& THE RAIN

MONAGHAN   LOUTH
MEATH   DUBLIN
WICKLOW   WATERFORD   CARLOW
KILKENNY   WEXFORD

OPPOSITE The ruined abbey at Trim is one of many relics of a
more tempestuous past in the Boyne valley. Both the abbey and
the nearby castle are well worth a visit.
ABOVE Photographed in Dublin, a very Irish variation of the
traditional Georgian door knocker.

MONAGHAN

A book of this nature has to follow a logical journey. I have chosen to start mine in County Monaghan and work my way clockwise around the coast, ending up with the central, landlocked counties. Many of these regions would be off the usual tourist route, but that only adds to their charm. Even if they lack the great country house hotels and restaurants which are the principal focus of the book, they all offer traditional Irish hospitality, no matter how simple, and each makes its special contribution to Ireland as a whole. The counties of the eastern seaboard and their near neighbours range from tiny Louth, where the twelfth-century ruins of Ireland's first Cistercian abbey, Mellifont, stand open to wind and rain, to the bustle and clamour and sophistication of Dublin; from the golden beaches of Wexford in the far south via the mountains of Wicklow to the architectural splendours of Kilkenny city.

A quiet county of neat farmhouses and market towns, Monaghan is hilly, with rough outcrops and good agricultural land, suitable for both tillage and livestock, elsewhere. The county is famous for its Carrickmacross lacemaking and also hosts the headwaters of that huge waterway that strangely flows northwards – the Erne.

Today Monaghan is the hub of Ireland's poultry industry: chicken, duck and turkey farms are in evidence throughout the county. In the village of Emyvale I found a remarkable young lady running the first and only EC-approved quail farm in Britain and Ireland – Ferndale Quails Limited. Fenella Steele started breeding the birds as a hobby in a converted outhouse next to the family home, and now she has a thriving business selling quails and quails' eggs to prestigious customers throughout the country. Among the numerous discerning recipients of her carefully reared produce are Colin O'Daly's Park Restaurant and the Lane Gallery Restaurant in Dublin, the Park Hotel in Kenmare, Arbutus Lodge and Ballymaloe House in Cork, and Patrick Percival's Rare Foods in County Mayo.

The obvious place to stay in Monaghan is Hilton Park. This magnificent Palladian-style mansion is part of the very appropriately named 'Hidden Ireland' group of country houses. Three miles out of Clones on the Ballyhaise road, it is entered through a set of imposing gates; as the house's handout informs guests, with the charm of Irish paradox, 'A word of caution – known as "the Green Gates", the entrance gates are in fact black with silver falcons'!

The rolling parkland dotted with sheep and horses suggests a working farm, which it is. It has been in the same family since the early eighteenth century when it was bought by Samuel Madden, a relative of the dramatist Oliver Goldsmith, and is now owned and managed by John and Lucy Madden. In this house the highest of old-world standards still obtain at every turn – beautiful old-fashioned half-poster beds, a lordly dining room illuminated only by candles, a vaulted breakfast room and everywhere exquisite arrangements of flowers.

With Lucy's good food and Johnny's affable nature one genuinely feels like a house guest, making a stay all the more special. Lucy's specialities are her home-produced cream cheeses and her delicious potato dishes. Hilton Park is also a favourite haunt where several other country house and restaurant owners 'go missing' from time to time. There is a small lake here offering boating and pike fishing, and there are facilities for golf and croquet.

For years I had been familiar with jars labelled

All the rooms at Hilton Park in County Monaghan are equipped to the highest standards, but this little old-world pantry – a proper cold pantry for storing game, cheeses and fish – is very much a favourite corner of the owners, Lucy and John Madden.

LOUTH & MEATH

The hospitality of an Irishman is not the running account of posted and ledgered courtesies, as in other countries; it springs, like all his qualities, his faults, his virtues, directly from his heart.
Daniel O'Connell

'Boyne Valley Honey' in shops around Ireland, and recently I decided to find out more about this much-praised product. I therefore visited the Cistercian monks at New Mellifont Abbey, Collon, in next-door County Louth, where the production of honey is one of their farm's commercial ventures.

It was a still, clammy afternoon. At first I could not find anyone: even the Press Office was closed. Eventually I encountered Father Peter, who explained the reason for the all-prevailing silence – the order was assembled not in prayer but to watch television: Ireland was playing soccer against Romania. Following his instructions I clambered through undergrowth and over fences until I approached a dark corner where twenty or so old wooden beehives were set amongst apple trees. The drone of thousands of bees disturbed the calm in a most sinister way, and there was no sign of Father Maurice, the beekeeper. . . . Suddenly, I got the fright of my life – a ghostly apparition with smoke swirling around its twisting, gesturing shape jumped up and shouted: 'Go away!' Father Maurice, shrouded in protective netting and brandishing a smoke-belching bee gun known as his bee special, had been collecting queens and feared for my safety. Then, to my horror, I saw a black cloud of bees descending. I was off like a shot, arms and feet flailing – negotiating any hurdles in my path like Roger Kingdom being chased by Colin Jackson.

Feeling somewhat deflated, I returned to the abbey and met the abbot – it must have been half time. He told me that Father Maurice does not like to be disturbed during his bee-tending chores; nor, unfortunately, was there any honey for sale. The blossom from which the bees were at that time collecting nectar was a second rape crop, resulting in thick, hard honey that the monks did not care to sell. I drove out of Mellifont with the windows of my car still closed and headed south to the village of Slane in County Meath.

Slane spans the historic River Boyne. This area, straddling the Louth–Meath border, is rich in history. Old Mellifont Abbey with its octagonal, Romanesque lavabo is just one of the spectacular ruins which lie alongside the river on the Louth side. To the south, in County Meath, the ancient mysteries of the megalithic tombs of Dowth, Knowth and Newgrange are still preserved in their awesome splendour. If you are lucky, the winter solstice at Newgrange will light up the cruciform interior in a spectacular way. This is rich farmland and the surrounding countryside includes King William's Glen, site of the Protestant–Catholic Battle of the Boyne in 1690; Tara, former stronghold of the High Kings of Ireland, Bective Abbey and Trim Castle are also in the vicinity.

Beauparc House at Slane is the ideal base from which to tour the Boyne valley and other parts of County Meath. This elegant eighteenth-century country house, full of antiques and fine works of art, now boasts all modern amenities. Its owner, Lord Mount Charles, lives at Slane Castle on the other side of the Boyne. For winter visitors, this general area of Louth, Meath and the region north of Dublin is good hunting country. The Fingal Harriers, the Louth Foxhounds and the Ward Union Staghounds all hold meets locally.

Back now to northern Meath. West of Slane, Martry Mill, built in the mid-1600s, still runs like poetry in motion and produces excellent stoneground flour on the 'rearranged' Blackwater River at Kells (known also by its Irish name, Ceanannus Mor). I have fond memories of the Blackwater in the seventies – before drainage began it was a superb trout stream and an excellent run for spring salmon. In those days Martry was a romantic little gem, the wooden waterwheel butted up against the main mill house, slowly going round and round, its paddles collecting and splashing – and trout rising everywhere to the 'grey flag sedge' or 'spring olive'. Then the mill was closed for seven years and the river's course changed a little, with the level dropping some eight feet. Public demand resulted in the mill being reopened, with the original wheel some eight feet lower and twenty feet away from the main building. The slow grinding of corn between two revolving stones generates very little heat, and the vitamin E-rich wheatgerm remains virtually undamaged in the resultant flour – one good reason why Ireland has a great reputation for good wholemeal bread. The Tallon family welcome visitors to Martry Mill where you can buy flour in tastefully designed packages.

When I die I want to decompose in a barrel of porter and have it served in all the pubs in Dublin.
J.P. Donleavy

DUBLIN CITY

If you travel down the Navan road you can enjoy the most spectacular entrance to Dublin – through the vast acreage of Phoenix Park with its herds of red deer, its bridle paths, its polo grounds, cricket and football pitches, its zoo and its gas-lit avenues. On the city side the River Liffey stretches a welcoming arm alongside, directing you into the heart of the capital. The distinctive smell of roasting hops wafts from the Guinness brewery across the river from Ryan's in Parkgate Street, where the knowing wise will stop for a pint. A pint, a pub and people – the essence of Dublin.

Dublin is two cities: a cosmopolitan metropolis thriving around the traditional heart of the 'old city'. And where is the old city? It is in Ringsend and the Liberties and several places in between. It is, even more, a sense of place; for real Dublin working-class values – wit, charm and generosity – are still expressed in a special colloquial accent. Look for it off the beaten tourist track.

Geographically, Dublin has a lot to be thankful for. It is a sea port, within twenty minutes of rolling mountain scenery, flanked to the north and south by sandy

The Dublin skyline at dusk, seen from the Forty Foot, the gentlemen's nude bathing pool at Sandycove. The city is blessed with good sandy beaches on its outskirts, as well as excellent fishing and two marinas.

RIGHT The quadrangle of Trinity College, Dublin, photographed on a late February morning after a snowfall. Trinity is the home of one of Ireland's greatest treasures, the Book of Kells – a magnificently illuminated ninth-century copy of the Gospels.

OPPOSITE ABOVE AND BELOW The face of Georgian Dublin: typical fanlights flanked by Ionic columns in Merrion Square. In the eighteenth century Dublin was one of the most elegant cities in Europe, and these squares, with their gracious façades, delicate ironwork and superb interior plasterwork, were the town homes of a cultured aristocracy and gentry. Alas, over the next hundred years they were deserted and began to decay. Today, although many houses first became tenements and then fell victim to property developers, the remnants are being carefully restored and turned to new and imaginative use.

beaches; and it provides good catches of salmon for the angler on the grand old River Liffey within its city limits – even as the rush hour traffic rolls by. Dublin also has two local fishing harbours and marinas – one at Howth and the other at Dunlaoghaire – as well as a series of fascinating little inlets and coves.

Mountjoy, Fitzwilliam and Merrion Squares stand at the heart of magnificent Georgian Dublin. Once their panelled doors opened on to streets where horses and carriages were the popular form of conveyance. Today you could be forgiven for thinking that little had changed, as many trusty Dublin workhorses still haul their drays over the cobblestones to deliver vegetables, turf, logs and coal and to collect scrap metal.

The Dublin Horse Show, held every August, is of course one of the most famous events in the equestrian calendar. The city has a modern and easily accessible racecourse at Leopardstown for flat and national hunt racing, and there are greyhound tracks at Shelbourne Park and Harold's Cross.

To complement the historical face of the city, Dublin today is a place for the young – half the population are under twenty-five. The new cosmopolitanism has led to the opening of many interesting new restaurants alongside the old-established names. One of these newcomers is Polo One in Molesworth Lane – an elegant restaurant with an immediately welcoming impression created by dappled light and hanging

I disclaim all fertile meadows, all tilled land
The evil that grows from it and the good,
But the Dublin of old statues, the arrogant city,
Stirs proudly and secretly in my blood.
Donagh MacDonagh

When money's tight and is hard to get
And your horse has also ran,
When all you have is a heap of debt –
A pint of plain is your only man.
AT SWIM-TWO-BIRDS
Flann O'Brien

baskets dripping with greenery in the airy stone and terracotta reception area. It is most suitable for lunch, for which one feels one should wear linen, preferably creased. The food here, under the direction of chef John Cooke, is light and elegant. Try the butterfly of wild salmon in a ginger and rosemary sauce, as good as any I have tasted in my life. The multi-cultured menu also includes parsley salads, prosciutto and osso buco.

Le Coq Hardi in Pembroke Road specializes in classic French cooking. Chef John Howard's speciality is the tasty, boned chicken dish after which the restaurant was named, but it was his brown bread that received a special accolade from President Mitterrand. Owner-chef Colin O'Daly's Park Restaurant is in the suburb of Blackrock, just ten minutes' drive from the city centre. His excellent track record started at Aer Lingus under the renowned Irish chef Jimmy Flahive, after which he worked at Ashford Castle, Newport House and the Park Hotel, Kenmare. Colin's particular speciality is seafood, including sea urchins. This confident and modern Irish cuisine is served in an expensively decorated restaurant where the only distraction is provided by a single olive tree growing beneath a circular skylight.

There are many other distinguished restaurants in Dublin, foremost amongst them being Locks at Portobello. The Lord Edward in the heart of old Dublin and the King Sitric in the charming fishing village of Howth on the north side of Dublin Bay are recommended for their fresh fish. Further north still, the Old School House at Swords still serves the traditional Dublin coddle – a tasty dish of boiled potatoes, bacon, sausages, onions and apples. Dublin has its gastronomic eccentricities too. Burdocks is a Dublin institution and the city's premier fish and chip shop. Here, when the mood takes them, the Burdock family serves fish, freshly dipped in batter and fried in the traditional manner on a coal-fired fryer. I can't help feeling that they would serve them wrapped in newspaper if the

law still allowed them to! Pasta Fresca in Chatham Street is a bustling café-style restaurant that makes and serves the best pasta this side of the leaning tower of Pisa. Capers, upstairs in Nassau Street, opens to evening diners with an imaginative and cheap menu, and it specializes in particularly good food for vegetarians. On St Stephen's Green, the Shelbourne stands as the last survivor of Dublin's grand hotels. Its Horseshoe Bar is a great meeting place and the Shelbourne is also an excellent spot for afternoon tea.

Indeed, Dublin has other eccentricities, too. Greer's, next to Mulligan's pub in Poolbeg Street, is the only saddle and harness maker left in the heart of the capital. This tiny shop, stepped down off the street, is full of leather straps and brass buckles and exudes the rich smell of saddle soap. The Forty Foot by Joyce's Tower in Sandycove is a gentlemen's nude bathing area; the tradition of diving into the sea here is preserved year round. I am not sure of the origin of the name and the water is certainly not forty feet deep when the tide is out. Something else peculiar to Dublin is the aroma of Bewley's coffee – the second most important smell in Dublin. A visit to Bewley's Oriental Café is still a special treat.

Like all good traditional Irish pubs, the best of the Dublin ones have a warm, casklike atmosphere, reflecting an amber glow reminiscent of good whiskey. The important ones include Kavanagh's in Glasnevin; Nesbitt's and O'Donoghue's (a great singing pub) in Merrion Row; Toner's in Baggot Street; the Bailey in Duke Street; Mulligan's in Poolbeg Street; the Docker on Sir John Rogerson's Quay; and the Brazen Head in Bridge Street (Dublin's oldest). No doubt you will find a few more on a good pub crawl. Before leaving Dublin, I must mention that the city is a starting point for two great canal systems – the Royal Canal and the Grand Canal – both structured in the mid-1700s. These arterial transport systems reached into the heartland of Ireland and were used for trading.

OPPOSITE Whiskey-toned Ryan's of Parkgate Street is one of Dublin's most popular traditional pubs – a perfect place for a lunchtime pint or a longer evening session.

Venus Clams with Fresh Pasta

'Clams can be cooked like mussels or scallops. Carpetshell and Venus shells – palourdes and praires in France – are my favourites.' John Cooke

SERVES 4

900 g (2 lb) fresh clams
100 g (4 oz) butter
4 garlic cloves, finely chopped
3 shallots, finely chopped
1 fresh chilli, seeded and finely chopped
300 ml (10 fl oz) white wine
100 g (4 oz) tomatoes, skinned, seeded and chopped
450 g (1 lb) linguine
1 tbsp olive oil
1 tbsp chopped parsley
tiny sprigs of thyme
salt and freshly ground pepper

Scrub the clams well, discarding any that remain open after tapping with a knife. Put them in cold water for 5 minutes.

Drain and re-cover with cold water. Rinse until the water is clean, then drain.

In a medium pot, add 25 g (1 oz) of the butter, the garlic, shallot and chilli. Sauté lightly, then add the clams and wine. Cover and steam until all the clams open. Discard any that remain closed.

Remove the clams with a perforated spoon and keep to one side. Quickly reduce the liquid in the pan by half by boiling without the lid. Lower heat, and add the tomato dice and remaining butter. Mix well with a wooden spoon.

Meanwhile cook the pasta until it is *al dente*. Strain, and then toss lightly in olive oil. Add the clams with their juices, and the sauce. Toss with the parsley, thyme and seasoning Serve immediately.

Wild Salmon with Ginger

To serve four people. Preheat the oven to 240°C, 475°F, Gas Mark 9. Arrange 4 fillets of wild salmon, skinned and boned (weighing about 200 g/7 oz each), in a clean, lightly oiled roasting tray. Scatter over 25 g (1 oz) fresh ginger, peeled and finely chopped, 300 ml (10 fl oz) medium/dry white wine, 7 small sprigs of rosemary, 50 g (2 oz) olive oil (not extra virgin) and some salt and freshly ground pep-

per. Bake until firm to the touch (about 8–10 minutes, depending on size of salmon pieces). Remove salmon and keep warm. Add 7 more small sprigs of rosemary, 1 tbsp chopped parsley and 50 g (2 oz) tomatoes, skinned, seeded and diced, to the liquid left in the tray. Stir well, heat gently and pour over the salmon. Serve with boiled potatoes and a mixed salad or vegetables.

Stuffed Breast of Chicken

A delicious way of serving chicken breasts – and of using one of Ireland's major products, whiskey. Serve with fresh young vegetables and, if you like, a tomato concassé (skinned, seeded and finely chopped tomatoes).

SERVES 4

4 × 175–225 g (6–8 oz) free-range chicken breasts
8 smoked back bacon rashers, rinded
2 tbsp Irish whiskey
150 ml (5 fl oz) Meat Glaze (see page 101)
mint leaves to garnish

STUFFING

75 g (3 oz) wild mushrooms, cleaned and sliced
25 g (1 oz) butter
225 g (8 oz) cooked potato, mashed
1 egg yolk
1 tbsp chopped fresh herbs
salt and freshly ground pepper

Preheat the oven to 180°C, 350°F, Gas Mark 4.

Remove the fillet from each breast of chicken and gently beat out flat. Beat out the breast as well.

For the stuffing, first sauté the mushrooms in the butter until soft. Mix with all the remaining ingredients.

Place stuffing in the centre of each chicken breast, and place the fillets on top. Reshape the breasts, and wrap each in two rashers of bacon. You may need to secure them with thread.

Place wrapped breasts on a baking tray and bake in the preheated oven for 25–30 minutes.

Flame the chicken breasts with the whiskey, then arrange on warm serving plates with a little Meat Glaze and accompanying vegetables. Garnish with mint leaves.

Poached Turbot with Noilly Prat Sauce & Caviar

'The vermouth in the sauce heightens the flavour and aroma of the turbot. My sister grows baby vegetables and pulls them freshly for the restaurant each day. My dishes reflect their origins – this reminds me of early morning fish markets and my sister's struggling endeavours to become a market gardener.' Colin O'Daly

SERVES 1
1 × 175 g (6 oz) fillet of turbot
salt and freshly ground pepper
25 ml (1 fl oz) fish stock
100 g (4 oz) prepared baby
   vegetables (see photograph)
5 g (^{1}/$_8$ oz) caviar

NOILLY PRAT SAUCE
1 shallot, finely chopped

^{1}/$_2$ garlic clove, peeled and
   crushed
about 8 thyme leaves
50 g (2 oz) unsalted butter
2 tbsp dry white wine
1 tbsp Noilly Prat (or any
   other good dry white
   vermouth)
25 ml (1 fl oz) fish stock
50 ml (2 fl oz) single cream

Preheat the oven to 160–180°C, 325–350°F, Gas Mark 3–4.

For the sauce, lightly sauté the shallot, garlic and thyme in half the butter until soft, but do not allow to brown. Add the white wine and Noilly Prat and reduce by half over a high flame.

Add the fish stock to the sauce reduction. Return to the boil, and allow to reduce again by half. Whisk in the remaining butter, and then add the cream. Strain (preferably through muslin) and season with salt and pepper. Keep warm, but do not boil.

Season the fillet of turbot, and place in a small dish with the fish stock. Cover with a little buttered greaseproof paper. Poach the fish gently for 4–5 minutes in the preheated oven until cooked. Steam the baby vegetables.

Spoon the sauce on to the base of a warmed serving plate and place the turbot in the middle. Sprinkle the fish with the caviar, surround with the steamed baby vegetables, and serve.

WICKLOW

Barges used to go as far north as Lough Key, as far west as Limerick and as far south as New Ross on the Barrow Line. The Grand Canal is still in use today for pleasure cruising.

County Wicklow, to the south of Dublin, is known as 'The Garden of Ireland' for our ancestors built great passage graves at Baltinglass during the megalithic period. For the early Christians, who in the fifth century carved a simple stone cross at Fassaroe in the valley of the River Dargle, this was a sacred place. The famous Irish lyricist Thomas Moore saw it as a place of peace, the setting for 'the meeting of the waters'. With its sea-sprayed coast roads, its safe, sandy beaches, its heather-clad mountain passes, its gorse-trimmed, rolling bogs and spectacular vistas, one could be forgiven for believing that Wicklow is where the rainbow starts. It is certainly where the River Liffey rises. Out of a shiny, black hole in the side of a bog, with an emerald-green fern guarding its entrance, the Liffey is born – 'a young, wee, slip of a thing' trickling her way down the mountainside to Ballysmutten and on into the Blessington Lakes.

In Wicklow, all routes are scenic routes. The county is criss-crossed by endless lanes, roads and pathways and provides facilities for every possible country pursuit and venture sport – from hillwalking to hunting and beagling, from pony trekking to canoeing and sea fishing. For those of a less active disposition the place is also rich in antiquities. The best-known are at Glendalough – the valley of the two lakes – where in the sixth century St Kevin founded a monastic city, the fame of which was to spread throughout Europe. Some remains on the eastern shore of the upper lake date back even earlier, to the Iron Age; however, the most impressive of the sights here are the eleventh-century cathedral, the 110-foot, thousand-year-old round tower, and St Kevin's church with its barrel-vaulted oratory and high-pitched stone roof.

In later centuries, Wicklow saw the development of large estates run from elegant mansions. The splendour of these places can still be enjoyed today at Mount Usher, with its extensive gardens at Ashford; Russborough, south of Blessington; and Powerscourt, in the northern foothills of the Wicklow Mountains at Enniskerry. Although the house at Powerscourt has been almost totally destroyed by fire, the exquisite surrounding gardens remain – still adorned with statuary, tessellated pavements and ornamental lakes.

Wicklow is sprinkled with tiny villages that make good lunchtime or refreshment stops, like Laragh, Ashford or Rathnew, where the eccentric Hunter's Hotel serves good old-fashioned afternoon tea. But if you need a base from which to explore this corner of Ireland at your leisure, I recommend Rathsallagh House. Just outside Dunlavin, Rathsallagh is a low-profile house with the warmth and character of a rambling, ivy-covered cottage, though it is the pastoral symphony of rolling fields and wooded brakes that stretch along the vast driveway that first takes your breath away here. Fine specimens of monkey puzzle trees, Scots pine, limes and beeches are strung like 'pearls of nature' over the five hundred acres. Sheep were grazing and horses being schooled on my recent visit, confirming Rathsallagh as a working farm.

Entering the house by a small back door off the courtyard you get an instant feeling of being at home – something especially dear to the hearts of the owners, Joe and Kay O'Flynn. 'Everyone is met and treated as a friend here,' says Joe, who once took ten of his guests to the local pub in a horsebox. The O'Flynns bought the house in 1979 and opened it as a guest house and restaurant seven years later. Now it is warm and welcoming, not over-opulent, the flickering firelight echoing the warmth of the greeting.

This is a sportsman's paradise, particularly if your sport involves horses. There is a choice of packs with which to hunt in the vicinity. Joe himself is a former Master of the Leix Foxhounds and hunted for over twenty-seven years; but after breaking every bone in his body he called it a day. Pony trekking in the hills

To the Irishman, the cow is his wife and the horse
his mistress.
Con Houlihan

Four ducks on a pond,
A grass-bank beyond,
A blue sky of spring,
White birds are on the
wing:
What a little thing
To remember for years –
To remember with
tears.
A MEMORY
William Allingham

roundabout is popular and can be enjoyed by all age groups. Finally, there is an international-size indoor riding arena adjacent to the yard where Diana Gilna runs her livery stables.

Maybe, despite being one of Ireland's passions, horses are not for you. No matter: Rathsallagh boasts its own clay pigeon shoot, a par three practice range for golfers and a man-made lake to which wild duck are attracted in the late evening. Alternatively, deer stalking and rough shooting in the hills can be arranged.

If all this is too much for you, why not just sit peacefully on the croquet lawn in front of the house and, like generations before you, gaze out across the ha-ha – that invisible ditch used by all self-respecting landowners to keep their livestock out of their pleasure gardens without interrupting the view. Be sure to find time to discover the 'secret garden' here – a two-acre patchwork of manicured lawns, elegant shrubbery, trees and a tennis court behind high walls fashioned from locally baked bricks. The herb garden here is complemented by acres of wild garlic and sorrel. Even after a hard hunting season, a horse that is let out to grass in the sorrel field will be as fit as a fiddle in less than two weeks.

Inside the house are twelve sunny, airy bedrooms, a billiard room, a gun room with its own private sportsman's bar, and a swimming pool. The old forge has been converted into a conference centre, and there can be few lovelier or more relaxing settings for a business meeting. And being Ireland, food receives proper attention: the small, intimate restaurant serves high-quality game, fish and lamb. Rathsallagh offers a delightful mixture of the elegant and the eccentric: Joe O'Flynn will even lay out a helipad on the front lawn, if required. It is an easy place to stay and make friends in the heart of a very beautiful part of Ireland.

A few miles south of here, just down the road near Baltinglass, two real Dubliners, Dennis and Hilary Healy, opted out of the rat race in the mid-eighties and now run one of the largest organic vegetable farms in Ireland. Working from sunrise to sunset during the summer months, with their gang of young pickeroons to help conquer those ever-stubborn weeds, they specialize in a wide selection of lettuces and red cabbages.

CARLOW

Most of their produce goes to special clients in Dublin who appreciate the incomparable flavour of produce grown in this way.

Continue south and you will enter County Carlow, a rather flat and somewhat anonymous agricultural county, best known for growing sugarbeet and wheat. But even here there are unexpected pleasures to greet the eye: the corn poppy still survives, and sometimes you will light upon glorious patches of scarlet where the farmer's herbicides have not penetrated.

Nowhere in Carlow is far from the Barrow, one of a trio of rivers known as the Three Sisters. This large, rich and somewhat sluggish waterway has always played an important role in the economy of the county, both as a source of power for milling and as a trading route. Along its course are a series of watermills; and where the river gets tricky to navigate, a canal system, the Barrow Line, runs parallel to the main flow. Both river and canal are used by boating enthusiasts and anglers seeking pike and perch; the river itself is a great survivor, having suffered pollution from the beet factories along its banks and major fish losses nearly every summer when wet weather follows a particularly dry spell.

South of Carlow town, which boasts an excellent golf course, turn left by the huge weir at Leighlinbridge to enjoy the drive through Bagnalstown (also known by its Irish name of Mhuine Bheagh), a well-kept, typical canalside mill town. Clashganny, a few miles further downstream, is the prettiest lock on the entire Barrow Line; with its sudden change of scenery it is best viewed from the height to which the road ascends here.

If you are limited by time and want to follow a logical route in this part of the world, you would now start to weave in and out of Carlow and Kilkenny. The latter county harbours Graiguenamanagh, the last stop on the Barrow Line. After this point the river broadens its banks to meander its way through dense woodland until it meets the tidal waters of St Mullin's and New Ross harbour, and thence flows on to the Irish Sea. St Mullin's was once a great ecclesiastical centre, and lovers of ruins will find a number of churches and abbeys in the area.

Great rivers washed by our door and if they swept away all the potatoes out of our field, sure there were often fish to be had at the roadside.
Myles Na gCopaleen

Lamb with Parsley Crust

Breda Coady serves this dish with Savoy potatoes (sliced and baked with garlic), and fresh garden peas with spearmint and/or a spearmint sauce.

SERVES 4

2 racks of lamb (best end of
    neck)
25 g (1 oz) butter

salt and freshly ground pepper
1 tsp chopped fresh rosemary
4 tbsp Dijon mustard
8 tbsp finely chopped parsley

Preheat oven to 200°C, 400°F, Gas Mark 6.

Remove any excess fat from the racks of lamb, and cut away the meat about 4 cm (1½ in) down from the top of the bones. Spread the racks with the butter and sprinkle with salt, pepper and rosemary.

Roast the racks in the preheated oven for about 35 minutes for pink, 10 minutes longer if preferred well done. Baste occasionally during cooking.

Remove from heat, allow to stand 5 minutes, then spread with Dijon mustard. Press on the parsley all over. Carve and serve at once with a gravy made from the trimmings from bones.

Eels Stuffed with Salmon Mousse

SERVES 4

2 × 450 g (1 lb) fresh eels,

SALMON MOUSSE
150 ml (5 fl oz) milk
25 g (1 oz) butter

40 g (1½ oz) plain flour
175 g (6 oz) salmon, minced
1 egg and 1 egg white, beaten
salt and freshly ground pepper
a pinch of ground mace
75 ml (2½ fl oz) double cream

For the salmon mousse, first prepare a *panade* by boiling together the milk and butter. Add the flour, off the fire, and beat until smooth. Put aside to cool.

Beat the *panade* into the fish and add the egg. Season with salt, pepper and mace, and then fold in the cream. Set the mousse aside.

Clean, skin and fillet the eels, removing the spine bone. You now have four long fillets.

Spread a thin layer of mousse along each fillet,

then coil along the length of the fillet, as if making a rope, each coil overlapping the other, resulting in a sausage-like shape. Wrap generously in cling film, sealing each end well.

Poach for 10–15 minutes until the mousse is firm in the centre.

Take fish out of the liquid and remove the cling film. Carve into six or seven slices and arrange on serving plates.

KILKENNY

Graiguenamanagh is a charming small town of medieval origin, famous for its turn-of-the-century temperance crusade and 'monster' meetings. However, that did not prevent a local man, Ned Prendergast, from becoming the fastest pint drinker in the world. He would take on anyone, anywhere, downing the standard four pints for such contests in around seven seconds. The legend goes (and it's easier to swallow after a few pints) that his encore included breaking the glass with a hammer and then eating it. The temperance meetings were not entirely negative – they provided a platform for the Graiguenamanagh Brass Band which, founded in 1760, is the oldest in Ireland.

Outside the town, Duiske Abbey, a former Cistercian monastery, has been lovingly and voluntarily restored by the townspeople at their own expense. This lovely, peaceful place rivals the famous abbey at Holy Cross in Tipperary, and is well worth a visit.

The architecture in the villages of County Kilkenny has its own particular stamp. An especially interesting series of these villages – Inistioge, Thomastown and Bennettsbridge – is strung together by the River Nore. This, the second of the Three Sisters, is a lowland river running in a fluctuating gravel basin. As a result, the life it supports within and around it is completely different from that of the Barrow, though it is fast-flowing and its shallows are good for trout and salmon. Inistioge is a chocolate-box town with an interesting river walk and a miniature village square. Further on, wander through the tiny streets of Thomastown, that side-step any attempt at symmetry. Its character is enhanced by a series of perfectly charming and colourful shop fronts and the promise of many a stout and sturdy bar. The derelict mills that surround the town are stark reminders of its wealthy commercial past. Nearby, the impressive ruins of Jerpoint Abbey have given their name to fine, locally blown glass.

A short distance from Thomastown stands Mount Juliet. Despite its size and amenities, this wonderful place is still a country house. It was built in the mid-eighteenth century by the then Earl of Carrick; in 1914 his successors sold it to the McCalmonts, who used it as a family home until its recent acquisition and

Land of ruined abbeys,
Discredited Saints,
Brainless senators,
Roofless castles,
Enemies of Joyce and Swift,
Enemies of Synge
THE DREAM SONGS
John Berryman

51

The antique gold image of Mount Juliet, bathed in a November sunset during the pheasant shooting season. The back of the house overlooks the salmon-filled River Nore.

conversion to a private hotel. Mount Juliet rests in a palatial setting at the end of an incredibly long driveway that winds its way slowly through 1400 acres of parkland. Portly pheasants strut and scratch nonchalantly around the grounds, which in early spring are filled with daffodils and oceans of bluebells. Much of the lifestyle and protocol of an old-fashioned country house have been carefully preserved here: a tailcoated butler waits to greet visitors, and an Irish wolfhound named Warlock is the house pet.

The estate provides organized pheasant shooting, clay pigeon shooting, pony trekking and salmon fishing on the River Nore in its own grounds; while the golf course is the only one in Ireland personally designed by Jack Nicklaus. The emphasis on outdoor sports is reflected inside in the Tap Room – the old kitchen, now a restaurant, which they are happy for you to enter in muddy boots and soaking raincoat after a long day on horseback, by the river or out with a gun. The executive chef at Mount Juliet is Chris Farrell, who trained with Gerry Galvin at Drimcong House and with Hans Peter Matthia at Chez Hans in Cashel. His specialities are roast pheasant and rack of lamb en croûte, as well as the luncheon favourite of shooting parties: Irish stew.

And so north to Kilkenny city (as its inhabitants insist on calling it), a fine town full of Tudor architecture. Shee's Almshouse, dating from 1581, and Rothe House, a wealthy merchant's town house of roughly the same date, are two of the best examples. Oliver Cromwell stabled his horses in St Canice's Cathedral, as he did in so many of the fine buildings of Ireland; fortunately the townspeople take a very different view of their heritage and in recent years the whole town has been painstakingly restored to its former glory. Be sure to visit Kytelers in St Kieran Street, a medieval inn where you can feast on locally caught trout or salmon, and the impressive, haunted Kilkenny Castle. For those with more thirst than hunger, Tynan's Bar is definitely the best example of how an Irish pub must have looked in former times.

The arts are no stranger to these parts: indeed Shee's Almshouse now displays the work of modern artists. Kilkenny produces its own crystal, sold through a

Roast Pheasant

A pheasant is the symbol of Mount Juliet. The birds are reared on the Estate, and there are plenty available during the season. They are hung for at least five days. This and the following dish are typical of the delicious, hearty Irish fare that is available in the Old Kitchen, one of Mount Juliet's two restaurants.

SERVES 4

1 well-hung brace of
   pheasants, plucked, cleaned
   and singed
2 tbsp maple syrup
salt and freshly ground pepper
about 225 g (8 oz) onion,
   carrot and turnips (or
   similar root vegetables),
   peeled and roughly chopped
2 tbsp olive oil

STUFFING

50 g (2 oz) shallots, peeled and
   chopped
50 g (2 oz) fresh herbs,
   chopped
225 g (8 oz) shelled chestnuts,
   cooked and finely chopped
100 g (4 oz) butter
225 g (8 oz) white
   breadcrumbs

GARNISHES

2 large potatoes, peeled
vegetable oil for deep-frying
550 g (1¼ lb) cranberries
2 tbsp maple syrup

Preheat the oven to 200°C, 400°F, Gas Mark 6.

To make the stuffing, sauté the shallot, herbs and chestnuts in butter. Add the breadcrumbs and season with salt and pepper to taste.

Stuff the brace of pheasants, and secure with larding needle and cord. Rub the maple syrup into the pheasant breasts and season well. Place pheasant on a bed of the chopped root vegetables in a roasting tray. Brush with olive oil and roast in the preheated oven for 35 minutes.

While the pheasants are cooking, prepare the garnishes. Pass the prepared potatoes through a vegetable mandoline to make game chips. Wash and dry well, then deep-fry in the hot oil until golden brown. Drain well, season and keep warm.

Wash the cranberries and simmer in boiling water for 3 minutes. Strain off most of the water and then caramelize the berries with the maple syrup.

Arrange pheasants and the garnishes on a warm presentation dish. Carve and serve.

Irish Stew

'This is a well-known traditional Irish dish. There is nothing fancy about it, but we do find it is particularly favoured by shooting parties who come to Mount Juliet in the winter to participate in the Estate's driven pheasant shoots.' Chris Farrell

SERVES 4
900 g (2 lb) gigot of lamb
    chops or breast of mutton,
    trimmed
675 g (1½ lb) potatoes, peeled
    and sliced

3 medium onions, peeled and
    sliced
salt and freshly ground pepper
1 tbsp chopped parsley
thyme leaves
450 ml (15 fl oz) water

Cut meat into fairly large pieces. Put layers of potatoes, meat and onion with seasoning and herbs into a suitably sized casserole, finishing with a layer of potatoes.

Pour the liquid over and bring to the boil. Cover and simmer gently for about 2 hours, or bake in a slow oven at 140°C, 275°F, Gas Mark 1. Check during cooking, adding more liquid if necessary. The crust of potatoes should be a rich golden colour and deliciously crunchy on top.

Serve accompanied by simple fresh vegetabels, if you wish.

We can feel the beauty of a magnificent landscape perhaps, but we can describe a leg of mutton and turnips better.
IRISH SKETCH BOOK
William Thackeray

LEFT The magnificent entrance hall at Mount Juliet, with its superb decorative plasterwork typical of so many of the Georgian country houses of Ireland. Here guests are traditionally met by the butler, Ted Richmond, and his Irish wolfhound, Warlock.

BELOW Detail from one of the many ornate classical marble fireplaces which embellish all the bedrooms at Mount Juliet.

showroom in Rose Inn Street, and the Design Centre offers a choice of excellent locally and nationally produced craftware. Late August sees the annual music and poetry festival that is Kilkenny Arts Week.

County Kilkenny has become a centre for modern Irish crafts, so it is no surprise to discover a potter of growing repute at Bennettsbridge. Nicky Mosse's stoneware became well established, encouraging him to experiment with ideas gleaned from his mother's extraordinary collection of spongeware. Today he exports around the world; visitors can call in at his shop-cum-pottery, where the turbines in the old mill have been refurbished to generate electricity to power his wheels and kilns. East of Kilkenny there is a charming tree-lined racecourse at Gowran Park. Evening meetings are a particular treat here in the summer.

At Borris, in the dower house of the MacMurragh Kavanagh estate, is a friendly, intimate restaurant and guest house run by Miss Breda Cody, who grew up in the house. Pre-dinner drinks by the open fire in the comfortable lounge are followed by a meal of delicious local produce. I can still recall the ambrosial taste of Graiguenamanagh eels stuffed with salmon mousse and chives, served to me on a recent visit.

WEXFORD

We enter County Wexford through the town of Enniscorthy, centre of the annual June Strawberry Fair, to drive northwards again, through Gorey to Regency Marlfield House. Here Ray and Mary Bowe have been entertaining guests at their restaurant and country house for over thirteen years. The house has an extensive Italianate marbled reception area that leads through to a classically decorated bar; a light and airy continental conservatory encloses most of the restaurant. There are flowers everywhere, carefully assembled arrangements by the loving hands of Mary Bowe. The food here is prepared using local fresh ingredients including Slaney salmon, monkfish and lamb. All the vegetables and herbs are grown in the Marlfield House vegetable garden – beautifully laid out, this makes for an interesting ramble.

Wexford is often referred to as the sunny south-east. Its extended hours of sunshine are complemented by miles and miles of fine sandy beaches. The coast road is the one for me now, past Courtown, maybe to pause at Cahore for some good fishing (for ray and rock salmon) and onwards by the golden mile through Curracloe to the strangely named Sloblands around Wexford town itself. This is an ornithological paradise where Greenland white-fronted geese graze side by side with other rare migrant birds. Almost every bird species in Ireland can be seen in Wexford, but the real enthusiast may wish to visit the Great or Little Saltee Islands off the county's south coast – no longer inhabited by humans now, and strictly for the birds.

Wexford town originated in the Middle Ages and lies at the mouth of the Slaney, a fast-flowing, gravel-bedded waterway that is one of the best spring salmon rivers in Ireland. The town's narrow, infinitely fascinating streets conjure up the atmosphere of an ancient seaside village. It has its fair share of good pubs and a market in the medieval square called the Bull Ring. In 1951 Wexford held a modest opera festival that has long since acquired an international reputation; now those twelve days in October are marked on the calendars of opera buffs all over the world.

For those travelling west to New Ross, I can recommend a worthwhile detour to the equestrian centre at Horetown House. Though fish find more favour with me than horses, I know that one day I will tread the steps to the top of the mounting block here – and never use a drop of petrol again! Horetown is essentially a large farmhouse of Georgian origin, providing lodgings and facilities for horsy folk. The food here is honest, hearty fare, and there is an excellent lunch buffet. The atmosphere is charged with the buzz of people enjoying themselves and you should drop by – even if only to be served in the standing and the staring.

After New Ross we descend into County Waterford, home of the famous crystal glass. Here the Three Sisters – the Barrow, Nore and Suir – become one and join the sea in Waterford harbour. Some of the coastal towns and villages, particularly Dunmore East and Tramore, are worth a visit; Tramore has what must be the smallest racecourse in Ireland.

Keeping to the coast road as far as Bunmahon, continue on through Dungarvan to Helvick Head and Ring, home of a superb Cheddar-type cheese. Alternatively, turn right into Kilmacthomas and on through Cappoquin to Lismore. Here you can visit Lismore Castle and gardens. For the most romantic, stirring sight of all, look back from the northern side of the bridge to see the castle suspended in the clouds above the weeping greenery that shades the banks of the dark Blackwater River. A trick of light on the leaded windows conjures up images of that legendary Celtic queen, Guinevere.

Ken Cummins, organic grower, sitting in a field of young red cabbages. Just before dark they give off a bizarre luminous glow. This picture was taken at 9.30 p.m. at his farm near Freshford, County Kilkenny, where he and Lynn Venables also grow fruit and flowers without the dubious benefit of chemical herbicides and pesticides.

Fillets of Salmon with Sorrel Cream Sauce

Sorrel is a tangy-flavoured perennial herb. It can be used as a sour salad leaf, and makes a delicious soup as well as a sauce. Adding the shredded sorrel at the end of the recipe ensures that the leaves retain their colour.

SERVES 4

4 pieces of salmon fillet, about 150–175 g (5–6 oz) each
salt and freshly ground pepper
juice of 1/2 lemon
1 tbsp clarified butter

FISH STOCK

2 celery stalks, chopped
1/2 leek, cleaned and chopped
1 onion, chopped
1 bay leaf

parsley stalks
2 or 3 small fish bones
25 g (1 oz) butter
4 peppercorns
150 ml (5 fl oz) white wine
600 ml (1 pt) cold water

SORREL SAUCE

about 100 g (4 oz) sorrel,
    washed and dried
150 ml (5 fl oz) fish stock
300 ml (10 fl oz) single cream

Preheat the oven to 200°C, 400°F, Gas Mark 6.

For the stock, sweat the celery, leek, onion, bay leaf, parsley stalks and fish bones in the butter in a pan. Add the peppercorns and continue to sweat without colouring until the vegetables are soft.

Add the wine and boil to reduce by half, then add the water. Bring the stock to the boil, skim, and pass through a fine strainer into a clean pan.

For the sorrel sauce, chop the sorrel very finely. Reduce the measured quantity of fish stock with the cream by boiling, then simmer for 5 minutes until sufficiently thick to coat the back of the wooden spoon. Add the sorrel, bring to the boil, then add salt and pepper to taste. Keep warm.

Place the pieces of salmon on a lightly buttered roasting tray and season with a little salt, pepper and lemon juice. Brush with a little clarified butter. Bake until firm but moist, about 8–10 minutes. To serve, pour some sorrel sauce on each warmed plate, then place the salmon pieces on top.

Terrine of Sweetbreads

Serve as a starter, accompanied by a little Cumberland sauce.
Sweetbreads have a delicate flavour which is enhanced here by being
marinated for a short time in cognac and port, and flavoured with
herbs and spices.

SERVES 10

275 g (10 oz) lamb's
    sweetbreads, soaked in
    water until clean (about
    2 hours)
85 ml (3 fl oz) cognac
150 ml (5 fl oz) port
20 g ($^3/_4$ oz) shallots, peeled and
    finely chopped
a sprig of thyme
1 bay leaf
a few parsley stalks
175 g (6 oz) lean pork
175 g (6 oz) veal

135 g ($4^3/_4$ oz) chicken fillet
125 g ($4^1/_2$ oz) goose, duck or
    chicken liver, soaked in
    milk
40 g ($1^1/_2$ oz) butter
400 ml (14 fl oz) double cream
25 g (1 oz) shelled pistachio nuts
1 tbsp Meat Glaze (see page
    101)
salt and freshly ground pepper
barding lard or smoked
    streaky bacon (about
    350 g / 12 oz)
a few thyme leaves

Trim the sweetbreads and cut in half. Marinate them for 2 hours in the cognac and port with shallot, thyme, bay leaf and parsley stalks.

Trim the pork, veal, chicken and liver very well. Chop, liquidize, pass through a sieve and reserve.

Drain the sweetbreads and dry them, then sauté in the butter until lightly browned. Add the marinade and simmer for 5 minutes. Remove the sweetbreads from the marinade and skin them. Keep to one side.

Remove the herbs from the marinade then reduce it to a glaze by boiling. Mix with the sieved meats, cream, pistachios and meat glaze. Mix well and season with salt and pepper.

Preheat the oven to 150°C, 300°F, Gas Mark 2.

Line a terrine (25 × 10 × 7.5 cm/10 × 4 × 3 in) with most of the barding lard or bacon (leaving enough for the top), and half fill with the meat farce. Press in the sweetbreads, and fill with the rest of the farce. Cover with the remaining lard or bacon, and top with thyme leaves.

Cover with the lid or aluminium foil, and place in a *bain-marie* with enough hot water to come halfway up the terrine sides. Poach in the preheated oven for about 35 minutes.

Leave to cool, then turn out and cut into slices and garnish with Cumberland sauce and a few salad leaves, if you wish.

THE GRAND ROAD
FROM THE MOUNTAIN
GOES SHINING
TO THE SEA

TIPPERARY
CORK   KERRY

OPPOSITE The Connor Pass penetrates the heart of the Dingle
Peninsula in County Kerry and makes splendid walking
country. Here, equipped with stout boots and a stick, you are
likely to come across more sheep than human wayfarers.
ABOVE Doyle's Seafood Bar, a must for seafood lovers, displays
one of the many brightly coloured shop fronts typical of Dingle
town in County Kerry.

TIPPERARY

Cork and Kerry poke out their bony fingers to make Europe's first contact with the surging, rain-laden Atlantic, while the Gulf Stream, swinging across from Florida, keeps out the winter frosts. Springtime here is a magical experience. Inland, Tipperary's pastures, mountains and river valleys give way to a broad central plain, known poetically as the Golden Vale; this is the most highly prized agricultural land in Ireland, and indeed some of the richest in the world. It flanks the winding course of the River Suir, on which lie some charming little towns in the south of the county, where one enters Tipperary from Waterford.

Leaving behind the Camelot images of Lismore, the steep ascent into the Knockmealdown Mountains leads through a forest of giant deciduous trees, impenetrable except for the twisting road that tunnels its way under the dense green foliage of midsummer. The roots of these monsters grip the craggy topsoil like eagles' talons clutching their prey. Suddenly one is confronted by a totally new geography. Hillside bogs are carved up by stone walls and green fields. There is a vastness here, broken once in a while by small outcrops of coniferous trees, breakaways from the main plantations, that interrupt the views across steep, bald mountains of blue and amber hue.

Heading towards the spectacular view known as the Vee, you can see white dots of sheep scattered across the vast stretches of moorland, and stone shepherds' huts that appear frozen in time. A suspended lake lies like a ladle in a small mountain to the left of the road before the first part of the descent. This is a wonderful place to walk on curlew-haunted sheep tracks through the mountains or simply along the roads that wind down to the villages of Clogheen and Ardfinan.

The Vee is a strange phenomenon – a power centre, for if you turn your car round it will be drawn uphill on a steep incline 'magnetically' at 30–40 miles an hour, with no assistance from the accelerator and in fourth gear. Get out of your car. Now the wind and light join forces to create a pulsating, dancing rhythm that illuminates one by one the myriad arable fields of the Golden Vale. As far as the eye can see are rolling fields like some majestic carpet of ochre, emerald, olive and old gold stretching out to the unimaginably distant horizon.

I returned to Ireland. Ireland green and chaste and foolish. And when I wandered over my own hills and talked again to my own people I looked into the heart of this life and saw that it was good.
Patrick Kavanagh

The Golden Vale in County Tipperary offers some of the richest agricultural land anywhere. The finest views in the region are now, alas, often concealed by that twentieth-century crop, mature plantations of coniferous trees. Here the sun races across just a tiny section of thousands of lush green fields stretching as far as the eye can see.

Four miles south of the town of Clonmel, rounding a sharp right bend and before crossing the River Suir, we come to Knocklofty House. Here there is everything that the visitor could want – an equestrian centre, squash court, swimming pool, sauna, gym, excellent salmon and trout fishing and – most important – excellent cuisine. Paddy and Joyce O'Keeffe endeavour to create a 'home-from-home' atmosphere in this fine house, formerly owned by Lord Donoughmore. It is surrounded by impressive stands of trees including rare hollies, several varieties of magnolia, five-hundred-year-old yews, giant oaks and the only golden poplar in Tipperary. Inside, the spacious hallway leads

A woman that's healthy
And loving and young
Gives pleasure for
months
Or a year, or a life,
When the throat's harsh
With smoke she's still
Sweet to the tongue
So who'd choose tobacco
In place of a wife?
HAPPY AS LARRY
Donagh MacDonagh

to a wood-panelled dining room and on to a galleried library, which in turn opens on to a terrace over-looking a lawn and the river.

Clonmel itself is an interesting town for a ramble, with some pleasant river walks, or you can go further afield into the Comeragh Mountains. A former mayor of Clonmel, Charles Bianconi, gave the town Ireland's first public transport service: his horse-drawn 'Bianconi cars' started running between here and Cahir, some ten miles west, in 1815.

A trip to Cahir by internal combustion engine will take you to Ballybroughda organic farm – a new departure for this agricultural region. Josef Finker came to Ireland from Germany in 1983; he arrived like a travelling road show, importing all the machinery needed to grow and harvest organic wheat, barley, oats and rye. By rotating his crops he can grow cereals without artificial fertilizers or any of the modern agricultural cocktails. Josef's organic flour is sold all over Ireland and abroad; a discerning customer closer to home is Otto Kunze at Dunworley Cottage Restaurant in west Cork, and a major Dublin bakery has recently become the first to use his flour commercially.

While in the Cahir/Clonmel area, Americans may like to make a detour to see Ballyporeen, the home of Ronald Reagan's ancestors. It is cradled below Cahir at the foot of the Knockmealdown Mountains.

From Cahir, now go north-west towards Tipperary, working your way across country (or via Limerick if you prefer main roads) up to Nenagh and on Dromineer on Lough Derg – the largest of the Shannon Lakes. This majestic inland sea, some twenty-four miles long and two to three miles wide, is steeped in angling history. 'Pepper's Ghost', a brown trout weighing 30 lb 8 oz, was caught by a Mr J. W. Pepper on a large copper spoon bait when pike fishing in 1861; and the famous 90 lb Lough Derg pike – probably the world record – was caught here on a common brass shoe horn by John Naughton and Patrick Sheehy in the following year. Alas – they don't seem to come that size any more!

Lough Derg and the rest of the Shannon are really for boating enthusiasts, but the drive along the shoreline that skirts the lake from Dromineer to Terryglass is very beautiful. At Ballinderry there is a wonderful place to stay, part of the 'Hidden Ireland' group of guest houses. The early nineteenth-century Gurthalougha House, set in extensive woodland, is approached by a higgledy-piggledy driveway that seems to go on forever. Log fires in both the sitting and dining rooms offer a warm welcome. Gurthalougha is a centre for pony trekking, walking, golfing, rough shooting and sailing. Boats and windsurfers are provided free to guests for use on the lake.

The round trip through Roscrea, with its Cistercian monastery, and Thurles takes us to Cashel (not to be confused with the village of the same name in Connemara) with its famous 'Rock' – a towering monastic ruin that commands extensive views over the Tipperary plain. The superbly restored medieval Holy Cross Abbey is also worth stopping for.

And if sight-seeing gives you an appetite, perhaps you should end up with a visit to Chez Hans, which occupies a former Methodist chapel. Hans Peter Matthia has been running his successful restaurant here for over twenty years. Understandably, this comfortable eating place has an ecclesiastical feeling: under a vaulted ceiling are an eclectic mixture of old and new oil paintings, tapestries and fresh flowers. The kitchen, incidentally, is one of the brightest and cleanest I have ever visited – it must be a real pleasure to work here. Chez Hans also has a proper cold room. Hans Peter personally supervises the cooking, and his specialities include the traditional Irish dish called colcannon – a mixture of potatoes and curly kale. Here it is raised to new heights of sophistication.

While on the subject of food, don't fail to taste – and buy – some of the famous Cashel Blue. One of the finest of the new Irish cheeses, it is widely available.

Down the road from Chez Hans is the Cashel Palace – a Queen Anne-style house that was once the residence of the local bishops. Obviously they lived well in those days: it is an impressive building indeed, and a former favourite hotel of Richard Burton and Elizabeth Taylor. Downstairs the old kitchens and wine cellars have been converted into the Bishop's Buttery – a cosy snack bar, perfumed with the smell of wood smoke, that serves good, tasty food.

Cashel without guests, rest-house abandoned and fire out, Packs of dark hounds growling on the battlements of Brian's tower, Duhallow without chief, leaderless the Dalcassian line now, These commanded me to this visit, Valentine Brown.
VALENTINE BROWN
Aogan O Rathaille

CORK

Travelling south via Cahir again towards the pleasant little town of Fermoy, we enter County Cork. Here I always veer eastwards to visit the small seaside town of Youghal, which has its own special place in history – and particularly in Irish history. To put it briefly – if not totally accurately in terms of the detail – in 1587 Walter Raleigh sailed home to Youghal harbour with a cargo of potatoes and tobacco leaves from the Americas. Stepping ashore, he planted in his back garden the first potatoes seen in Europe. This done, he sat down to relax: he rolled a tobacco leaf, set light to it and smoked it. The maid entered the room, saw smoke rising from behind the master's high-backed chair, panicked and rushed out for a bucket of water. She may well have extinguished the cigar, but not the habit. Myrtle Grove, Raleigh's house in Youghal, is now open to the public and the town celebrates his landfall with an annual potato festival in early July.

But Raleigh is merely a digression; the reason I turn aside and make for Youghal is Aherne's Seafood Bar on the wide Blackwater River, which merits a detour on any southern journey. For me, and for many others, it is a kind of pilgrimage of patronage – or, more bluntly, a love of good food. Don't be put off by the 'Bar' in the name. True, it was originally a pub, but since 1969 the brothers John and David Fitzgibbon, together with their wives Kate and Gay, have transformed it into an internationally renowned restaurant. David previously worked at Arbutus Lodge in Cork city and with the Roux brothers.

Due to Aherne's proximity to the sea and a well-cultivated relationship with the local fishermen, all the fish here is superb. The prawns which are the house speciality are served out of their shells on escargot dishes, covered in garlic and mixed herb butter and breadcrumbs, and baked in the oven. Every time I leave, my taste buds are already dragging me back. Indeed every time I look at prawns, I think of Aherne's. I remember their simple, friendly, happy approach and their maxim, 'Fish will cook in your hand – leave it alone.' They don't even have a tin opener here for pet food. Maybe the reason for their success is that to the Ahernes their restaurant is more than a business: it is a sense of place.

Prawns in Garlic Butter

In 1924 Jimmy Aherne bought a pub which has been known ever since as 'Aherne's'. When Dublin-born Gerry FitzGibbon, married to Betty Aherne, retired from the Army in 1965, they both came into the business full-time. Gradually various dishes evolved from the local produce, especially the seafood so close at hand. Twelve prawns per person can be served as a main course (twelve-hole escargot dishes are perfect for this) or six as a starter.

SERVES 12

12 large raw prawns each

salt

fresh breadcrumbs

GARLIC BUTTER

450 g (1 lb) butter, softened

1 small garlic bulb, cloves
  peeled

65 ml (2$^{1}/_{2}$ fl oz) red wine

1 tbsp mixed fresh chopped
  herbs

freshly ground pepper

$^{1}/_{2}$ onion, finely diced

Preheat the oven to 200°C, 400°F, Gas Mark 6.

Tail the prawns and place in a pot of boiling salted water. When they float to the top, remove and place in iced water. Shell when cool.

For the garlic butter, blend all the ingredients together well.

Place a little of the butter in each hole in your escargot dish, then put a prawn on top. Cover each prawn with some more butter, and sprinkle breadcrumbs over the top. Place the escargot dish in the preheated oven for approximately 10–15 minutes.

Serve hot, with garlic bread.

Beauing, belle-ing,
Dancing, drinking,
Breaking windows,
Damning, sinking,
Ever raking,
Never thinking,
Like the rakes of
Mallow.
Living short
But merry lives;
Going where
The devil drives;
Having sweethearts
But no wives,
Live the rakes of
Mallow
THE RAKES OF MALLOW
Anon

Its position on the mouth of the Blackwater makes Aherne's an excellent starting point for a memorable journey up through the Blackwater valley itself, as this full-bodied, broad-shouldered and masculine waterway winds its way casually through vast stretches of rich pasture and arable land. This is the principal salmon river of the south, and it can certainly hold its own against any of the reputable western rivers. Heading northwards through Tallow to Fermoy, and then west via Ballyhooly to Mallow, you may be lucky enough to catch an afternoon or evening meeting at the wonderful Mallow racecourse. Meetings here are only held in the more temperate seasons, as the course is liable to flooding in winter. The hinterland, as well as being the nicest part of the Blackwater valley, embraces two of Ireland's finest country houses.

The first of these, three miles west of Mallow, is the Georgian Longueville House: watch out for the abrupt warning sign on the main Mallow to Kanturk road. A typically long Irish drive leads one past sheep manicuring the front pastures under a shady and impressive stand of oak trees. The five-hundred-acre estate is owned and managed by the O'Callaghan family, and once again this is a working farm.

When the house finally presents itself it is elevated, standing to attention, respectfully saluting the ruins of massive Dromineen Castle, the original seat of the O'Callaghan family on the other side of the river. Longueville appears larger than most mansions of its period: the original house dates from 1720, but additions and alterations have been made over the succeeding centuries. Its impressive architectural details include an elegant and regal portico of about 1800 and a fine Victorian conservatory nurturing an explosion of colourful plants and hothouse palms.

Combining the farming side of his life with his interest in wine has led owner Michael O'Callaghan to plant up some three acres of the garden as a vineyard; in years when the weather is good the grapes produce a characterful light, dry wine. The extensive kitchen gardens provide a plentiful supply of fresh vegetables and fruit, which take on a special quality in the hands of his son William, who trained with master chef Raymond Blanc.

ABOVE The gracious façade of Longueville House overlooks the River Blackwater and ruined Dromineen Castle. The elegant portico dates from about 1800 and is later than the early Georgian core of the building, built around 1720. On the right the fine Victorian conservatory, added in 1866, provides ideal conditions for exotic plants.

LEFT A bit of a wine fanatic, owner Michael O'Callaghan makes a delicious light dry German-style white wine from grapes grown on the estate. Coisreal ('Beside the black water') Longueville is served with pride to guests, who come here for some of the best salmon fishing in Ireland.

Escalopes of Turbot with Shellfish

This delicate fish dish is served in a wine sauce thickened with carrageen moss, a seaweed found on most of Ireland's rocky shores.

SERVES 4

1 × 2.25 kg (5 lb) turbot, cleaned, filleted and skinned

20 mussels, washed and beards removed

20 cockles, washed

4 shelled scallops

4 shelled oysters

7 shallots, peeled and finely chopped

25 g (1 oz) butter

50 ml (2 fl oz) dry white wine

10 g (¹/₄ oz) dried carrageen moss

50 ml (2 fl oz) single cream

salt and freshly ground pepper

Preheat the oven to 240°C, 475°F, Gas Mark 9.

Cut the fish into four portions. Discard any mussels or cockles that do not close when tapped sharply with the blunt side of a knife. Cut the scallops horizontally into three.

Sweat the shallots lightly in butter in a casserole until transparent, then add the wine and a dash of water. Place the fish portions on top of the shallots along with the mussels and cockles. Cover with butter paper, place in the preheated oven and cook for about 8 minutes, removing the mussels and cockles after 4–5 minutes. Keep warm.

Meanwhile, soak the carrageen moss in cold water to cover. Drain.

When the turbot is cooked, remove from the casserole and put on a warm plate. Cover with butter paper and keep warm.

Pass the juices from the casserole through a sieve into a saucepan, and reduce a little. Add the cream and salt and pepper. Add the scallop pieces and the oysters, and simmer for 1–2 minutes until cooked.

To serve, arrange the fish and all the shellfish on warm plates. Put the drained moss in the sauce for 30 seconds, then pour the sauce over the fish.

Gâteau of Provençal Vegetables with Lamb Fillets & Herb Vinaigrette

The fillets required for this dish come from best end of neck or loin of lamb. Ask the butcher to cut the eye of meat away from the bones.

SERVES 4

4 lamb fillets, 200 g (7 oz) each
butter
salt and freshly ground pepper
fresh herbs to garnish
1 each of green, yellow and
   red peppers
1 aubergine (see below)
1 large courgette
900 g (2 lb) tomatoes

4 tbsp olive oil
1 small onion, chopped
1 garlic clove, crushed
a little grated orange zest
300 ml (10 fl oz) olive oil
4 basil leaves, finely chopped
1 sprig thyme and rosemary
1 garlic clove, crushed
4 tbsp white wine vinegar
a pinch of sugar

Preheat the oven to 240°C, 475°F, Gas Mark 9. Butter a baking tray lightly, arrange the lamb fillets on it and dot with butter. Halve the peppers lengthwise and put them on a baking tray in the oven alongside the lamb. Bake until the meat is pink, about 9 minutes. Remove from the oven. Season the lamb and leave to cool.

Put the peppers in a lidded pot for a few minutes. Skin them, then dice the flesh very finely. Fry briefly in 1 tbsp of the olive oil, then drain on absorbent paper, season and leave to cool. Reduce the oven temperature to 180°C, 350°F, Gas Mark 4.

Choose an aubergine with roughly the same circumference as 7.5 cm (3 in) rings. Cut it crosswise into four 2.5 cm (1 in) round slices. Colour on both sides in 2 tbsp olive oil, then place on a wire rack in the oven until soft, about 10 minutes. Remove, drain on absorbent paper, season and leave to cool.

Slice the courgettes into circles of coin thickness. Fry off in 1 tbsp of olive oil, then drain on absorbent paper, season and leave to cool. Put the tomatoes in boiling water for 10 seconds, then drain, skin, remove seeds, and dice the flesh. Fry the onion and garlic in the remaining oil until soft, then add the tomato and orange zest, and stir-fry briefly.

Line the four rings tightly at one end with aluminium foil to form a base. Place the aubergine slices in the bottom of each, then overlap the courgette slices around the ring, each slice resting half on the aubergine, half up the sides of the rings (see photograph). Add 1 tbsp of the tomato mixture to the centre, top with half a lamb fillet, then cover with another tbsp of tomato. Top off with some of the pepper dice. For the vinaigrette, heat the olive oil gently with the herbs and garlic. Whisk the remaining ingredients, adding salt and pepper and a cup of water, and then whisk into the oil. Strain.

To serve, place a little of the vinaigrette on each plate. Unmould the gâteaux, and place in the centre of the plate. Slice the remaining lamb fillets and arrange around the gâteaux, with little mounds of pepper dice and herbs.

Assolas House, near Kanturk in County Cork, is perhaps the most peaceful of all Ireland's delightful country houses. It is very much a family concern, and the Bourkes have run the house and farm for many generations. A leisurely game of tennis on the court in front of the house, or a stroll along the beautiful riverside walk before dinner, is the perfect way for guests to unwind. The Ring of Kerry and the whole of Cork can be toured comfortably from here in a day.

Jane O'Callaghan, Michael's wife, runs front of house with effortless ease born of experience, and contributes greatly to Longueville's special atmosphere. The food here is classic but cooked in a contemporary manner, and the menu is notable for its succulent lamb, reared on the estate.

The O'Callaghans are a good-humoured couple with a spirit of adventure. In the off-season, Michael particularly likes to go wine hunting in France, and therein lies a tale. Some years ago, with horsebox in tow carrying their latest finds home, Michael and Jane found themselves trapped in the middle of a chaotic

jump on travellers and dispossess them of their valuables. In those days the owner helped those in danger from robbers and floodwaters, and hung a guiding light in his window. As a result the house became known in Gaelic as Ata Solas, meaning ford of light, which was later corrupted to Assolas.

Crossing a small bridge over the river, one gets a first glimpse of the house – a medium-sized chateau that forms the backdrop to immaculate lawned gardens, set off to perfection by the riverside walk that borders the grounds. This is the home of the Bourke family, who manage it with great affection: a visit to Assolas quickly becomes a real family affair. Along with Longueville and Ballymaloe, Assolas was a founder member of the Irish Country Houses and Restaurants Association.

The first time I came to Assolas it was a perfect summer's day – still, sunny and warm. I entered the open hall door to be greeted by Eleanor Bourke topping and tailing a huge bowl of garden-fresh gooseberries and watching tennis from Wimbledon on TV. Her husband, Hugh, was appropriately re-marking the tennis court in front of the house. I was introduced to their son, Joe, then in charge of the kitchen. We all sat down, out of doors, to afternoon tea and a chat about the house. There was perfect quiet, for guests do not normally arrive until later in the afternoon. The mid-morning to mid-afternoon break gives the Bourkes time for family life and to get on with the gardening, preparing the evening meal or simply making a fuss of their pair of resident swans.

Hugh and Eleanor have recently handed over the running of Assolas to Joe and his wife Hazel – formerly second chef. When he discovered her full capabilities in the kitchen, Joe smartly hung up his apron, put on a suit and now manages front of house. He himself was trained in Kinsale by master chef Gerry Galvin, so needless to say, the quality of the food gets top priority here. The cuisine is simple but rewarding: keep an eye out for some excellent preserves, chutneys and, of course, Granny Bourke's marmalade.

Since the sixties County Cork has enjoyed a strong and ever growing reputation for good food, with restaurants of all complexions being opened all over

Paris traffic jam with an overheated engine. As concern turned to despair, with not a drop of water in sight, clever Michael foraged in the horsebox for a bottle of wine with which to fill the searing radiator. It did the trick, and they brought back the rest of their booty without further problems.

A little further west of Longueville, still following the upstream course of the Blackwater and a couple of miles off the main Mallow to Kanturk road, lies Assolas House. The curious name derives from its geographical position: here in the eighteenth century the road forded the river, a prime place for highwaymen to

Granny Bourke's Marmalade

'We are giving you our own special recipe, which was originally my grandmother's. The interesting thing about Granny Bourke's recipe is that while all the different members of our families make it to exactly the same recipe, it always has an individual character, and so every man claims his wife makes the best edition. I certainly am no exception.'

Joe Bourke

MAKES 9–10 KG (20–22 LB)
12 Seville (bitter) oranges
2 sweet oranges
1 lemon
9 l (16 pt) water
6.5 kg (14 lb) granulated sugar

Wash all the fruit well, then cut in half and squeeze out the juice into a large glass or porcelain bowl. Remove all the pips and tie them in a piece of muslin. Slice all the fruit peel thinly, removing the bitter-tasting white pith. This may be done by hand or in a food processor.

Leave the fruit and muslin-wrapped pips to soak in the orange juice and water overnight.

Next day, transfer the fruit, pips, juice and water to a preserving pan. Bring to the boil and allow to reduce by half. At this stage the fruit peel should be tender when cut with a knife.

Reduce the heat, add the sugar and stir until completely dissolved. Bring back to the boil and boil quickly for 20 minutes or until it has reached setting point. To test this, put a spoonful on a cold saucer; if it wrinkles after a few minutes when a finger is drawn through it, it is ready.

Remove the muslin bag of pips. Pot and seal in the usual way.

the place – from Youghal to Cork city, through to the gourmet centre of Kinsale and right around the coastline of seemingly endless bays, inlets and creeks: in fact all the way down to Mizen Head, which is as far as you can go. This coastline, full of safe moorings and small harbour villages, has always been a favourite with passing yachtsmen, especially the French and the British, as well as a host of other visitors. With a plentiful supply of good-quality produce and strong demand from the public, it is not surprising that an awareness of good food and ways of cooking it superbly have evolved here.

In Cork city the Arbutus Lodge restaurant has not only stood the test of time but has been responsible for spawning a 'new' lineage of Irish chefs. Rory O'Connell and Canice Sharkey (Ballymaloe), Michele Flamme (Ashford Castle), Michael Clifford (owner of Clifford's, also in Cork), Michael Peters (owner of Skippers in Kinsale) and Moira Foley (owner of the Lime Tree in Kenmare) are just a few of the chefs who have formerly worked at Arbutus Lodge. This very fine restaurant (and, indeed, small hotel too) is owner-managed by Declan and Michael Ryan (known to many as Ireland's Roux brothers) and has enjoyed an international reputation for serving excellent food for over twenty years.

Arbutus Lodge, named for the arbutus or strawberry tree growing in the lovely garden, was built in the late 1700s by one Thomas Beale. He eventually sold it to a master cooper who made barrels for the Cork butter market. (Once the largest market of its kind in the world, it is still worth a visit today for a ramble around its stalls of fresh produce.) Later residents included Major Charles O'Sullivan, father of the actress Maureen O'Sullivan and grandfather of Mia Farrow. The house was purchased in 1961 by the Ryan family and converted into a hotel. In the early years Mrs Ryan did all the cooking while her husband, Sean, continued to run the other family business – the Blackthorn House in Patrick Street. Predictably, he sold stout blackthorn sticks as well as ladies' accessories and military buttons and insignia. After his day's work at the shop, however, for several more hours he often assumed a wider range of roles back at Arbutus Lodge – barman, porter, waiter.

The couple's hard work and long hours paid off, and as their reputation spread their son Declan was co-opted into the business after having completed hotel school and on-the-job training at a number of major London hotels. But he quickly realized that good chefs were less plentiful in Ireland than good hotel managers. Meanwhile in 1974 Declan's brother Michael began to take seriously his father's advice: 'Learn to cook and you can work in any town in the world.' After gaining working experience in France he took over the running of the Arbutus Lodge kitchens, releasing Declan to manage the hotel and its related services. These two young men are passionate about food, and proud to be able to cook fare of outstanding quality that is uniquely Irish.

There is no better place to talk to Michael Ryan than in the engine room at Arbutus – the kitchen. You quickly learn from his friendly and articulate banter the two reasons why his food is so consistently good. One is the sheer quality of their suppliers: over the past few years the Ryans have been working very closely with their good friend Simon O'Flynn, Cork's designer butcher, who under their guidance has perfected the art of producing *kassler* (smoked loin of pork) and put new life into that traditional old Irish dish of bacon and cabbage. Simon also supplies them with first-class fresh beef, what he uniquely labels in his shop window as 'low-mileage pigs' trotters' (also known as crubeens) and perhaps the finest spiced beef available in Ireland. All three feature strongly on the menu. Dot Haynes from west Cork makes a daily run to provide them with such rarities as sea urchins and periwinkles – the latter served as a kind of Irish *tapa* at the bar. Jim Teehan from Tipperary sells them the very best venison. Local free-range ducks come from Mrs Barry at Fort Farm. The back door is always open here (as it is in any good restaurant in Ireland) to 'knockers' (those unexpected casual suppliers of good ingredients who arrive unannounced), and the Ryans have learnt to be endlessly adaptable. A surprise arrival of fresh brill or turbot, wild duck, a box of field mushrooms or a punnet of succulent berries could change the night's menu at an instant.

Roast Wild Duck with Elderberries

Wild duck of all varieties are shot locally, and Michael Ryan buys as many as he can handle. Elder grows in the garden; earlier in the year, he makes elderflower sorbet as well.

SERVES 4

4 mallard or 6–8 teal/wigeon, plucked and gutted

SAUCE

1 carrot, peeled and diced

1 celery stalk, diced

1 onion or 2 shallots, peeled and diced

40 g (1½ oz) butter

300 ml (10 fl oz) red wine

100 g (4 oz) elderberries

salt and freshly ground pepper

To start the sauce, first cut the legs off the ducks.

Sweat the vegetables in 25 g (1 oz) of the butter in a medium pan, then add the legs. When coloured, pour over the red wine and enough water to cover. Simmer for 2–3 hours.

Remove the bones, and press the liquid, meat and vegetables through a strainer. Reserve.

Preheat the oven to 220°C, 425°F, Gas Mark 7.

Roast the duck breasts on the carcass in the pre-heated oven for 15–20 minutes. Remove and rest in a warm place for a further 10 minutes.

To finish the sauce, add the elderberries, the remaining butter and some salt and pepper. Cook gently only until the elderberry juice starts to run.

To serve, take the duck breasts off the bone, and arrange on heated plates. Cover with the finished sauce which will look dark and glossy from the juice of the elderberries.

Bacon & Cabbage

'This is our version of traditional Irish pork and cabbage. Kassler, smoked pork loin, is of German origin, and ours comes from Simon O'Flynn in Cork. The loin of young pork is first marinated for 24 hours with juniper berries, peppercorns and cloves. It is then dry-smoked for 6 hours in a mixture of soft and hard woods.' Michael Ryan

SERVES 4
4 Kassler 'chops'
1 cabbage, or head of spring
  greens, finely shredded
2 carrots, peeled and sliced
  (optional)
vegetable oil
salt and freshly ground pepper

Preheat the oven to 220°C, 425°F, Gas Mark 7. Brown the chops in a pan in a little oil. Place in the oven for 10 minutes. Blanch the cabbage in boiling salted water for 3 minutes. Do the same, separately, with the carrots. Drain well and season lightly.

To serve, place the cabbage in the centre of a warmed plate, and arrange the carrot around (if using). Discard the bone and any fat from the chops, then slide on to the lightly cooked cabbage. Serve at once.

Blackcurrant Leaf Sorbet

SERVES 4–6
450 g (1 lb) granulated sugar
450 ml (15 fl oz) water
20–30 young blackcurrant
  leaves, washed
lemon juice to taste

Make a sugar syrup by dissolving the sugar in the water over gentle heat, then bringing to the boil. Cool. Make a mix of two parts of this sugar syrup and one part water. Place a little in a food processor. Add the leaves and process them quickly with the syrup. They should be just finely shredded.

Strain the mixture through a fine strainer and add lemon juice. Add the rest of the syrup and freeze in a sorbetière if you have one. If not, place in a container in the freezer and freeze until mushy and part frozen around the edges; stir well, then return to the freezer and freeze until firm.

Traditional Cork Crubeens

*'Cork was a major provision centre in the nineteenth century,
Wellington's army marching on the salted pork, beef and butter exported
from there. The offal was left for the people of Cork, so grew a tradition
continuing to this day. You will need two "splints" of wood from a
vegetable box or similar, and some bandage to tie the crubeens together,
otherwise the knuckles pop when they're cooked.'* Michael Ryan

SERVES 4

4 crubeens (pig's trotters),
    salted for preference
4 tbsp white wine vinegar
1 carrot, peeled
1 onion, peeled
75 g (3 oz) butter

a pinch of mixed spice or
    ground pimento
at least 100 g (4 oz) dried
    breadcrumbs
simple oil and vinegar dressing
    to serve
lemon wedges to serve

Tie two crubeens at a time lightly to a splint (see photograph). Place the pairs of crubeens in a pan and cover with cold water. Bring to the boil, then discard the water. Cover with fresh cold water and add the vinegar, carrot and onion. Simmer on a low heat for 5 hours approximately until tender. (This can be done the day before needed.) Leave to cool. When cold, remove bandage and cut each crubeen in half down the middle.

Preheat the oven to 230°C, 450°F, Gas Mark 8, or preheat the grill.

Melt 50 g (2 oz) of the butter in a shallow dish. Add the spices to the breadcrumbs. Dip each half crubeen into butter, then coat with spiced breadcrumbs.

Place the half crubeens on an ovenproof dish, and put a knob of the remaining butter on each. Heat in the hot oven or under the grill for 8–10 minutes, until the breadcrumb coating becomes crispy and the crubeen is heated through.

Serve on hot plates with vinaigrette and lemon wedges on the side.

Simon O'Flynn, prize-winning butcher (and cellist) of Cork city, makes delicious spiced and smoked beef as well as *kassler* – smoked loin of pork. He also sells pig's trotters, known locally as crubeens, Irish veal and venison. His excellent meat features strongly on the menu at Arbutus Lodge, where owners Michael and Declan Ryan are pleased to attribute part of their success to superb-quality ingredients from suppliers such as Simon.

The other reason for the brilliance of the food is the cold room. Here at Arbutus this is a huge, walk-in affair where all meat, poultry and game are hung to perfection. Nothing comes to the kitchen for preparation until the time is right. The food here has a general lustiness about it that I particularly like. The *carte*, cleverly including an eight-course tasting menu, will never let you down. And as for the wines, this restaurant has won an Egon Ronay award for the single best wine list in Ireland and the UK: much of its stock was purchased at auction from the cellars at Ardnagashel House, whose former owner had lovingly collected wine for nearly thirty years. At Arbutus there will always be something and a bit more to make another visit worth looking forward to.

Not long ago, one of the Lodge's former chefs, Michael Clifford, opened yet another addition to Cork city's more serious restaurants. The eponymously named Clifford's occupies a two-hundred-year-old building that was once the County Library. It has been unusually decorated in purple, lilac and soft greys, but in combination with the hard-edged modern furniture the decor works surprisingly well. Modern Irish paintings are hung in an eccentric patchwork, while batik blinds diffuse the light in a spectacular fashion.

Clifford's is a husband-and-wife partnership. Michael trained at Claridge's and the Connaught in London and in the south of France before returning to Arbutus Lodge and White's in Dublin. In Irish gastronomic circles he is now a *cause célèbre*, and his food is very much of the new Irish school. He has an extremely friendly approach – his restaurant and his kitchen are his home; this attitude is emphasized by the vivacious hospitality and attention that his wife Deirdre lavishes on their guests. Michael's presentation is thorough but unfussy, often displaying a finely textured Mediterranean touch.

Cork, built like Rome on seven hills, is a surprisingly busy city with newly pedestrianized streets full of tiny shops, coffee bars and cafés. It has its fair share of interesting pubs like the Mutton Lane Inn and the Oyster Tavern off Patrick Street, and Cork's at Jurys Hotel; in bars and pubs like these you will find the real spirit of Ireland. This spirit, and in particular Cork's fierce pride, are pithily summed up by an exchange between two local comic 'characters':

'I read in the paper the other day that Cork is being described as the Paris of Ireland,' says the first.

'Is that so?' comes the reply. 'And why are they not calling Paris the Cork of France?'

To many regular travellers in Ireland, a visit to County Cork is not complete without a visit to Ballymaloe House, south-east of Midleton at Shanagarry; Midleton itself lies about twenty miles east of Cork, on the Youghal road, and is the Irish whiskey capital – Ballymaloe is situated on a three-hundred-acre farm where, according to Ivan Allen, 'we grow sheep'. On a further hundred acres just down the road they grow fresh vegetables for use in the kitchen and in the famous Ballymaloe Cookery School, which is run by Darina Allen.

The house itself is well weathered and full of inviting character: it looks comfortable in its middle age. A giant chestnut tree stands guard over the entrance and shades the car park in front of a craft shop – not trinkets and tat, but a treasure trove of genuine Irish craftwork including spongeware by Nicky Mosse at Bennettsbridge and work from the nearby Shanagarry pottery. A swimming pool, croquet lawn and golfing facilities are all available to help the visitor relax. The quiet, calm atmosphere is disturbed only at mealtimes by the sudden mustering of both guests and staff taking delight in the ritual of dinner or the wonderful lunch buffet – for once a welcome rush hour. However, the

confident control inspired by Myrtle Allen – the *grande dame* of Irish cookery – is never broken. She has lived here with her family for nearly thirty years, but each day still brings her joy and surprise – at the time of a recent visit by me she was delighted at the discovery of two full buckets of fresh field mushrooms, despite the fact that it was only early July.

Myrtle Allen is the executive chef at Ballymaloe, orchestrating the menus that will be supervised by Rory O'Connell and his second chef Canice Sharkey. She has organized her kitchen into a well-disciplined series of departments, capable of handling over 120 guests for dinner. Over the years Myrtle has developed at Ballymaloe a food culture relying on classical and locally available ingredients presented in a contemporary style that is uniquely Irish. The success of her approach is reflected in the highly acclaimed books she has published and in tremendous popularity of Darina Allen's cookery school.

The restaurant has everything at its disposal – free-range geese, ducks, chickens and turkeys are available locally as well as smoked mackerel, herrings and eels and fish from Ballycotton; the local catch, taken in a fleet of small boats, is delivered only hours old by six every evening. While talking to Ivan I noticed four bottles of wine – gorse, honeysuckle, sloe and pear – beautifully labelled with the name of O'Neill's of Kenmare: something to buy and look forward to on the journey ahead. Overnight guests can tuck into a particularly fine Irish breakfast before sallying forth to nearby Midleton to sample one of Ireland's greatest and best-known products – whiskey. No doubt you will want to purchase a bedfellow or two for O'Neill's country wine.

Ireland is best seen when you have no particular place to go but lots of time to discover it. I therefore recommend passing through Cork city again and leaving it by the secondary, southern route to Kinsale. Although only eighteen miles from Cork, Kinsale is in a world of its own – a fishing port and haven for yachtsmen, with medieval streets and quaint sea-town houses. It also has the bonus of many continental villages of its type, being chock-full of intriguing restaurants, bistros and hotels.

Gâteaux of Summer Fruits

This is a fairly complicated recipe, but it looks and tastes magnificent for a very special summer occasion. Many of its elements can be prepared in advance, however. The stock syrup – made by first dissolving 275 g (10 oz) granulated sugar in 600 ml (1 pint) water, then boiling until sticky – keeps well for days.

SERVES 4
4 nest-shaped choux buns
4 scoops ice cream
225 g (8 oz) summer fruits

FRUIT COULIS
300 ml (10 fl oz) stock syrup
100 g (4 oz) strawberries

100 g (4 oz) gooseberries
juice of 4 oranges
25 g (1 oz) arrowroot

MERINGUE
2 egg whites
75 g (3 oz) caster sugar
a pinch of salt

Make a strawberry coulis by liquidizing the strawberries together with 150 ml (5 fl oz) of the stock syrup (see above); pass through a fine strainer. For a gooseberry coulis, cook the gooseberries in 150 ml (5 fl oz) stock syrup until soft; liquidize, cool and pass through a fine strainer. To make the orange coulis, simply boil the orange juice in a small saucepan, then dilute the arrowroot in a little water and whisk it into the orange juice until the mixture thickens; cool and pass through a fine strainer.

Make the basic meringue mixture by whipping the egg whites until stiff, then folding in the sugar.

Place in a piping bag with a star tube.

Preheat the grill.

To assemble, fill each choux nest with a scoop of ice cream, then top with a little of the mixed summer fruits, chopped if necessary. Pipe the meringue on to the top of each choux gâteau neatly. Place on a heatproof plate and dust with icing sugar, glaze under the preheated grill until light brown.

To finalize the dish, cover the base of a plate with a little of each coulis as in the photograph. Place the glazed choux gâteau in the centre, and arrange the remaining fruits around it. Serve immediately.

Mushrooms à la Crème

'This is a good way to cook cultivated mushrooms. It reheats very well in its sauce, so it is very suitable for advance cooking. Flat field mushrooms are, of course, wonderful cooked this way.' Myrtle Allen

SERVES 4
450 g (1 lb) mushrooms, sliced
175 g (6 oz) onions, finely
   chopped
at least 40 g (1½ oz) butter
1 tbsp chopped parsley

1 tbsp chopped chives
200–250 ml (7–8 fl oz) single
   or double cream
lemon juice
salt and freshly ground
   black pepper

Fry the onion in the butter until soft, then remove from the pan. Fry the mushrooms a few at a time, just enough to cover the bottom of the pan. Take them off as soon as they go limp. Add more butter if necessary, but never too much.

When cooked, add herbs, cream, cooked onion and a squeeze of lemon juice. Taste for seasoning. Thicken if necessary with a roux (a little flour cooked out in some butter) or some beurre manié (equal quantities of butter and flour mixed).

Ballymaloe Brown Bread

FOR FOUR 13 × 20 CM (5 × 8 IN)
LOAVES
1.5 kg (3½ lb) wholemeal flour
1 tbsp salt

1–2 tsp black treacle
1.25 l (2¼ pt) water at blood
   heat
110 g (4 oz) fresh yeast

Mix flour with salt and warm it. Mix treacle with some of the water in a small bowl and crumble in the yeast. Put the bowl in a warm position. Grease bread tins and put them to warm, also warm a clean tea-towel. The yeast will take about 5 minutes to rise and will be frothy on top. Stir it well and pour it with remaining water into the flour to make a wet-tish dough. Put the mixture into the tins and put them in a warm position or in an airing cupboard with the tea-towel on top. In about 20 minutes the loaves will have risen by twice their original size. Now bake them at 230°C, 450°F, Gas Mark 8 for 45–50 minutes or until browned and hollow when tapped.

A mouth-watering selection of organic charcuterie made by Otto Kunze at his Dunworley Cottage Restaurant. Here salami is seen at different stages of maturity, accompanied by home-smoked bacon. Every May Otto, a true believer in the organic movement, holds an extremely popular 'pig party' – an open-air festivity with spicy sausages and salami and other goodies from organically reared saddleback pigs, served with salads and home-made bread. Book early to avoid disappointment.

The restaurateurs here have formed the Kinsale Good Food Circle, with the aim of working in co-operation and yet preserving their own individualities. A gourmet festival is run here each October and deservedly attracts lovers of good food and wine from all over the world. Some of the restaurants I would personally recommend are Man Friday, the Vintage, Doyle's Seafood Bar and a recent addition – Skippers.

Driving westward from Kinsale not long ago my attention was suddenly distracted by a huge stone-carved inscription declaring: 'I am the Immaculate Conception'. I should have known. I was in Ballinspittle – home of Ireland's legendary moving statue of the Virgin Mary. I reversed the car to take a look – alas, the only thing that was moving was the mass of blue and white bunting flapping in the breeze.

I went on my way, for I was off to visit Otto Kunze just outside the village of Timoleague, where his Dunworley Cottage Restaurant perches on top of the headland. Otto, who learned his trade as understudy to Gerry Galvin in his days at the Vintage in Kinsale, is a champion of organic produce: his ultimate ambition is to use only organic ingredients. His small restaurant, opened in 1984, is now a very popular place despite its out-of-the-way location; the extraordinary 'pig party' held every summer has been particularly responsible for his ever-increasing reputation.

The centrepiece of Otto's party is a charcoal brazier on which organically reared saddleback pork from Vicky Heslop's farm in Tipperary is barbecued; it is then served with an intriguing selection of Otto's own handmade sausages and smoked salamis. And visitors to Dunworley need never leave empty-handed – a selection of these mouth-watering delicacies may be purchased to take away.

Nettle soup is another speciality here. Made to Otto's mother's recipe, it has a delicious flavour and texture; it is also, of course, very good for you! Otto's belief in nettles as an organic food source is so strong that he is seriously investigating the possibility of commercially farming them. For those in doubt, I can personally recommend them: Otto's soup tastes like a more sophisticated version of spinach soup.

Just a mile or so down the road is the next town, Clonakilty. I have always found it a little confusing that this part of the world is referred to as the west of Cork, when in fact it is the southern coastline of the county. It is, more correctly, south-west Cork and west of Cork city. The countryside now takes on a different, pastoral character. It is rich farmland, though the light soil and winter winds from the Atlantic conspire to make it, for the most part, a treeless place. Much of the landscape is divided into comfortable-sized fields bordered by low hedges, where cattle graze gently. There is a stillness here, an ease and warmth in the air, the gift of the Gulf Stream.

Clonakilty is the first in a series of small towns where the painted shop fronts take on an identity that is forever Ireland. Visit the local butcher, Twomey's, famous for black pudding locally known as 'drisheen'. Go on through Rosscarbery to lunch or to stay the night at beautiful Glandore, in a simple, family-run place, the Marine Hotel. Situated on the waterfront, it is owned by Sean and Teresa O'Brien and was chosen by Joe and Hazel Bourke from Assolas House for their wedding reception: now there's a recommendation! The food in this spotlessly clean hotel is simple and good, relying heavily on Sean's expert knowledge of the local fishing grounds. He has his own fishing boat and even pots his own prawns in specially imported large pots to guarantee a good-quality catch. While in Glandore, visit the fishing village of Unionhall across the quiet inlet – an unspoilt port of call for yachts.

All the towns in these parts have good delicatessens, so delicious picnic lunches are easy to shop for. If you prefer to let someone else do the work, Ballydehob, fifteen or so miles west of Glandore, boasts a good restaurant – Annie's Bistro. My next favourite port of call is Schull on the edge of the evocatively named Roaringwater Bay; for me it is the most interesting of all the small towns in the whole area.

Schull is sheltered from the north-west winds by Mount Gabriel, rising over thirteen hundred feet into the Cork sky. The nucleus of the town is Denis and Finola Quinlan's Courtyard – a complex including a bar, a delicatessen, a coffee shop, a restaurant, a craft shop and a traditional bakery. The delicatessen carries an excellent selection of Irish farmhouse cheeses including Gabriel, a Gruyère type made locally by Bill Hogan, and Dereenatra, a low-fat garlic and herb soft cheese. Both have recently won awards. Another award-winner, Gubbeen cheese, handmade by Tom and Giana Ferguson, is also to be found here. The delicatessen carries a fascinating selection of fine foods including organic vegetables. As I rooted deeper and deeper in this Aladdin's Cave I was intrigued to discover various Irish country meat pies and sausages – labelled real sausages and made by a Cumbrian girl, Gill Boazman, in Rosscarbery.

Like myself, Gill's husband John discovered Ireland by accident. When the couple came to live here, Gill – a sausage fan – was disappointed with the poor-quality sausages available in local shops and started to make

Most Corkmen know a lot; but this one knew everything. I tried many times to catch him out on some bit of esoteric information but it was no use. Invariably he was ready for me.
CARPATHIAN DAYS – AND NIGHTS
Nichevo (Robert Maire Smyllie)

her own. After ten years of experimentation, in 1987 she decided to set up her own business, manufacturing preservative-free home-made sausages containing no false colourings or flavourings. She now produces a range including pork and sage, traditional pork with coriander, spicy sausage with chilli and garlic, and tomato and basil. She also makes two pies – smoked venison and pork.

The most interesting part of the Courtyard, however, is the bakery, which uses an old, traditional Perkins coal-burning brick oven installed in 1919. It burns coal because of the scarcity of trees – and therefore of good firewood – in the locality. The only other similar oven remaining in Ireland is at the Cistercian monastery in Roscrea – and that is a turf-burning version. The one at Schull had been closed down for years

until one day Denis Quinlan came across a man named Jack Bennett, now in his eighties, who had worked for over forty years at the bakery in its heyday. Denis persuaded Jack to return to his old job of baking the traditional way, using the original recipes that are now a closely guarded secret. The bakery turns out two hundred pieces a day for the delicatessen and the restaurant: work starts at 6.30 in the morning and finishes at midday.

On leaving Schull it is a must to continue along the coast and visit Crookhaven, a small village which has always been a favourite watering-hole for those who are not in a hurry. A little suntrap, this quaint harbour has its fair share of cottage-type restaurants and good bars that specialize in lobsters and other fresh seafood. Now, after this pleasant interlude, maybe it is time for

Even in his eighties Jack Bennett is as good a kneader of dough as you'll find anywhere in Ireland. The old-fashioned bakery in the Courtyard at Schull, County Cork, produces a wonderful array of rolls and loaves and scones and buns, and the smell wafting from the old coal-fired oven is out of this world. Jack, who had worked at the bakery for more than forty years, was brought out of retirement by its present owner, Denis Quinlan, who wanted to revive the business. Among the bakery's neighbours is a first-rate delicatessen.

a refreshing swim at Barleycove. On a sunny day this, the most southerly inlet in Ireland, with Mizen Head at its tip, conjures up images of Aegean landscapes or the northern part of Corfu. Here you can walk off a white strand and bathe in crystal-clear water.

At the head of Dunmanus Bay, a little further north – but definitely west of Cork – is Durrus. Here you will find Blair's Cove Restaurant, run by Philippe and Sabine De Mey in a large converted stone barn attached to a Georgian manor house. The focal point in this candlelit setting has to be the cold table displaying a tempting variety of pâtés and soused and pickled fish, closely followed by a wonderful array of desserts which are usually set out on top of the grand piano. The subtle smell of wood smoke from the open barbecue grill at one end of the great barn lends the place an Elizabethan atmosphere. In the same complex as the restaurant is a garden courtyard containing beautifully finished self-catering apartments and a craft shop.

Just outside the little town, at Coomkeen, Jeffa Bates produces the farmhouse cheese also known as Durrus – now firmly established as one of the better hand-made Irish cheeses. Semi-hard and somewhat flaky, it is certainly one of my favourites. When I first visited Coomkeen, some years ago, Jeffa regaled me with a lovely history of Irish traditional cheeses that by now appears to have gone full circle. I think that we in Ireland would all like to believe this one.

The story goes that St Gall left Ireland in the sixth century with his monks to bring Christianity to Europe. They traipsed across rivers and mountains and finally settled in a remote corner of the Alps where they built a monastery; in due course a town grew up, which was named St Gallen. His followers brought with them their wonderful cheese recipes, which were quickly adopted by the Swiss and French. Over the centuries both countries have rightly been proud of their traditional cheeses; but now, by a twist of fate, Ireland is again producing cheese worthy of yesteryear – to the admiration and envy of its European partners, especially the French.

The final few miles into Bantry are on a main road. Bantry House, overlooking the bay of the same name, is full of antique furniture, paintings and *objets d'art*. It

has been in the hands of the White family since 1739 and the present owner, Egerton Shellswell White, has recently opened the east and west wings to overnight guests. His taste in refurbishing the house is obviously inherited from his ancestor Richard White, 2nd Earl of Bantry, who collected many of its treasures during his European travels in the nineteenth century.

The dining room at Bantry House is essential viewing, with its elaborate tapestries, silver and porcelain, and can be made available to visitors by special arrangement for dinner parties – a treat that I would dearly love to indulge myself with. The Italian gardens and the walks surrounding the house are worth a visit in themselves.

For the historically minded, for almost two hundred

LEFT Bailey Cove at Mizen Head, County Cork, the southernmost inlet in Ireland. Kissed by the Gulf Stream, this bay remains warm for most of the year. The gently sloping, sandy bathing beach feels more like Corfu than Ireland.

OVERLEAF The magnificent dining room at partly Georgian Bantry House overlooks the garden on the shores of Bantry Bay. The restrained elegance of Georgian mahogany – the dining table and chairs, and the sideboard and wine coolers in the window – contrasts vividly with the rococo swirls and cherubs of the sideboard underneath the tapestry. The portraits, by the Scottish artist Allan Ramsay (1713–84), are of King George III (to whom Ramsay was official painter) and Queen Charlotte, and were given to the 1st Earl of Bantry at the time of the Act of Union between Britain and Ireland in 1800.

years a French frigate, the *Surveillante*, a member of an eighteenth-century mission to invade and 'liberate' Ireland, has lain 140 feet underwater in Bantry Bay. The Bantry 1796 French Armada Trust has now been formed to attempt to salvage and preserve the vessel; it is hoped to house the ship in a special museum at Bantry House.

If you are travelling onwards round the coast to Glengariff, I recommend that you call on my friend Kathleen O'Sullivan and enjoy the homely comforts at the Sea View Hotel in Ballylickey. She serves the largest breakfast in Ireland – pancakes, boxty, coddled eggs and kippers are on offer as well as the more usual morning fare. Her dinner menu is unpretentious and excellently cooked.

KERRY

Bantry House looks out over extensive gardens on one side and over the sun-warmed expanse of Bantry Bay on the other. This fine house has been in the hands of the same family – the Whites, Earls of Bantry – since 1739. After admiring the sumptuous interior visitors can enjoy the equally famous Italian gardens, filled with classical statuary.

For nearly twenty-six miles Kenmare Bay etches its way inland to form a divide between the Bere and Ring of Kerry Peninsulas. Crossing the bridge at the head of the bay one arrives at Kenmare. This is one of three thriving towns in Kerry, the others being Sneem and Dingle, that have preserved a special atmosphere and sense of place, self-contained, that epitomizes the true Irish town. Contributing to this sense of place is the Park Hotel, a piece of High Victoriana that makes a perfect first stop in County Kerry.

Originally opened as a railway hotel in 1897 for well-to-do English tourists en route to sub-tropical Parknasilla, the Irish Riviera, it was then known as the Great Southern. The hotel remained in business until 1976; after considerable refurbishment it was reopened four years later as the Park Hotel, under the management of Francis Brennan. Most of the 'new' furnishings were auction bargains: not many people wanted to accommodate large Victorian and Edwardian pieces, but they were perfect for the hotel. In 1984 Francis bought the place, and in a few short years turned it into one of the best hotels in the world. In 1988 it was voted the Best Hotel in Britain and Ireland.

Francis is still a young man with an endless supply of enthusiasm and energy. His staff of sixty are also very young – their average age is less than twenty-five. This appears to be a key factor in the hotel's success. Like a good football manager, Francis coaches his team to a professional level of performance, and after three or four years good transfers are usually forthcoming.

The hotel has fifty bedrooms, but to give his guests the proper comfort and service Francis pretends there are only twelve. This helps to maintain the cosiness and personal touch of a country house, but involves very hard work. The workaholic himself does, however, manage to find a little peace and quiet. From time to time he can be found pursuing his favourite therapy of trimming and cutting flowers for the lavish arrangements in the hotel. The raking of the bedroom carpets, to give the impression that no one has ever stood there before, and the early morning washing of car windscreens so that visitors may enjoy a clearer view of Kerry, are just two of the eccentricities that make the Park Hotel a special place.

OVERLEAF This kind of miracle of light is typical of the West of Ireland. After continuous rain the skies are torn apart and a shaft of light illuminates Glengariff and Garinish Island – but only for the length of time it needed to take this photograph. Five minutes later it started to rain again.

The food here lives up to expectations and is under the supervision of Matthew Darcy, who has worked at the Park for several years. His first two years were spent as second chef to the one they are all talking about at present in Dublin – Colin O'Daly. The fish dishes are especially good and include local sea urchins. I have never met anyone who can present crab claws with no trace of cartilage as Matthew can, though he is reticent about demonstrating his secret technique.

Almost next door to the Park is a small, two-hundred-year-old converted schoolhouse, now a restaurant called the Lime Tree – named after the two fine specimens growing in what was once the school playground. The bustling town of Kenmare provides more than adequate custom for Tom and Moira Foley's restaurant, so booking is advisable. The Lime Tree is open for dinner only and offers a robust and varied menu for a restaurant of its size, with a choice of eight starters, two soups, twelve main courses (eight of which are fish dishes) and six puddings. I was pleased to hear that Moira's own herb garden started life with stock purchased from those pioneers at Eden Plants, nearly three hundred miles away in County Leitrim. The organic vegetables are supplied by a local grower, Billy Clifford. The Foley family also owns a local pub called the Purple Heather that serves great pub grub: try it for lunch some time.

The town of Kenmare, dating from 1775, is set amidst an outdoor enthusiast's dream – particularly if you are interested in hillwalking and climbing.

Walking is fast becoming an important alternative leisure pursuit in Ireland, and an annual walking festival is held here over the June bank holiday weekend. There is space and a place for everyone, whether you want to take a short stroll around the quaint town and its surrounding country lanes or ramble through the foothills of the MacGillycuddy Reeks. Facilities for cycling, sea fishing and bathing are all within easy reach. For those who enjoy riding, at the Dramquinne stables, three miles out along the road to Sneem, horses and ponies are available for trekking in the mountains and along the local beaches.

The obvious route now would seem to be north towards Killarney to see the famous lakes. However, I prefer the more leisurely journey, going by the route that is known as the Ring of Kerry, where only flocks of sheep cause traffic jams. The coast road takes one in the footsteps of the Victorian travellers to Parknasilla. Sheltered from the north-west winds, it is wrapped in rare, lush vegetation: mimosa, eucalyptus and twenty-foot-high silver ferns embellish this delightful place.

Passing through the colourful town of Sneem and Caherdaniel you will arrive at Waterville, home of a renowned championship golf course. Fishermen will find salmon and sea trout fishing of the highest quality free on Waterville's legendary Lough Carrane; while for those for whom history holds a fascination this area of Ireland contains a rich archaeological heritage of standing stones, hill forts, beehive huts and Romanesque ruins.

There is a lake in every man's heart . . .
and he listens to its monotonous
whisper year by year, more and more
attentive until at last he ungirds.
THE LAKE
George Augustus Moore

Quail with Morel Stuffing & Madeira Sauce

Quail weigh between 100 and 150 g (4–5 oz) each, and are occasionally found in the shops already boned. It is rather a fiddly business to do at home, but well worthwhile.

PER PERSON
1 large quail, boned
salt and freshly ground pepper
butter
175 ml (6 fl oz) Meat Glaze (see
    page 101)

STUFFING
25 g (1 oz) fresh morels
175 ml (6 fl oz) Madeira

1 large shallot, peeled and
    finely chopped
1 tsp fresh chopped herbs
25 g (1 oz) fresh breadcrumbs

BEETROOT TARTLET
1 thick slice of toasting bread,
    crusts removed
2 baby beetroots, cooked,
    skinned and diced

If you bone the bird yourself, leave in the shin bones only. Lay the bird flat, and season.

For the stuffing, soak the morels in the Madeira for 1 hour. Remove morels and chop finely, retaining the Madeira. Melt 15 g (½ oz) of the butter in a pan, and sauté the shallot, morels and herbs for a few moments. Mix in the breadcrumbs. Season and leave to cool. Preheat the oven to 220°C, 425°F, Gas Mark 7.

For the tartlet, flatten the slice of bread with a rolling pin. Dip both sides in 25 g (1 oz) of melted butter, and set into a tartlet mould (or similar). Place another mould on top, and cook in the preheated oven for 4 minutes. Remove from the oven and leave to cool and set. When ready, fill with the beetroot dice. Heat through just before serving.

Stuff the bird and sew it together with fine string, or use wooden cocktail sticks. Melt 25 g (1 oz) butter in a pan and brown the bird on all sides before roasting for 8–12 minutes. Wrap in foil and keep warm for 10 minutes. Deglaze the pan with the leftover Madeira. Boil to reduce by half, then add the Meat Glaze.

Reduce again, then pass through a fine sieve. Season and swirl in a knob of butter.

To serve, slice the bird and place on a warm plate covered with sauce (or serve the latter separately). Garnish with the warmed beetroot tartlet.

Pan-fried Monkfish with Spinach Tomato Timbales

Glazed shallots, little spinach timbales and almond-coated monkfish served with a light beurre blanc – a delicious combination of colours, textures and flavours. This dish is a good example of the versatility of beurre blanc.

PER PERSON

175 g (6 oz) monkfish tail, skinned and cut into 3 noisettes

about 15 g (¹/₂ oz) plain flour

salt and freshly ground pepper

1 egg, beaten

50 g (2 oz) almonds, chopped

1 large tomato, skinned, seeded and diced

50 g (2 oz) fresh spinach, stalks removed, blanched and finely chopped

olive oil

15 g (¹/₂ oz) butter

2 tbsp beurre blanc (see page 87)

GLAZED SHALLOTS

2 shallots, peeled

7.5 g (¹/₄ oz) butter

¹/₂ tsp demerara sugar

Season the flour with salt and pepper and lightly coat the monkfish pieces. Dip the floured fish into the egg wash, and then coat with chopped almonds. Set aside.

Season the tomato dice and shredded spinach, then press into a lightly oiled timbale mould (or similar), tomato first. Place in a steamer over boiling water and steam for about 10 minutes.

Place the shallots in a small pan, and just barely cover with water. Add the butter, sugar and a little salt, and bring to the boil. Continue boiling until the water evaporates, then reduce the heat. Shake the pan until the shallots brown on all sides.

Heat 1 tbsp of oil and the butter together in a pan, and cook the noisettes on both sides until golden brown. Place them in a semi-circle on a warm plate. Turn out the timbale, and place alongside the fish. Garnish with the beurre blanc and glazed shallots.

Roast Loin of Lamb on an Oyster Walnut 'Stuffing'

Ask your butcher to cut the fillet from the loin or best end of neck. Keep the bones to make a stock: roast for a few minutes in a hot oven, then simmer with vegetables and flavourings for 3–4 hours. Strain and boil to reduce to a meat glaze for the sauce.

PER PERSON
1 lamb fillet, about 200 g (7 oz) in weight
salt and freshly ground pepper
diced raw tomato, diced cooked beetroot and parsley to garnish

STUFFING
25 g (1 oz) butter
1 tsp finely chopped onion
25 g (1 oz) walnuts, finely chopped

2 shelled oysters, finely chopped
2 basil leaves, finely chopped
25 g (1 oz) fresh breadcrumbs

SAUCE
1 garlic clove, crushed
1 small sprig of rosemary
$^{1}/_{2}$ tomato, skinned, seeded and diced
75 g (3 oz) butter
175 ml (6 fl oz) meat glaze (see above)

Preheat the oven to 240°C, 475°F, Gas Mark 9, or as high as possible. Season the lamb, and seal it all over in a hot, lightly oiled pan. Place in the very hot oven for 5–8 minutes (depending on how rare you like it). Remove, wrap in foil, and leave in a warm place to rest. (The lamb continues to cook in the foil, retaining all its juices.)

For the stuffing, melt the butter in a pan, and briefly sauté the onion, walnuts, oyster and basil. Season and stir in the breadcrumbs. Keep warm.

For the sauce, in another pan sauté the garlic, rosemary and the tomato dice in half the butter. Add the meat glaze, and boil to reduce by half. Season and pass through a fine sieve. Swirl in the remaining butter.

To serve, place the stuffing neatly in the centre of a warm plate. Carve the lamb, and arrange the slices on top of the stuffing. Either surround with sauce, or serve it separately, and garnish with tomato and beetroot dice and parsley.

'A man who is not afraid of the sea will soon be drowned,' he said, 'for he will be going out on a day he shouldn't. But we do be afraid of the sea and we only do be drownded now and again.'
THE ARAN ISLANDS
J. M. Synge

Driving through Cahirciveen and Glenbeigh gives a further opportunity to experience the special magic of Kerry – painted against a backdrop of impressive blue mountains highlighted by golden seams of sandy beaches, the glimmering crystal of rushing cool hillside streams and vast and distant seascapes. After all, beyond the Skellig rocks the next town is Boston or New York. Nature here takes on extravagant proportions – everything in Kerry seems larger than life, from the enormous, remote vistas to the tall tales of giant and swarthy men.

If you visit Killorglin in early August you may be lucky enough to coincide with the annual Puck Fair – a famous three-day sheep, cattle and horse show. This is a thoroughly Irish affair: the festivities include a hunt through the mountains by local men to capture a wild male goat, which is then crowned to preside over his often bruised subjects for the duration of the event!

Rounding the corner at Castlemaine, as it were, into the Dingle Peninsula, a new maxim applies: 'Rain at seven, sun by eleven.' I have been to the Dingle Peninsula on seven or eight occasions when seemingly relentless morning drizzle has given way before noon to soft banks of light that expand into clear, sharply blue, cloudless skies. One cannot help noticing how the tenderness of the morning rain has endowed the local fields with a rich greenness, not typical of other parts of Kerry. The spectacular strand at Inch, a natural breakwater that reflects the changing light of the dramatic skies over Dingle Bay, fingers its way for miles straight into the ocean. The beach has a dual personality, either humoured by fine, calm weather or pounded by the full force of the Atlantic on a windy day. The place was captured for posterity in David Lean's beautifully photographed movie *Ryan's Daughter*.

Slightly out of character, a flat pocket of land along the coastline of the Ring of Kerry somewhere between Waterville and Cahirdaniel. After a recent shower the sun has transformed this little plateau into a carpet of green.

*M*illefeuilles of *W*arm *O*ysters in Guinness Sauce

Stella Doyle invented this dish in order to include the national drink and the oysters which are so popular in the Seafood Bar. She makes a similar dish with cubes of salmon, steaming them for 5 minutes before placing in larger squares of pastry. With the salmon, instead of Guinness sauce she serves a sorrel sauce (see photograph), adding 100 g (4 oz) sorrel purée to the beurre blanc recipe below.

SERVES 6

450 g (1 lb) prepared puff
    pastry
1 egg yolk
36 shucked oysters
6 tbsp Guinness

GUINNESS SAUCE

6 shallots, peeled and chopped
40 g (1^1/$_2$ oz) butter
300 ml (10 fl oz) Guinness
400 ml (14 fl oz) single cream
6 tbsp hollandaise sauce
salt and freshly ground pepper

Preheat the oven to 220°C, 425°F, Gas Mark 7.

Roll the pastry out to a thickness of about 3 mm (^{1}/$_8$ in). Cut into six 4 cm (1^1/$_2$ in) squares, and arrange on a baking sheet. Chill well. Lightly cut the tops in a simple pattern, and brush with the beaten egg yolk. Bake in the preheated oven until lightly browned and risen, about 12–15 minutes.

Make the hollandaise sauce (see opposite).

For the Guinness sauce, sauté the chopped shallot in the butter for about 5 minutes. Add the Guinness and boil to reduce down to about 2 tbsp. Add the cream and reduce until it coats the back of a spoon. Strain and keep warm to one side.

Put the oysters into a pan with the 6 tbsp Guinness and just bring to the boil, then remove from the heat. Split the cooked pastry in half horizontally and reheat in a hot oven for a few moments if necessary. Place a few oysters on each of the bottom halves. Meanwhile, add the hollandaise sauce to the Guinness and cream reduction, warm through and season to taste. Pour over the oysters and place the pastry lids on top. Serve immediately.

Beurre Blanc

Stella Doyle serves this sauce with claws from the crabs she buys for the Seafood Bar, the remainder being used in crab cocktails. The combination has proved rather successful! Some supermarkets now sell peeled and cooked crab claws. If raw, cover with boiling water, add a lemon cut in half, and simmer for 10 minutes.

To make enough beurre blanc for six people, put 300 ml (10 fl oz) dry white wine, 1 tbsp black peppercorns, 1 tbsp chopped parsley and 1 bay leaf into a saucepan, and reduce by boiling to one-third of its original volume. Strain, return to the pan, and add 100 g (4 oz) cold butter, cut up into small pieces, whisking all the time. When all the butter has been added, finish by stirring in 150 ml (5 fl oz) single cream.

Serve immediately.

This simple but delicious sauce is equally good with many other fish recipes.

Hollandaise Sauce

This classic, velvety sauce is now part of the repertoire of most good cooks. It makes a perfect partner for salmon and, as in the recipe opposite, can also form a base for more inventive sauces.

Mix together 2 tbsp water, 1 tbsp crushed white peppercorns and 1 tbsp white wine vinegar. Set over a high heat and reduce by two-thirds. Take the pan off the heat, and beat in 1 tbsp water and 3 egg yolks. Place the pan over a gentle heat, or in a *bain-marie*, and continue beating. After 8–10 minutes, the mixture should be creamy. Whisking continuously, beat in 200 g (7 oz) melted butter, a little at a time. If it should become too thick, add a little more water. Season to taste with salt and the juice of $^1/_2$ lemon. Remove from the heat and keep warm until needed.

Grilled Black Sole

Some of the best dishes in Ireland – or anywhere else for that matter – are the simplest. The secret lies in being able to obtain the very best and freshest ingredients, which at Doyle's is no problem at all.

Simplicity itself. Put a fresh black (or Dover) sole of about 450 g (1 lb) in weight per person on to a greased baking tray, and brush with butter. Cook under a hot grill until golden, about 10 minutes.

Serve hot, garnished if you like with parsley and lemon wedges. A salad or some lightly cooked fresh garden vegetables are all that is needed to accompany it.

BELOW Racing currachs in Dingle harbour. Traditionally these were fishing vessels but today they are used for racing by oarsmen – Dingle Races are famous. It is claimed that the men in these parts are so strong that they can pull the gunwales off a boat.
RIGHT Colourful nets nowadays made of synthetic fibres, lend colour to the grey stone of Dingle harbour.

And so to Dingle town itself; this vibrant fishing village was founded in the Middle Ages, though most of its buildings today date from late Georgian or early Victorian times. It was an important trading post for both the Spanish and French wine trades in former centuries, and an export centre for linen and fish until the First World War. For its size, Dingle has more pubs than any other town in Ireland – one for every week of the year. The town presents a helter-skelter of interesting streets, and is definitely worth two or three days if you can spare them. In summer it acquires a distinctly cosmopolitan population – Italian, French, German, American and Scandinavian visitors mingle freely with the native Irish in the tiny bars and characterful streets that are never far from the sound and smell of the sea.

Doyle's Seafood Bar and Town House is my favourite restaurant in Dingle. It was set up on a whim by Stella Doyle, who found herself with time on her hands when her husband John, who had dropped out of the advertising business in Dublin in the early seventies, was out fishing on his own trawler. Rather than see the entire local catch exported, she decided to establish a small restaurant specializing in seafood. It was such a success that John soon joined her to run the expanding business. He never went back to sea.

Doyle's is open for lunch and dinner, but it seats only forty people at a time and so booking is essential. Although service is speedy and efficient, great care and patience are taken to ensure the quality and standard of the ingredients, which vary from day to day according to what the catch is, and of their cooking. In recent years the Doyles have added a series of well-furnished guest rooms.

West of Dingle, the surrounding area encompasses some of the most spectacular seascapes to be seen anywhere in Ireland, particularly during stormy weather. Some breathtaking tricks of light can be caught at sunset, and from Slea Head there are views of the largely uninhabited Blasket Islands, lying wild and lonely out in the ocean. Beyond that, as thousands of Irish men and women discovered in the past, there is nothing but the green Atlantic rollers until you reach the New World.

Will you come to the bow'r o'er the free boundless ocean. Where the stupendous waves roll in thunderin' motion. Where the mermaids are seen and the fierce tempest gathers. To lov'd Erin the Green, the dear land of our fathers, Will you come, will you, will you, will you come to the bower?
COME TO THE BOWER
Anon

Where Grasses Grow & Waters Flow in a Free & Easy Way

LIMERICK
CLARE   GALWAY

OPPOSITE A barren, treeless view over the bogs surrounding the Screeb fishery, Galway. The tiny hut provides 'a little bit of comfort' for sea trout fishermen on wet days such as this. ABOVE Fruits of the land – St Tola goat's cheese salad as served at Drimcong House. OVERLEAF Adare Manor, with its Gothic arches and pinnacles, has a unique atmosphere. Carved baronial ravens bearing the coat of arms of the Dunraven family stand guard over the great oak staircase.

LIMERICK

The Midwest of Ireland, divided by the estuary of the salmon-rich Shannon and bordered by the green Atlantic, is a region of sharp visual contrasts. The lush green landscapes of Limerick are but a short journey away from the curious moonscape of northern Clare and the desolate but beautiful expanse of Connemara. This is stone wall country, and for centuries masons and other craftsmen have used the same stone to fashion the castles for which much of the area is famous. Here, unusually, these great monuments to Ireland's past and her great warrior chieftains are not roofless ruins staring into the sky but are frequently still inhabited. Fittingly, therefore, the region preserves the ancient language: it is one of the main *Gaeltacht* (Gaelic-speaking) areas of Ireland.

The Midwest encompasses two of Ireland's major cities – Limerick, where the Shannon starts to widen on its way to the sea, and the university centre of Galway. Yet the ancient face of the land is still evident: men still go to sea in the wooden-framed boats, covered in tarred canvas, known as currachs; and the blackened square rigs of lovingly restored 'Galway hookers' describe an elegant silhouette far out into Galway Bay. The coasts of these western counties are famous for shellfish, including the native Galway oyster. In fact one is never far from water in these parts, and the whole region is a paradise for fishermen – capital sport can be had pitting one's rod and wits against sea trout and salmon.

At the turn of the century the pretty village of Castleconnell on the main Dublin road just outside Limerick offered perhaps the best salmon fishing in Europe. The record books testify to regular catches of enormous fish weighing some 40–50lb. In those days anglers would have been wielding the massive 17-foot greenheart fly rods made famous by the local Enright family; these are now collectors' items. But time moves on, even in Ireland; and since the construction of the hydroelectric scheme at Ardnacrusha the Castleconnell fishery has diminished considerably. However, a little further downstream at Annacotty, where the Mulcair River joins the Shannon, it is still possible to stand and witness the extraordinary, wonderful sight of hundreds of salmon leaping the falls in early autumn, on their annual spawning run.

For the tourist, Limerick city forms a crossroads: from here one travels south to Cork, south-west to Kerry, north to Galway or east to Dublin, and for those without too much time on their hands there would seem very little reason to tarry. The one exception is Adare, nine miles south of the city on the main Killarney road. Situated alongside the River Maigue, this village, more English than Irish in character, is considered to be among the prettiest in Ireland: it has a charming row of thatched and rose-hung cottages, as well as a traditional coaching inn and an eighteenth-century manor house, all surrounded by ruined castles, abbeys and priories.

Several years ago Daniel Mullane had the foresight to purchase a two-storey cottage for conversion into, in his words, 'an Irish restaurant in the new style'; he called it the Mustard Seed. This small, busy and attractive place is well served by its chef, Thomas O'Leary. Having discovered that there was a renaissance in fine food taking place in Ireland, he returned from working in Switzerland and Bermuda to develop a cuisine that is 'a variation on traditional and country house recipes, governed by the availability of fresh, seasonal produce'. He takes care to use organically grown vegetables – a scarcity in this area except for those foraged from local small farmers or available in Limerick's Saturday market. The menu includes both black and white puddings from the local organic butcher, Tony Sheehey. Harking back to Limerick's former reputation for excellent ham and bacon, Tony has recently set up a business specializing in preservative-free, hand-made sausages, black and white puddings and smoked hams.

Delightful though the village is, its focal point is undoubtedly the great Adare Manor. This, the former seat of the Earls of Dunraven, boasts a splendid room which is the second longest gallery in Europe. The architecture is modelled on that of the Palace of Versailles, and the house is filled with magnificent, ornately carved wooden and marble fireplaces of monumental proportions. Like several Irish manor houses and estates it has recently entered a new era, having been converted into a hotel of the highest standard.

BELOW One of Ireland's greatest architectural jewels, Adare Manor, set amid a thousand-acre estate, is the proud possessor of the second longest gallery in Europe.

OPPOSITE Now glassed in, the former cloisters have become a dining area much favoured for candlelit suppers. Flowers, sparkling glass and crisp white linen add to the ambience.

The Manor is set in rolling parkland with an eighteen-hole golf course; riding, shooting and hunting are among many other activities on offer. For less active guests who just want to stroll and enjoy the view, the thousand acres of parkland include a magnificent stand of trees along the west side of the house, with copper beeches, cedars of Lebanon, Irish peach apples and evergreen and cork oaks.

The aura and architecture of Adare Manor present a rare opportunity to savour a piece of history. The hall and reception area are set under 1830s' Gothic arches, and in the evenings late sunshine may steal through the windows, dappling the light and shimmering on the superb crystal chandelier. Carved ravens stand guard on the massive oak staircase that leads to the famous gallery and the spacious suites. The dining rooms, one of them adapted from the original cloisters, demonstrate fascinating dual character: in part rich and dark and serious in nature, in part sharply light – the richness of Burgundy set side by side with the flintiness of Sancerre.

The chef, Ian McAndrew, has brought with him to Adare Manor an immaculate pedigree, having written several important books on fish and game. He is now busy restoring the estate's extensive walled gardens, so as to improve the quality and extend the variety of vegetables and herbs available for his kitchens. Although a relatively new arrival on the hotel scene, Adare Manor, with its ambience, comfort and fine cooking, is surely one of the finest country house hotels in Ireland and a marvellous base from which to enjoy the sights and pleasures of Limerick.

Veal Fillets with Leek Tagliatelle

Adare Manor's Michelin-star chef, Ian McAndrew, has a reputation for imaginative recipes using the freshest ingredients. Flavours, textures and especially colours play an important part in his cooking. Here he has used contrasting green leeks to complement the veal. He keeps vegetables simple – the leeks have just been blanched and tossed lightly in a little butter.

SERVES 4

4 × 75 g (3 oz) veal fillets, cut 2.5 cm (1 in) thick
4 medium leeks, cleaned, washed and cut into strips 7.5 cm (3 in) long and 6 mm (¼ in) wide
75 g (3 oz) unsalted butter
1 tbsp vegetable oil
50 ml (2 fl oz) Noilly Prat or other dry white French vermouth
450 ml (15 fl oz) hot veal stock
4 tbsp skinned and chopped walnuts
salt and freshly ground pepper

Blanch the leek strips in boiling salted water for 30 seconds. Remove them with a slotted spoon and plunge immediately into a bowl of iced water to refresh them and preserve their colour. Drain the leeks well and set aside.

Heat 50 g (2 oz) of the butter and the oil in a heavy non-stick frying pan and fry the veal fillets for 4 minutes each side until they are lightly browned and still slightly pink in the middle. Remove the fillets and keep warm.

Pour off half the fat in the pan, then add the vermouth and stir well for 1–2 minutes over medium to high heat to deglaze the pan and burn off the alcohol. Add the hot stock and continue stirring, uncovered, until the liquid is reduced by half. Add the chopped walnuts, season with salt and pepper, remove from the heat and keep warm.

Melt the remaining butter in a small pan, toss in the leek strips and season lightly with salt and pepper.

Place each fillet on a warm serving plate and pour the sauce over. Garnish with the leeks and serve with steamed vegetables such as carrots, broccoli and new potatoes.

Rillettes of Pork with Red Wine & Shallot Vinaigrette

This version of rillettes is a cut above the old peasant dish which, in the old days, was prepared at the beginning of winter and stored in stone jars for use throughout the season. The layer of cabbage adds a nice contrasting colour as a garnish, and as in the recipe opposite the vegetable has been cooked in a very simple fashion.

SERVES 6

900 g (2 lb) shoulder or belly pork, rind and bones removed

sea salt and freshly ground black pepper

1 tbsp juniper berries, lightly crushed

1 sprig of dried rosemary, chopped

1 medium Savoy cabbage

chervil to garnish

VINAIGRETTE

300 ml (10 fl oz) red wine

300 ml (10 fl oz) red wine vinegar

6 tbsp peeled and chopped shallots

3 tbsp extra virgin olive oil

First prepare the red wine and shallot vinaigrette. In a medium saucepan, boil together wine and vinegar, uncovered, until they have reduced by half. Meanwhile, in a small saucepan, sweat the shallots in the olive oil for 2 minutes. Add the shallots and oil to the red wine mixture, stir well and cool slowly to allow the flavours to infuse, then season with salt and pepper.

Preheat the oven to 140°C, 275°F, Gas Mark 1.

Trim away any excess fat from the meat and rub it well all over with sea salt. Cut into thick strips with a sharp knife and place in an appropriately sized earthenware dish. Season with the juniper berries, rosemary and freshly ground black pepper. Add a soup ladle of water, put on the lid, and bake in the very slow oven for about 4 hours until the meat has become very soft and tender and all the fat has been rendered down.

Stand a wire sieve over a bowl and turn the contents of the dish into the sieve, allowing the fat to drip through. Purée the pork lightly in a food processor, seasoning with salt and pepper again if necessary. Do not over-process.

Pack the meat tightly into a 600 ml (1 pt) rectangular terrine, keeping warm a small quantity (enough for one thin layer in the terrine). Allow the meat to get cool, and set aside the reserve pork fat for use another time.

Remove any damaged outer leaves from the cabbage, then pull apart the inner leaves. Blanch the leaves for 30 seconds in boiling salted water, remove with a slotted spoon, plunge into iced water and drain immediately. Purée the cabbage and season lightly with salt and pepper.

Once the meat in the terrine has cooled completely, spread a layer of the cabbage purée over the top with the blade of a knife. Top with a thin layer of the reserved rillettes, and set aside to cool again.

To serve, cut the rillettes into slices and arrange on individual serving plates surrounded by the shallot and red wine vinaigrette and garnished with chervil. Serve with toast or just bread.

CLARE

*There's not one girl in the wide, wide world
Like the girl from the County Clare*
THE DARLIN' GIRL FROM CLARE
William Percy French

County Clare, Limerick's neighbour, is bounded on the west by the pounding Atlantic, on the north-west by Galway Bay and in the south-east by the estuary of the Shannon. It is a perfect place for fishermen and seafood lovers, for birdwatchers and those in need of recharging their spiritual batteries.

Almost at the gateway to Clare off the Limerick road is the village of Bunratty, where the local pub and restaurant, the evocatively named Durty Nelly's, and the folk park at Bunratty Castle provide welcome refreshment and entertainment. Alternatively, try MacCloskey's Restaurant run by Gerry and Marie MacCloskey in the old kitchen quarters and cellars of the nineteenth-century Bunratty House. Thanks to Marie, the restaurant is flower-filled and pleasantly cottagey in feel; as for the food, soufflés, both sweet and savoury, are a house speciality. For those with more time on their hands, just a cock's step up the road stands the fairytale turreted Dromoland Castle, now a superbly appointed hotel set gemlike amid expansive woodland. Once the home of the Earls of Inchiquin, it now boasts an eighteen-hole golf course and offers tennis, pheasant shooting, horse riding and other sports. This is the patrician face of Ireland; pampered guests may also like to experience the more rustic side at the local Ballycasey craft centre, where the workshops feature traditional skills including pottery, leatherwork and basketmaking.

Nearly on the coast lies the delightful place popularly known as the Town of the Cascades – Ennistymon. The chief attraction of this pretty little market town on the River Inagh is its two-hundred-metre stretch of waterfalls: when the river is in full spate the normally gentle cascades turn into a spectacular roaring torrent that crashes and tumbles its rocky way to the sea. The Georgian and Victorian shop fronts help to give this town its particular character; many have

been carefully restored while others, still charming, peel and crumble in colourful dereliction. The townspeople treasure their heritage and work tirelessly for its preservation, encouraging shopkeepers to retain the atmosphere that has remained virtually unspoilt for some two hundred years.

In the hinterland of Ennistymon two special local cheeses are made: St Tola, a goat's cheese, and Kilshanny, a Gouda type. At Inagh Lodge, since 1980 Meg and Derrick Gordon's herd of sixty goats have been producing the milk that goes into the delicious white, soft St Tola and the oval, hard Lough Caum. The Gordons produce about two tons of cheese every year and supply it to some of Ireland's leading award-winning restaurants, including Drimcong House in County Galway and Adare Manor in County Limerick. Meg and Derrick also keep bees, and Derrick

LEFT The herd of Saanen goats at Inagh Lodge in County Clare are snow-white, in pristine condition and, like all goats, very curious about everything! From their milk Meg and Derrick Gordon make St Tola and Lough Caum cheeses, eagerly sought after by the best restaurants and cheesemongers in the region.

BELOW LEFT Kilshanny, a Gouda-type cheese, is made in a range of flavours by Janette and Peter Nibbering from unpasteurized cow's milk. Here Peter towels the rind of one of this maturing cheeses. The cheese can be bought from Limerick market or at the farm itself, where visitors can also obtain bed and breakfast.

recommends eating St Tola Greek-fashion with his favourite honey, derived from the nectar of the whitethorn blossom.

Kilshanny, the other speciality of these parts, is a firm, full cream cheese that comes in several sizes and flavours including garden herb, garlic, green and red pepper, and cumin seed. Janette and Peter Nibbering make their cheese in the coolness of three converted north-facing rooms in their small guest house and, despite the limitations of space, the cheesemaking is conducted in spotless conditions. Peter takes immense care at every stage, personally turning and towelling the maturing rounds one by one until they are ready for market.

The local Liscannor stone features strongly in the architecture of these parts, and has spread its influence to other parts of Ireland too. Further north the great windswept cliff faces of Moher raise their thousand-foot wrinkled brows to gaze out over the Aran Islands and onwards to the mountains of Connemara. The breathtaking view is best at sunset or in stormy weather, but all too often a fog or drifting sea fret denies the expected drama. Along their meandering five-mile span these cliffs are alive with the raucous clamour of countless colonies of seabirds – puffins, fulmars, kittiwakes and shags. For sportsmen, the waters at the feet of the cliffs and around Liscannor Bay provide good shark fishing for porbeagle and spectacular views of the rock face towering majestically above.

Doolin is a centre of Irish traditional music, for which County Clare is famous. Here, in the legendary Gus O'Connor's pub, you can spend an enjoyable evening listening to the sound of *Port an Bheal* (unaccompanied traditional Irish singing), the beat of the *bodhran* (a traditional Irish drum) or the lilt of the pipes, fiddles, flutes and concertinas. Several bars and restaurants flourish here, offering a selection of good fish, game and vegetarian fare; one I liked is Bruach na hAille, meaning bank of the river.

After a hectic night in Doolin, taking the waters in Lisdoonvarna may be the best advice! Since the eighteenth century this small town has been famous for its sulphur and iron spa, and nowadays it offers entertainment, too. During July visitors can take part in the

local folk music festival, while in September a more curious ritual – a match-making festival – is held here. For those in search of a different kind of cure I can recommend the Curtin family's roadside tavern with its eccentric mural and its good, honest pub grub. And at Brigitte and Peter Curtin's newest venture, the Lisdoonvarna Smoke House, you can treat yourself to finest-quality smoked salmon, trout and mackerel.

From here there are a number of ways of getting to Ballyvaughan on Galway Bay. There is a scenic coast route to the west by Black Head, and a corkscrew road through the middle of that extraordinary stretch of landscape called the Burren. However the one that I prefer turns south, passing the ruins of Leamaneh Castle, and continues by an ancient burial chamber, the Poulnabrone portal dolmen, to the top of the Burren.

The great cliffs of Moher facing the broad Atlantic are a haven for seabirds and a paradise for ornithologists. For those with other interests, good shark fishing can be enjoyed in the waters round about. Mist and fog frequently obscure this magnificent natural feature on the Clare coast – here they have been caught in late afternoon against a calm sea, awaiting their evening blanket of mist drifting in from the ocean.

Perhaps the most fascinating feature in County Clare, the Burren is a rocky botanical wonderland littered with pewter-coloured karst, shale and tumbling stone walls that create a sense of primitive, almost Stone Age remoteness. This effect is broken only by patches of peaty topsoil lying thinly on the limestone bedrock. The day's sunshine is stored up within the limestone and combines with a softly moist, frost-free climate to nurture an abundance of rare and exotic plants not found together anywhere else in Europe: tiny alpines from the mountain passes jostle for growing space with sun-lovers from the Mediterranean.

From the silent marvels of the Burren one descends to earth in the form of the village of Ballyvaughan, nestling snugly in a little fishing bay on the north coast of Clare. Yet here too are found quiet and privacy, and the place is fast becoming a favourite of those who value these qualities and wish to preserve them. For the afternoon visitor Mrs O'Donoghue, a fanatical gardener, runs a splendid cottage tea room. Those staying on into the evening can make a booking – to avoid disappointment, for it is justly popular – at Claire's Restaurant. Several years ago Claire Walsh and her husband opened a shop selling local crafts, and since it did not occupy all her time Claire decided to open a restaurant in the rear of the shop. Its comprehensive menu includes excellent fresh soup of the day, followed by main courses with a bias towards local fish and seafood. On a recent visit I was too early for dinner and Claire guided me to Monk's Quayside Bar; it was full of several nationalities feasting on very fine dishes of fish chowder, mussels, crab claws and salmon.

GALWAY

Heading north again one passes through the village of Kinvara, famous in the summer for the Galway hooker regatta. Before any reader starts to use his or her imagination too freely, I should perhaps explain that in Galway hookers are picturesque, masted fishing vessels!

Still in this area, barely a good Irish mile west of Kilcolgan, make the detour to Moran's of the Weir to sample the best of the local native oysters, reared in the unpolluted Atlantic waters. During the autumn Galway Oyster Festival – a time for merriment everywhere, for simple slurping of oysters and quaffing of Guinness in unpretentious pubs, to the sound of buskers in the street outside – people from all over Ireland and abroad make an annual pilgrimage to Willy Moran's riverside bar. This former world champion oyster opener prises open his succulent molluscs backwards, using a small bandaged penknife. In July he marshals the local fishermen to draw the seabed for oysters, transferring them to his holding beds in the tidal shallows close to his pub. At low tide during the season, which starts in September and runs to the following April (remember the old adage: 'Eat oysters only when there's an ''r'' in the month'), he gathers them in buckets for sale to regular customers and passers-by.

Oysters as fresh and as good as these and still smelling saltily of the sea are supposed to have weird and wonderful effects on the eater. One local woman, considerably younger than her husband, told me that he had proposed to her in Moran's after just such a feast. Ever since then, their monthly visits to the pub during the season have (who can say?) helped them to produce and rear an expanding, happy family. Apart from the oysters the Moran family serves one of the best pints of Guinness in all Ireland and excellent pub food.

Back on the main road, look out for McDonagh's charming thatched pub at Oranmore en route to Galway city. Standing at the mouth of yet another salmon-teeming river, in the summer months Galway is a vibrant, cosmopolitan place – many languages, including Irish, can be heard in the streets – and it is very much a favourite with the young. Fortunate in having its industry concentrated on the outskirts, and

'Little fields with boulders dotted./Grey-stone shoulders saffron-spotted,' wrote John Betjeman of the Burren, Clare's fantastic moonscape region. The limestone rock, known as karst, is typically this dull pewter colour. Between the cracks slivers of soils are warmed up by the sun, and this apparently barren area gives birth to thousands of wild flowers in spring and summer.

Perhaps only in Ireland could graffiti be raised to the level of an art form. This is a fishing supplies store in Kinvara, County Galway – as if there could be any doubt of that.

in having no sprawling suburbs, it is also blessed with a one-way traffic system that really works. The tiny side streets are peppered with fascinating little shops, bars and restaurants; it also boasts quaint quayside walks and 'The Bridge'. Sited near the cathedral, and spanning the famous salmon fishery, 'The Bridge' is definitely the local *paseo*. Here people from all over the world mingle and congregate with the locals to peer into the Corrib River's crystal-clear water and see the salmon queueing up, often in thousands, to ascend into the quieter flats above the weir. From the gallery parapets they witness the take or rejection of the anglers' fly – taking partisan sides with cheers of *olé!* or simply 'ah'! – in the captivating battle of wits between fish and fisherman.

Galway's most famous landmark is the Spanish Arch, all that remains of the city's former ancient fortifications. It is a reminder of the days when Spanish merchant ships unloaded their casks of wine and Andalusian treasures here. And – a more accidental Iberian connection, this – some say that Connemara's famous ponies are the descendants of Arab stallions which scrambled their way ashore after ships of the ill-fated Armada were wrecked on the rocky shores.

The social event of the year is Galway Races. It is as much a carnival as a race meeting, and some racegoers spend all their time among the sideshows and in the beer tent and never get near the horses. No matter – the point is to get into the spirit of this colourful occasion.

West of Galway city is an area steeped in the oldest folklore and culture, still preserving the Gaelic traditions of speech, story-telling, music, drama and dress. This whole area, up as far as Killary Harbour, is known as Connemara. Spiddal is the nerve-centre for those wishing to tour this still wild region or to sail to the Aran Islands, sitting far out in Galway Bay; these rugged barren islands, where Gaelic is still spoken and traditional costume often worn, are the site of Dun Aengus, one of Europe's finest prehistoric monuments. The village of Barna, on the way to Spiddal, provides an appropriate stop to savour the tradition of fine hospitality shared by Celtic cousins: a Breton restaurant called Ty Ar Mor, housed in a converted cottage near the tiny pier, is well worth a visit.

PREVIOUS PAGES The fruits of
County Galway. Clockwise,
from top left: clams;
langoustines, known in
Ireland as Dublin Bay prawns;
Pacific oysters – now
commercially farmed here,
they grow to at least double
the size of the natives; mussels;
giant king scallops; lobsters;
winkles; and finally the true
native Galway Bay oysters.
Michael Reynolds of Sawer's
in Dublin's Chatham Street
always has a fine supply of
Galway seafood when
available.

In winter, Connemara is carpeted in ginger-brown
and amber and wrapped in a shroud of haunting,
romantic mist. In summer this giant rockery is bordered with stretches of white, gold and coral beaches,
darts of copper reflecting the acid waters of dozens of
peat-stained rivers and lakes. Rocky and barren, treeless and divided by a maze of flinty, rambling walls, it
has a coastline peppered with rock pools full of pela
crabs, winkles, mussels, shrimps and sea urchins, in
sight of dolphins riding the huge Atlantic breakers that
roll endlessly towards the coast. During a trip along its
coastline you can stare into the infinite distance as if
standing on the edge of the world. Inland is the spectacular vista of the Inagh valley, wrapped in its lush
shawl of coniferous forests and falling between two
mountain ranges, the Twelve Pins and the Maamturk.

County Galway is the home of the mighty Lough
Corrib, known familiarly as 'The Corrib'. At over 68
square miles in area the biggest lake in the Irish Republic, it is dotted with hundreds of islands edged by
reed-fringed shallows and is the most popular trout
and salmon lake in the country, particularly at mayfly
time. It draws many visitors, especially those who
enjoy sailing, to its lakeside villages. Fishermen – as
virtually everywhere in Ireland – are also attracted like
moths to a lamp, for throughout history the Corrib has
yielded catches of leviathan trout. As far back as 1860
one of 24 lb was landed, and it is still quite common for
trout with weights in double figures to be caught here.
Usually these huge fish are accidentally caught by fishermen trolling for salmon, but more consistent catches
of large trout certainly result from adopting a specialist
approach.

Just off the road through Moycullen and close to the
Corrib is Drimcong House. This is the domain of
Gerry Galvin, unquestionably the chef laureate of Irish
cuisine. Gerry first came to prominence at the Vintage
Restaurant in the gastronomic honeypot of Kinsale,
where he was a leading light of the local Good Food
Circle. With his wife Marie he then moved to Moycullen and opened the superb restaurant at the lovely
seventeenth-century Drimcong House. In less than a
month they had converted it from a run-down private
home to a restaurant with its present comfortable at-

Galway is Irish in a sense in which Dublin and Belfast and Cork and Derry are not Irish but cosmopolitan. Its people, their speech, their dress, their swarthy complexions, their black hair, their eyes like blue flames, excite the imagination with curious surmises.

Galway city – technically, it is only Galway town – is to the discoverer of Ireland something like what Chapman's Homer *was to Keats. It is a clue, a provocation, an enticement.*
GALWAY OF THE RACES
Robert Wilson Lynd

mosphere – surely a record. The surrounding gentle gardens include extensive lawns and a small lake, home to perch, carp and pike, which Gerry uses at his discretion. The sweetly flowing stream that feeds the lake also helps to feed the house: from one tiny original plant, luxuriant and carefully tended watercress now flourishes, waiting fresh for the kitchen table. The vegetable garden produces a crisp and succulent crop of salad vegetables, a wonderful array of scented herbs and an abundance of juicy summer fruit. Marie has laid out her herb and vegetable garden in a clever and visually impressive series of small beds, while the front of the house is embellished with carefully manicured flower gardens. If you are there in summer you cannot fail to admire the fanned climbing rose trained over the wall – an imposing backdrop to the discipline and fastidiousness of the whole garden.

The old courtyard adjacent to the house is like a Galway version of the Ark. If Noah had been an Irish farmer, he certainly would have loved to live here amongst the chickens, Muscovy ducks, dogs and cats, donkeys and sheep; and, like Gerry, he too would have taken in an injured barn owl if he had found one. Home-produced food abounds, and Mrs Keady, an old and faithful member of the team at Drimcong, is often seen crossing the courtyard with a basket laden with fresh eggs for the house.

Inside, polished oak, fine Irish glass and turf fires in the winter months create the perfect ambience to complement the fine cooking. Today Gerry Galvin's name is on the tip of every gourmet's tongue in Ireland; he is quietly fanning the flames of a gastronomic revolution, born of his understanding of the potential of the country's fresh produce – cheeses, fish, game and wildlife. He is also generous enough to share the secrets of his kitchen: the four-day cookery course that he runs in November each year is justifiably popular among both men and women.

This quiet, softly spoken chef oversees his tiny kitchen with ball-bearing precision. His gentle gestures rise and fall like a seasoned choreographer directing his corps de ballet. To him each night's dinner is treated as a gala performance, an opening night, his dining room a stage for dramatically fine food.

OVERLEAF The view southwest across a small section of the mighty Corrib between Conn and the village of Maam in County Galway. Twenty miles long, Lough Corrib is the largest lake in the Irish Republic. All around are villages where fishermen stay – for this, justifiably, is the most popular lake in Ireland among anglers. The trout are of vast proportions, and the salmon fishing is free.

Roulade of Rabbit with Nettle & Mustard Sauces

*'Rabbit has a fine, mild, gamey flavour and is inexpensive to buy.
Nettle tops should be picked only when young in the spring, with scissors
and rubber gloves. They make a flavoursome, nutritious alternative to
spinach in soups. In Ireland today the nettle is very little used in
cooking, although it appeared in old Irish cookbooks.'* Gerry Galvin

SERVES 4

1 × 1.4 kg (3 lb) wild rabbit,
  skinned and boned

1 egg

2 tsp grain mustard

2 tsp Irish whiskey

2 tsp marrow (or similar)
  chutney

100 g (4 oz) young nettle tops,
  well washed and dried

50 g (2 oz) softened butter

150 ml (5 fl oz) dry white wine

salt and freshly ground pepper

12 back bacon rashers

12 shelled pistachio nuts or
  hazelnuts

NETTLE SAUCE

100 g (4 oz) young nettle tops,
  well washed and dried

300 ml (10 fl oz) single cream

$1/4$ tsp freshly grated nutmeg

2 tsp lemon juice

MUSTARD SAUCE

300 ml (10 fl oz) single cream

1 tbsp grain mustard

Preheat the oven to 200°C, 400°F, Gas Mark 6.

Prepare the nettle sauce first. Bring the nettles and cream to the boil, then turn off the heat. Leave to infuse.

Make a savoury mousse by processing together the rabbit leg meat, the egg, the mustard, the whiskey and the chutney.

Soften the nettle tops in a pan with 25 g (1 oz) of the butter and the white wine until the mixture is a green colour and resembles cooked spinach. Season to taste with salt and pepper.

Spread a sheet of aluminium foil 45 cm (1$1/2$ ft) square on your worktop, and brush all over lightly with the remaining butter. Lay the rashers side by side on the foil and spoon the mousse across the middle of the rashers like a long sausage. You want the ends of the rashers to be able to fold over and contain the mousse.

Sprinkle the nuts evenly on top of the mousse. Spoon the thick nettle mixture along the length of the mousse, on top of the nuts.

Place the remaining rabbit meat, from the saddle, on top of and at either side of the nettles and mousse. Season with black pepper only.

Enclose the rabbit 'joint' in the rashers by rolling up the foil into a cylindrical shape and pinching the ends tight. Roast for 45–50 minutes.

Finish the nettle sauce by bringing the infusion of nettles and cream back to the boil, then flavour with nutmeg and lemon juice. Liquidize, taste and season if necessary. Make the mustard sauce by mixing the cream and mustard with plenty of freshly ground pepper, then reducing to a pouring consistency.

When the joint is cooked, peel off the aluminium foil and carve. Serve accompanied by the nettle and mustard sauces.

Marinated Dried Apricots with Sherry & Almond Liqueur

A handy winter standby for serving hot or cold with custard or ice cream, or cooked in a crumble. It's delicious with Honeyed Cream Cheese (below). Gerry Galvin offers an array of marinated fruits in winter and this one is always a great success.

FILLS A 450 G (1 LB) JAR
225 g (8 oz) dried apricots
50 g (2 oz) caster sugar
zest of $^1/_2$ orange

zest of $^1/_2$ lemon
50–85 ml (2–3 fl oz) dry sherry
1 tbsp Amaretto (almond liqueur)

Put the apricots, sugar, orange and lemon zest with 600 ml (1 pt) water into a saucepan and bring to the boil, stirring occasionally.

Simmer for 5 minutes to thicken the syrup, and for another 20 to soften the fruit.

Sterilize the jar, and keep warm until ready for filling with the apricots, sherry and Amaretto.

Leave the apricots to mature for at least 10 days before use. This will allow all the subtle flavours to blend together in the most delicious way.

Honeyed Cream Cheese

This cream cheese mixture goes well with most fruit, and is a useful substitute for whipped cream.

For four people, simply cream together 225 g (8 oz) fromage blanc or curd cheese, 1 tbsp runny honey, 1 tbsp single cream, juice of 1 lemon and $^1/_4$ tsp salt. Keep cool. Obviously if you use a herb-flavoured honey, it will add more interest to the finished dish. Or you could flavour the mixture with a liqueur of your choice, or with a pinch of spice such as cinnamon or mace.

Goat's Cheese Salad & Herb Pesto

This simple recipe uses a 50 g (2 oz) slice of a St Tola log (made by Meg Gordon in County Clare).

Make a herb pesto by blending together 50 g (2 oz) fresh basil leaves, 3 tbsp pine kernels, 3 peeled garlic cloves and 175 ml (6 fl oz) olive oil. When smooth, season and mix in 2 tsp grated Parmesan.

Top the slice of cheese with a teaspoon of pesto, and cook under a hot grill for a minute. Place the cheese on a serving plate and surround with selected salad leaves, vegetables and herbs (see photograph).

Grilled Lake Trout with Wild Garlic

The wild garlic in this dish is properly called ramsons, a broad-leafed garlic which grows liberally in the damp woodland round Drimcong in late spring. If ramsons is unavailable, use a mixture of young leeks and some garlic.

SERVES 4

4 trout fillets, each about 175 g (6 oz) in weight

65 g (2¹/₂ oz) butter

2 shallots, finely chopped

225 g (8 oz) wild garlic leaves, roughly chopped

freshly grated nutmeg

juice of ¹/₂ lemon

SAUCE

50 g (2 oz) wild garlic leaves

100 g (4 oz) soft butter

4 tbsp single cream

2 tbsp dry white wine

juice of ¹/₂ lemon

To start the sauce off, roughly chop the wild garlic. Then place the soft butter and garlic in a food processor and process until well mixed. Chill in the refrigerator until it has solidified a little.

Bring the cream and wine for the sauce to the boil and reduce by half.

Then over a low heat swirl in the chilled wild garlic butter, little by little. Season to taste with a little lemon juice and keep warm.

In a separate pan, heat 50 g (2 oz) of the butter and cook the shallot for a minute or two, then toss in the garlic leaves for a further minute. Season with freshly grated nutmeg, salt and pepper. Keep warm.

Preheat the grill.

Melt the remaining butter, mix in the lemon juice, and brush this over the trout fillets. Season them with salt and pepper. Grill the fish fillets for about 5 minutes, turning them over halfway through the cooking time.

Serve the grilled fish on a wild garlic and shallot bed with the sauce in a circle around the trout.

Leaving Drimcong, to the north-west, on the main Clifden road at Oughterard, I often turn off to travel by the side of the Corrib to visit a friend and fellow photographer. Here, too, is Currarevagh House. If you like an element of surprise it is a definite advantage to arrive at Currarevagh after dark, and in late spring. At first light you will hear the dawn chorus of what seems like just about every known songbird, prompting the sun to carve its way across the Corrib. Gradually it peers through a gap in the trees to illuminate the exotic displays of rhododendrons, azaleas, camellias and sweet-smelling laurel blossom in the gardens and on the lawns that slope off gently to the shore of the Corrib. Gazing out towards the horizon and the tiny islands of this mighty lake, you may be slightly confused by a clump of palm trees to your right. Is this the tropics? Suddenly a trout rises, and a definite statement by a blackbird warning off a cuckoo reminds you that you are in Ireland.

Currarevagh House, run by Harry and June Hodgson, is an Irish country house in the true sense. An early Victorian manor in the Italian style set in some 150 acres of woodland that skirt the Corrib, it has been in the hands of the Hodgson family since it was built and has been run as a guest house for the past fifty years. It represents the type of country house that is my personal favourite, reminding me of the qualities and richness of an old tweed jacket, handed down from father to son, getting a little frayed at the edges, but developing an indefinable, unique patina.

Harry, ensconced in the hallway which doubles as reception area and bar, takes care of welcoming the guests and is a very good host indeed. June, apart from looking after the kitchen, gets up at 5.30 every morning to collect flowers and shrubs from the garden, delighting visitors with colourful and ever-changing displays. Hospitality here reflects a special feeling of being 'at home' – but what a home! This is like being a guest at a country house party in the palmy days before the First World War. Deep, comfortable chairs and open fires make afternoon tea a real pleasure; and in the bright and airy dining room, with its range of curious table shapes, the Art Deco coffee pots contribute to the delightful air of eccentricity.

The food at Currarevagh is very traditional and quite simple, but of the highest standards. At 9 a.m. a gong is struck to summon the guests to breakfast – an Edwardian-type breakfast, laid out on a sideboard, that includes such classic dishes as kedgeree. The traditional bacon and eggs here have an inimitable flavour, which is particularly noticeable in the accompanying delicately fried bread. June told me how she preserves the good old-fashioned taste: she renders down lamb's fat, and uses that in the frying pan instead of the late twentieth century's ubiquitous vegetable oils.

Dinner, too, is heralded by the gong – punctually at 8 p.m. There is a five-course menu, with 'seconds' for those who still have room after June's generous helpings first time round. The cooking is complemented by a good wine list, which always contains excellent house wines. Main courses usually include a good roast or fresh fish, followed by such delicious greed-encouragers as steamed treacle pudding, a monumental bombe alaska or white chocolate mousse.

To help wear off the effects of all this good living – and indeed to work up an appetite for more – all the expected sports and pastimes are available in the vicinity. Tranquil Lough Corrib awaits the fisherman eager to tempt brown trout, salmon, pike and perch to his rod, and boats and professional ghillies can be hired by those who have not brought their own. Indeed, one of the distinguishing features of the house is a group of several large specimens of the aforementioned Corrib trout, stuffed and encased in the hallway. But if fishing is not for you, why not take one of Currarevagh's hearty packed lunches and go swimming in the clear, unpolluted waters of the lake, or else potter around the many islands.

Continuing the lakeside drive from Currarevagh is particularly worthwhile, for despite the fact that it ends in a cul de sac it offers a spectacular view. The unmissable traditional thatched cottage near the end of the drive is owned by my friend Liam Jordan, who wisely keeps it as an enviable private retreat.

After leaving Oughterard travel through Maam Cross to the pleasantly Victorian Cashel House, situated – with its own small beach – on the rocky tidal

The snug at Cashel House, on the shores of Cashel Bay. With its warm-hued decor, comfortable furniture and turf fire, surely there could be no more welcoming place for tea on a chilly winter afternoon. The fifty-acre estate includes prize-winning gardens and a hard tennis court, and the whole place is a haven of tranquillity.

inlet of Cashel Bay on the south-western edge of Connemara. Here, amidst award-winning gardens that in spring are a riot of brilliant azaleas and rhododendrons tempered by the cool elegance of camellias, Dermot and Kay McEvilly have nurtured a hotel that well deserves its international renown. Since the visit of Charles de Gaulle in 1969, Cashel House has become especially popular with French visitors, who know a thing or two about good food and wine and are quick to recognize excellence wherever they find it. They have contributed in no small way to an atmosphere in which a whole new style of cooking, still using excellent fresh Irish produce, has evolved.

The house speciality is lobster; Dermot and Kay also have a way with oysters and serve a superb fish soup. A sharp apple sorbet is served between courses to cleanse the palate and prepare one for the next delicious offering. Behind the facade of this efficiently run hotel good-humoured Dermot, cigar dangling from his lips, stands in his office, bespectacled, slightly rakish, surrounded by the bits and pieces of his small computer which show that modern methods can be accommodated in this kind of enterprise without in any way detracting from the personality of the place.

Serious sea trout country from July to the beginning of October, the region includes the famous Ballinahinch River and Lake. From amidst the beautiful scenery of the Twelve Pins and the Maamturk Mountains they are fed by tumbling streams through a descending series of pools and flats that flow to freedom in Cashel Bay below Toombeola Bridge. The Ballinahinch River has always been superb for salmon, and today it offers a good example of the way in which a river can be properly groomed to suit the fly fisherman; fishing on the river can be arranged at Ballinahinch Castle, now a hotel but once owned by an Indian maharajah. For non-fishermen, the trip through Roundstone and Ballyconneely to Clifden provides a series of fine beaches and rewarding landscapes to walk among, photograph or simply delight in. The English nineteenth-century novelist Thackeray was certainly delighted, describing it as 'the most beautiful district it is ever the fortune of a traveller to examine'.

Clifden is a prosperous, busy town with a charming character. I recommend it as a stop either for lunch or dinner at O'Grady's Seafood Restaurant. This is an unpretentious, modestly priced little restaurant serving superb food: the specialities include seafood chowder and garlic mussels. It is run by the enterprising and friendly O'Grady family who have their own small trawler, guaranteeing a continuous supply of the best fresh fish. For some gentle exercise after lunch or before dinner, wander through the town to shop for some of the traditional tweed. The town's other claim to fame is the annual Connemara Pony Show.

From simple restaurant move on now to gracious living – though always, being Ireland, with good food and a friendly welcome. Paddy and Anne Foyle's Rosleague Manor, at Letterfrack, overlooks Ballinakill Bay and 'The Diamond', a small mountain in the Connemara National Park (so called because it glistens in the rain). The views from the summit are well worth the climb. Rosleague is a favourite of mine with its elegant, masculine dining room, hung with oil paintings and candlelit for dinner. The charming Regency house is discreetly comfortable, with tastefully furnished public rooms and plenty of lovingly polished antique pieces that you feel are part of a well-cared-for family home rather than a hotel. Paddy and Anne Foyle (brother and sister) were literally born into the hotel business. The family have had a hotel nearby in Clifden for over a hundred years.

Some Connacht garb
Around me clings,
Some savage strain,
An uncouth air;
I'd rather hear
The fiddle strings
Of tinker folk
At Galway Fair.
BALLADE OF A DUBLIN SALON
Michael Joseph MacManus

Baked Stuffed Mussels with Garlic

'This is a simple dish, which has stood the test of time. Shellfish and molluscs were cooked by our ancestors in their own juices in the half-shell on an open fire on what was then known as a griddle. By using contemporary flavourings and seasoning and following the old method, this recipe combines past and present.' Jack O'Grady

SERVES 4–6

1.8 kg (4 lb) wild mussels	225 g (8 oz) butter
salt	6 shallots, finely
120 ml (4 fl oz) white wine	chopped
parsley stalks	4 tbsp chopped parsley
1 tbsp fresh lemon juice	4 garlic cloves, crushed
	225 g (8 oz) breadcrumbs

Clean the mussels well, and discard any that remain open after tapping sharply with the blunt side of a knife. Place mussels in a large pan with a little sea-water (or salted water), the wine, parsley stalks and lemon juice. Add the lid and cook only until they open, a few minutes. Discard any that remain closed. Discard top halves of mussel shells. Reserve the mussels in the half-shell.

In a sauté pan, melt half the butter and sweat the shallots, chopped parsley and garlic for a few min-utes. Add the breadcrumbs and mix thoroughly, adding the remainder of the butter to bring it to a coating consistency. Simmer for about 5 minutes to allow the garlic to infuse.

Preheat the grill.

Place mussels in the half-shell on a heatproof plate and cover with the breadcrumb mixture. Glaze under the preheated grill until golden brown. Serve immediately with lemon wedges and a sprig or two of parsley to garnish.

The dining room at Rosleague Manor has an elegant, old-world look that belies its age – it was only built some twenty years ago. The effect is achieved with mellow furniture and chandeliers, while oil paintings and an arrangement of plates embellish the walls.

Here you can go painting under the skilled eye of a local artist; alternatively you can burn off the huge, traditional breakfasts by riding, cycling, playing tennis or swimming from the beautiful beaches; and, of course, my favourite sport of fishing can be indulged! The local fishermen from Cleggan provide wonderful fresh fish for the kitchens at Rosleague, supplemented by superb Connemara lamb and beef, while herbs and vegetables come from the hotel garden or from growers in the locality.

Since Ireland – and particularly regions such as the West of Ireland – is famous the world over for horse breeding, it would be improper to leave Galway without a few words on the great October Fair at Ballinasloe, supposedly the oldest horse fair in Europe. Originally a huge market fair firmly rooted in the times when Ireland still had its own High King, it now provides an annual gathering point for gypsies, tinkers and all varieties of travelling people. Once, like all fairs, it was where labour was hired; and, since communications were then much poorer and people met up much less frequently, it was where match-making took place. Legend tells of one farmer who set off in a pony and trap with his daughter but returned home with the daughter but minus the pony – the prospective bridegroom obviously liked the horse better! Even at the end of the twentieth century the almost medieval feeling remains, with booths and sideshows and shysters, and horses showing their paces up and down the streets to the shouts and whistles of onlookers, and bargains being struck in the time-honoured way – for the first week of October, the horse fair *is* the town.

Ragoût of Shellfish

'All our fish is caught locally and loaded on the pier in front of the hotel,
so it's almost on the doorstep. The recipe is one of several we have that
use local produce.' Patrick Foyle

SERVES 4

1 small lobster, about 900 g
  (2 lb) in weight
4 × 50 g (2 oz) pieces fresh
  wild salmon
about 20 large prawns
8 scallops, sliced horizontally
4 × 50 g (2 oz) fresh fillets of
  white fish
(turbot, brill, sole or a mixture)
150–200 ml (5–7 fl oz) fish
  stock (see method below
  and page 60)
at least 50 g (2 oz) butter
150 ml (5 fl oz) dry Martini
1 tbsp dry white wine
150 ml (5 fl oz) single cream
lemon wedges to garnish

It would be better to add the lobster raw to the pan after the other fish and shellfish have been briefly cooked, but it can prove a bit tricky to extract the meat quickly. So instead, lightly boil the lobster separately first – about 10 minutes – then carefully split the tail and claws without breaking up the meat too much. Extract the meat and keep warm. Reserve all the juices which run out while shelling.

Keep the lobster cooking water too, as the basis for the fish stock; use all the trimmings of the lobster and other fish and some flavourings, then reduce it down to about 150–200 ml (5–7 fl oz).

Cook the salmon pieces gently in butter until *almost* done, about 1–2 minutes. Remove and add the prawns and sliced scallops, and again only cook until *almost* done, another 1–2 minutes. Remove,

and add the white fish fillets to the same pan juices. Remove these as soon as you feel they are on the point of being done, about a couple of minutes. Keep all the fish warm.

Add the Martini, fish stock and lobster juices to the buttery pan. Boil fiercely until the liquid starts to reduce. Make sure the Martini doesn't overpower the flavours; if so, add a drop of dry white wine. Finally add the cream, and boil a little more, but gently, and it should thicken a little. If it doesn't, add a little butter and stir into the sauce.

Add all the fish pieces and reheat *very* gently, taking care that the fish does not break up.

Arrange equal amounts of fish on four deepish plates. Spoon over the sauce and serve straightaway, garnished with lemon wedges.

*The town of Ballinasloe is seated upon a river, the
name of which I neglected to inquire. It is much
frequented by saints and cattle-dealers, carries on a
smart trade in sheep and proselytes, and Bibles and
bullocks are 'thick as leaves on Vallombrosa' . . .
pigs and popery are prohibited.*
WILD SPORTS OF THE WEST
William Hamilton Maxwell

The place derives its name from the Gaelic *Beal Atha
na Sluaighe* – mouth of the ford – the point where the
former kings of Connacht crossed on their journey to
Tara, seat of the High King. A small tribal village grew
up around the ford, and by the fifth century it had
become an important bartering place for the large
numbers of horses in the locality: the surrounding
limestone pastures are rich in calcium, which help to
create sturdy stock with strong, healthy bones.

Perhaps the most famous horse sold here was
Marengo, Napoleon's mount at Waterloo. Thousands
of cavalry horses were bought here for the many wars
of the nineteenth century; sadly, the Irish draught
horse was nearly wiped out at the time of the First
World War, for it was purchased in vast quantities to
pull the heavy guns through the mud of Flanders.

The first official fair was held in the early eighteenth
century, but its peak years were in the 1850s, when the
building of the railways made it accessible to far
greater numbers of people. At this time an estimated
thirty thousand would pack into the little town in Fair
Week, during which some four thousand horses,
twenty thousand cattle and a hundred thousand sheep
would be sold. The story is told that one visitor,
unable to use the road because it was completely
blocked with sheep, walked from the station to the site
of the fair along their backs! Even if, being Ireland, the
tale is somewhat apocryphal, it makes the point that,
then as now, the occasion was not just a horse fair but
an agricultural fair too. Today show-jumping, livestock and other agricultural produce, dog shows and
fashion parades all contribute to the business and bustle
and excitement at Ballinasloe.

But the old nomad spirit still lingers on. The fair has
always had its quota of travellers, tramps and thieves.
Today the traveller will as often be dealing in cars as in
horses, for modes of transport have changed. Gleam-
ing Range Rovers and ornate chrome-bedecked

mobile homes with acid-etched windows stand wheel to wheel with barrel-topped caravans over which a riot of painted roses scramble for footing – smart double-glazed bungalows side by side with homely thatched cottages. A mixture of modern-day nomads, their drivers form the core of the hand-slapping and wheeler-dealing. Rumours abound of all sorts of trickery, known to old hands and handlers of horses – of ginger suppositories giving renewed vigour to a tired old nag, or lame horses being led by a man with an even more distracting and dispirited limp. Showmen strut in striped suits with waxed gold locks and huge 22-carat rings. Be careful – the pubs stay open until well past midnight.

OPPOSITE Horses of all kinds change hands rapidly during the week-long livestock market at Ballinasloe.

ABOVE Horse trading is thirsty work and during the Fair the thirty or so pubs in Ballinsloe are open well over sixteen hours a day.

BELOW LEFT Two old hands in deep discussion about the day's bargains.

LEFT They say, 'When it rains it rains' in these parts, and today it's every man for himself.

In Ireland, all you need to make a story is two men with completed characters — say, a parish priest and his sexton.
THE CAT AND THE CORNFIELD
Bryan MacMahon

$\mathscr{I}$T'S HOME, SWEET HOME WHERE'ER I ROAM THROUGH LANDS & WATERS WIDE

MAYO   SLIGO
DONEGAL   LEITRIM
ROSCOMMON

ABOVE Organic strawberries and raspberries from the walled garden at Temple House, Ballymote, County Sligo. OPPOSITE Hargadon's in Sligo town must be one of the nicest pubs in the whole county. Thankfully, unlike many of its brethren it has resisted 'improvement' and has therefore retained its delightful, genuinely Irish atmosphere. It is deservedly a favourite watering-hole for the thirsty traveller.

MAYO

Lacking the southern warmth of the Gulf Stream enjoyed by the likes of Cork and Kerry, and battered by persistent north-west winds, this is perhaps the wettest part of Ireland. It is an area of mild winters, though the summers are unreliable. But in compensation for the rain there is no intensive farming here, nor mass tourism; it is also an area of great trout lakes and prolific salmon rivers. For me, it is at once the wildest and the richest part of the country, and without doubt it is the area with which I feel the deepest affinity. Like much of Ireland it is a place of marked contrasts, from the rugged mountain fastnesses of Mayo with its vast loughs to the Lake District and County Sligo – the far gentler landscape of Yeats Country.

Here, too, are Donegal's seascapes, her thrashing breakers and endless miles of deserted beaches where no wandering footprints have yet been recorded. Leitrim, often denigrated as the Cinderella of the twenty-six counties of the Republic, cradles the birthplace of the great Shannon River; its mere two miles of seashore force a tiny wedge between Sligo and Donegal. And for landscape-lovers the magnificent and abundant hedgerows where the Leitrim, Sligo and Roscommon borders meet are unforgettable.

Whether you are using the Regency splendour of Connemara's Rosleague Manor as a base, or whether you opt for more simple accommodation in the village of Letterfrack, you may well be entering County Mayo from Leenane. On the way you will pass Kylemore Abbey, now a convent school, and a number of lakes before reaching Killary Harbour; Ireland's only fjord, it is home to a rich variety of marine life. Alternatively, if you are coming from the majestic, turreted Ashford Castle at Cong you could skirt the northern shores of Lough Corrib through Maam Bay to come upon the most commanding view of this great lake. Remember to check your fuel gauge before you set out, for this is remote country and petrol stations are few and far between.

There are now two options for the journey to Westport. One route is through the Erriff valley, sandwiched between the Sheaffry Hills and the Partry Mountains; the other goes by the northern side of Killary to the Doolough Pass.

On the gentle route through the Erriff valley, the river, now state-run as a superb salmon fishery, winds its way downwards for more than eleven miles through the hills, collecting the rainfall and depositing the day's takings over the Ashleagh Falls into Killary harbour. This is an area of immense beauty and drama with olive, beige and brown velvet mountains: Ben Gorm stands at the head like the Colossus of Rhodes. These mountains have never seen anything but hardship; yet today, dotted with sheep, they have a splendid beauty.

On the other route, passing the falls, following the northern coast road on to Finn Lough and Doolough along the course of the Bundorragha River, one comes to the area known as the Delphi Fishery, famous for its

Ashleagh Falls on the River Erriff, in full spate in midsummer. Incredibly, in the foaming white water beneath the falls lie dozens of salmon, waiting to go through the fish pass in their journey upstream on this, one of Ireland's premier salmon rivers. For those who do not fish, the surrounding mountainous countryside is breathtakingly beautiful and well worth a tour. It is, however, very wild, remote terrain – so go equipped, whether on foot or by car.

sea trout and salmon. Delphi Lodge, beautifully restored in 1988, is run as a premier guest house by Jane and Peter Mantle. Originally built in 1830 on the sporting estate of the Marquess of Sligo, the Lodge is now popular with shooting parties and ramblers. Local seafood is a speciality, and is served in the superb oak dining room. The house also contains an extensive fishing library. On a wild, wet, windy day the spectacular scenery at Doolough, which includes sixty-foot 'phantom' water sprays skating across the crest of the waves, is accentuated by the silver threads of fresh rainwater streams rushing down off the cliff-edged Mweelrea Mountains.

Both northward journeys wind by the mist-wreathed pilgrimage mountain of Croagh Patrick,

whose rough scree slopes thousands of the faithful climb every year in atonement for their sins. According to legend, this is also the place from which St Patrick banished the snakes from Ireland. The two routes meet in the elegant and prosperous town of Westport, largely eighteenth-century in character; the town and its environs contain many delightful places for an overnight stay, from which the whole of scenic north-west Mayo can be toured.

The first option is to travel ten miles north to the historic Georgian Newport House, overlooking the Newport River and quay. Famous as an angling centre, it offers salmon and sea trout fishing on the river and on Lough Beltra. The hotel is also known for its splendid cuisine, based on fresh produce from its own fishery, garden and farm. Newport House is run under the personal supervision of its proprietors Kieran and Thelma Thompson. Their efforts and those of their long-serving staff pay a special bounty towards the end of the season when the house looks particularly

OPPOSITE Magnificent lacy wedding-cake plaster crowns the brilliantly top-lit staircase at Newport House, County Mayo. Perhaps the grandest of all Ireland's country house hotels, Georgian Newport House is much patronized by the fishing fraternity.
RIGHT Fine decorative plasterwork at Enniscoe House, County Mayo, in the process of restoration. The use of a special organic paint allows the plaster to breathe and preserves it better than conventional chemical-based paint.

Guests at Enniscoe House receive a daily reminder of the former glory of Lough Conn as a pike fishery. This superbly mounted 38 lb monster is on display in the hall at the house, surmounted by a stuffed pheasant and trout fishing rods. For those who now come to fish for trout and salmon, Enniscoe has a private jetty on the lough.

splendid in its mantle of crimson ivy. Pride of place has to go to Owen Mullins for his patient contribution and attention to the house, the staff and its visitors over the years. The smoked salmon is the finest I have ever tasted, and is prepared according to his own recipe.

A few miles further inland one can enjoy the hospitality at Enniscoe House. It has a private jetty on the shores of Lough Conn and lies under the shadow of Nephin, Mayo's highest mountain. Enniscoe is another country house that has passed by inheritance to its present owner, Susan Kellett, and is protected by the Irish Georgian Society. Inside, the most striking feature is its winding staircase leading to an elliptical skylight. When I visited it not long ago a German artist was restoring the ornate detail of this skylight – surprisingly with organic paint, it helps the plaster to 'breathe' and protects it for much longer than conventional paint. Enniscoe specializes in fishing parties and has recently appointed a new fishing manager.

During my visit I also met Patrick Percival, whose Westport business, Rare Foods, supplies Irish cheeses, venison, quail and smoked eel to the local country houses. Patrick is a great forager and supplier of the gastronomically unusual. He introduced me to Ring cheese – a hard, mature Cheddar type; his sample offer led me to try a second chunk that firmly established it as my current personal favourite.

Constance Aldridge presides over one of the most popular of Irish country houses, Mount Falcon Castle in County Mayo, and serves excellent local produce to her guests. Here a 17 lb spring salmon lies ready for rinsing and cleaning before its journey to the kitchen to become the delectable centrepiece of that night's dinner. The house was bought by Constance and her late husband over fifty years ago, and they have always run it as a guest house.

Driving north, beyond Castlebar, Loughs Conn and Cullin are joined by a neck of water at Pontoon. This large expanse of water charts some of the most important chapters in Irish angling history and to this day, together with the River Moy, it is somewhat of a fishing phenomenon. Lough Conn was once renowned for its monster pike, including those caught by John Garvin, amongst them his famous Irish record 53-pounder landed in 1920. Today it is a place for not very large but free-rising brown trout, and as such it probably has no peers as a wet fly lake; since the draining of the Moy, this stretch of water's principal river, it has become a great salmon fishery as well. The Moy itself is now perhaps the most prolific Atlantic salmon river in Europe and is worth millions in terms of tourism. Never the most handsome of rivers, since its drainage in the sixties it has become rather ugly, with large canal-type rock banks scarring the landscape.

Mention of the Moy brings to mind the enigmatic Constance Aldridge and her Mount Falcon Castle. Connie, as she is known to her friends, is in her early eighties but still runs with great enthusiasm and energy what is certainly one of the most popular Irish country house hotels. She came to Ireland with her husband, the late Major Aldridge, in the thirties to purchase Mount Falcon, primarily as a fishing lodge and guest house; the house now has some eight miles of fishing

*R*oast Woodcock

*The woodcock shoots in County Mayo mostly comprise visitors from the
Continent escaping to the west coast of Ireland and its winters, which
are warmer than those of mainland Europe.*

The birds must be carefully plucked, head and all, because the entire bird is roasted, undrawn (ie not gutted). They are best if they are hung for 4–5 days. Woodcock must not be cooked too fast, so that they remain juicy and slightly pink. Season well, then wrap a large rasher of bacon around each bird. Skewer the rasher with the long beak. Place each bird on a lightly buttered piece of bread to catch the juices during roasting. Preheat the oven to 200°C, 400°F, Gas Mark 6.

Roast the birds for 20–25 minutes in the pre-heated oven, then serve with a thin gravy, made from the juices of the roasted birds, enlivened with a squeeze of lemon and a dash of red wine.

*Now with the coming of Spring, the day is
beginning to stretch, And after the feast of St Brigid
I'll rise up and go, Since the notion came into my
head I'll not even stop for a second Till I set my
foot down in the middle of County Mayo.*
CILL AODAIN
Antoine Raifteiri O Reachatabhra

Hare Soup

Hares are in season in Ireland from August to March, and they are shot locally for the kitchen of Mount Falcon. The soup is wonderfully warming in winter, being a particular favourite with French guests. The marmalade adds a unique flavour.

SERVES 10
1 hare, cleaned and skinned
plain flour
salt and freshly ground pepper
100 g (4 oz) butter, or 100 ml
    (3$^1/_2$ fl oz) vegetable oil
2 onions, peeled and sliced
2 carrots, peeled and sliced
$^1/_2$ turnip, peeled and sliced
2 celery stalks, sliced
3.5 l (6 pt) good chicken stock
1 bouquet garni
12 black peppercorns
4 garlic cloves, peeled
300 ml (10 fl oz) red wine
1 tbsp marmalade
lemon juice (optional)
croûtons to serve

Cut the hare into small joints and roll in seasoned flour. Melt the butter or oil in a large saucepan and add the hare and vegetables. Fry gently until slightly brown. Add the stock, herbs, peppercorns and garlic, and simmer for 3–5 hours.

Strain and remove the meat from bones. Liquidize the meat and vegetables. Put this purée into another large saucepan with the liquid, and add the red wine and marmalade. Boil gently together, adding more wine or a squeeze of lemon juice to help bring out the taste. Test for seasoning.

Serve hot, garnished with small croûtons.

Elderflower Sorbet

'In June, the hedgerows of County Mayo are fragrant and creamy with elderflowers. Later, the small black berries are used to make wine and syrup. Shake the flower heads well, but do not wash them. It is difficult to measure the quantity of elderflower heads needed for this recipe, so I use this rather imprecise method.' Constance Aldridge

SERVES 6–8
elderflower heads (a wine box
    full)
1.2 l (2 pt) water
225 g (8 oz) sugar for every
600 ml (1 pt) liquid
2 lemons for every 600 ml
    (1 pt) liquid
2 egg whites for every 600 ml
    (1 pt) liquid

Remove flower heads from stalks as much as possible. Put two huge handfuls of them (using both hands) into the water in a large pan, bring to the boil, and simmer for 15 minutes. Strain and cool, then measure liquid obtained.

Add the required amount of sugar, and heat gently until melted. Boil fast for 20 minutes, then leave to cool.

Place in a suitable container in the freezer and fast freeze for an hour or until firm.

Remove and add the strained juice of the required number of lemons. Whip the required number of egg whites and fold into the mixture.

Return to freezer for 20 minutes, then blend again to be sure egg whites are totally absorbed. Return to the freezer and freeze until firm.

At Portacloy in County Mayo every exposed rock seems to be covered in tarmacadam at low tide. Upon close inspection, however, it turns out to be thousands of mussels ripe for the picking.

on the Moy. Major Aldridge was himself a fanatical fisherman, and looking through the extensive memorabilia at Mount Falcon one can marvel at the amazing salmon catches landed by him and his guests. Connie still remembers the draining of 'her' river and its remorseful effect on her husband. But even at her remarkable age her *joie de vivre* rings throughout the house, where visitors are privileged to share her extraordinary love of fresh food and good cooking. Connie Aldridge is very fond of dogs. Her springer spaniels, Gail and Dudley, her 'page boy and lady in waiting', follow her everywhere. She also loves to visit the Art Deco hot seawater baths at Enniscrone, County Sligo. Despite the fact that she says the heat makes her tired it must be the effects of the seaweed that make her look so youthful. Connie has a way of life in which she is still queen of her castle and a gracious hostess to the many dedicated and eager guests who gather round her table. A lasting image to many will certainly be of her seated at the head of the table serving soup from a silver tureen or carving a roast on the antique sideboard.

Mount Falcon is a traditional Irish country house, with a casual but efficient atmosphere, punctuated with colourful arrangements of fresh, seasonal flowers. Apart from the fishing, the place is also a base for woodcock shooting parties managed by Salmon and Woodcock from nearby Foxford. Both pursuits give ample clues to the quality of fare. In the summer gravad lax and elderflower sorbet and in the winter jugged hare soup and roast woodcock are typical, accompanied by year-round fresh garden vegetables.

Using one of these three country houses as a base, I can recommend travelling at one's leisure to discover the whole of this wild and remote north-west country. Start from the mountains at Clew Bay in the south and descend to the boglands north of the Nephin Mountains; then travel onwards to the Mullet Peninsula, a haven for whole colonies of migrating birds. Here is the remarkable inlet of Portacloy, at first sight a peaceful, surf-washed beach, ideal for picnicking or simply for taking a swim in total privacy; but some find different treasures here – I was taken by a marine biologist to see the place where to his delight he had found fifteen types of seaweed and over twenty species of fish.

Such a wonderful array of freshly caught fish would seem more at home in a Mediterranean market than anywhere in the British Isles – yet all these were caught with rod and line in Killala Bay in the north of County Mayo. They include dogfish, ling, pollack, codling, grey and red gurnard, cuckoon wrasse, coalfish, whiting, ponting, ray, black sole and many more.

SLIGO

BELOW A bucket of large juicy cockles raked up on the shore at Strand Hill in County Sligo. Cockles and mussels are very plentiful all along the shoreline in these parts – truly food for free – and the name 'Sligo' derives from the Gaelic word meaning 'shell'.

OPPOSITE A corner of the inner hallway at Temple House after a day's woodcock shooting. The odd hare and a few wildfowl are usually bagged as well. Out of sight on the other side of the hall, steaming dogs snore and wheeze in their sleep like old men, legs still running.

OVERLEAF A collection of shooting memorabilia at Temple House, including old Victorian game books used as daily logs for the shoots, and a meerschaum pipe in the shape of a woodcock. For over a century the Percival family have nurtured three hundred acres of lowland bog and woodland as an ideal place for migrating woodcock, en route to Siberia, to overwinter.

At Knockacreagh you are entering Sligo, the Yeats county. My first stop here is often at Strand Hill at low tide to rake a bucket or two of cockles and mussels off the beach. Sligo, by the way, means 'shell' and once there were huge oyster beds here. It is but a moment's work, and the kitchens of many country houses would be pleased to cook your catch for you.

In this part of the country, there is again a good choice of special places to stay and one or two very fine restaurants. Perhaps the most interesting is Temple House at Ballymote, a Georgian mansion set in a thousand acres of farmland and woods; the Percival family have lived in houses on the site since 1665. The present house boasts its own walled garden, where produce is grown for family and guests – organic food is a major feature here. Sandy Percival runs the farm while Deborah, his wife, looks after the house.

TEMPLE HOUSE
GAME BOOK
DAILY REGISTER
Pheasants
Woodcocks
Snipes
Hares
Rabbits
Grouse

On entering, one steps into the incredibly dark outer hallway with its nostalgic hunting trappings. This is the place to discard muddy boots and weatherwear under the gaze of a monstrous stuffed pike which rests over the fireplace. Inside, Temple House offers a splendid dining room, a marvellous gallery and several rooms furnished to the best of old-world standards. One of these bedrooms is so large that it has been christened 'The Half Acre'.

The house caters for both the summer and the winter visitor. Over three hundred acres of primeval woodland and rare bogland have been nurtured by the family as a preserve for woodcock shooting, which is conducted with great discipline three or four times a year. In the dampness of winter these woodlands are carpeted with pale green, sponge-like mosses and the bare branches are festooned and dripping with some of the rarest lichens to be found south of the Arctic Circle. For naturalists it is a fascinating place.

Temple House Lake is a well-known pike fishery and Deborah occasionally includes pike among the house specialities. Not far away is the awe-inspiring Carrowkeel, site of the ancient passage graves perched on the Bricklieve Mountains; whether you care for prehistoric remains or not, it is worth the climb for the spectacular view of Lough Arrow below, and through

LEFT Within the magnificent two-acre organic kitchen garden at Temple House garlic of enormous size and superb quality are lovingly grown by Frances Bell. Organic produce is an important element in the cooking here.

BELOW The staircase at Temple House is softly lit by a skylight and hung with family portraits. The house is Georgian, with Victorian additions, and has more rooms than any other private house in Ireland.

the distant haze the surroundings of Counties Mayo, Leitrim and Roscommon. This view in itself is a must on any serious explorer's agenda.

Lough Arrow, the most beautiful of island-studded lakes, is fed mainly from underground springs that have taken water from the surrounding limestone; as a result the lake nurtures large brown trout of a high average weight, pink-fleshed and of excellent flavour. It was here that the pre-eminent turn-of-the-century angler John Henderson pioneered the art of dry fly fishing on Irish lakes. Today it is one of the great mayfly lakes, with dry fly fishing one of its most attractive assets.

OVERLEAF Lichens such as these only grow in the purest of atmospheres, and here at Temple House the winter woods are dripping with them like some fantastic, primeval forest. Some are very rare, and are not found anywhere else outside the Arctic Circle.

Dust covers sadly shroud the drawing room at Temple House, which is now little used. The once sumptuous drapes, now in tatters, are original to the house.

OVERLEAF Cromleach Lodge looks out over Lough Arrow, probably the best dry fly lake in Europe towards the Bricklieve Mountains and the megalithic tombs at Carrowkeel.

Facing westwards, with an incredible elevated position overlooking the lake, the Bricklieve Mountains and most of Yeats Country, is a modern hotel – Cromleach Lodge, run by Christy and Myra Tighe. Like an observatory, Cromleach Lodge offers the most exciting views through the gentle hills and valleys of County Sligo, and it is fast earning an enviable reputation for excellent cuisine. It is popular with discerning local residents, and anyone wanting to fish Lough Arrow can arrange accommodation and boating facilities locally. Eating is a breathtaking pleasure here for the view alone – whether watching the sunrise burst through a morning haze or the moon passing quietly over the lake below.

Nearer to the town of Sligo, travelling north, is Coopershill, a further fine example of an elegant country mansion. It was built in the Palladian style by Francis Bindon in the mid-eighteenth century, using local sandstone which was hand-crafted into blocks on what is now the front lawn. Set in five hundred acres of farm and woodland, this gracious yet homely place – it has remained in the hands of the O'Hara family since the very beginning – offers a warm welcome and very good food. The rooms are packed to capacity with a fascinating collection of old photographs, paintings and other memorabilia.

With its four-posters or half-posters in most bedrooms, and log fires in the drawing room, Coopershill is a comfortable and comforting house. Candlelight adds an extra dimension and authenticity to the genuine, classic country house food served under the personal supervision of Brian and Lindy O'Hara in the small but elegant dining room, which houses a lovely collection of pewter, silver and decanters. Many of the windows in the house still contain the original Georgian glass, and the outer hallway displays an eye-catching original fanlight and architrave over its inner door. The wooden staircase leads up into the light of half a dozen windows to where the heads of several proud stags gaze, preserving memories of the former deer park. At one end of the gallery, a free-standing Victorian shower and bath still function: the bizarre shower-head is surprisingly powerful and has massaged away the weariness of many a traveller.

Kebabs of Cockles
with Herb & Almond Butter

'Michael McGowan is one of the older children of the McGowans – the last remaining family on Coney Island. When he has time free from making the hay he rakes the cockles on the island shore. His father rows the children across to Rosses Point each morning to catch the school bus to Sligo and when Michael passes the restaurant, he drops the bag of cockles at the back door. They are cooked and eaten within 12 hours.' Paula Gilvarry and Sarah Speares

SERVES 4 AS A STARTER

12 or more cockles per
   person
a pinch of oatmeal
1 bunch of large spring
   onions, cut into 1 cm ($^1/_2$ in)
   pieces

COATING

100 g (4 oz) soft butter
1 tsp chopped almonds
1 garlic clove, chopped
1 tsp finely chopped parsley
freshly ground pepper
50 g (2 oz) white breadcrumbs

Soak the cockles overnight with a pinch of oatmeal, discarding any that do not close when sharply tapped.

The next day, drain and cook in 600 ml (1 pt) fresh water until they open. Shell the cockles, discarding any that have remained closed.

Thread the cockles and the pieces of spring onion on to small thin skewers about 15 cm (6 in) long.

Make up a paste using all the coating ingredients. Season it well.

Roll the skewered cockles in the breadcrumb coating, and grill until hot, a few moments.

Or you could, if you wish, serve the grilled cockles off the skewers in a ramekin, with the heated butter, in which case do not add the breadcrumbs to the coating paste before grilling.

Lettuce & Lovage Soup with Cockles

Lovage grows wild in some places but it can be grown from seed, or plants can be bought from most good nurseries. It has a strong celery flavour, and apart from using it in soups and sauces, the large mid-green leaves make a wonderful garnish.

SERVES 6–8

450 g (1 lb) fresh cockles in their shells
a pinch of oatmeal
1 l (1³/₄ pt) stock (see method)
25 g (1 oz) unsalted butter
white part of 1 leek, cleaned and chopped
200 g (7 oz) butterhead or other round lettuce, shredded
14–16 medium lovage leaves
150 ml (5 fl oz) single cream
salt and freshly ground pepper

Soak the cockles overnight in salt water with a little oatmeal to cleanse them. Discard any that do not close when tapped sharply with a knife.

The next day drain the cockles and boil in fresh water to cover until they open, a few minutes only. Pick them out of their shells, reserving any liquor. Strain this through muslin to remove any sand. Make this liquor up to 1 l (1³/₄ pt) with good fish or chicken stock.

Melt the butter, add the leek, and cook for 4–5 minutes. Add the shredded lettuce and half the lovage leaves, also shredded. Stir into the leeks with the stock. Bring to the boil then simmer for 5 minutes. Purée, then return to the pan and blend in the cream.

Add the cockles and heat gently. Taste, season and serve in a flat soup bowl, garnished with remaining lovage leaves.

Confit of Duck

'We use Aylesbury ducks, reared for us by Ken Moffat on his family's farm at Blacklion, County Cavan. We joint the ducks, and roast the breasts with various sauces.' Paula Gilvarry and Sarah Speares

SERVES 6

12 duck legs
600 ml (1 pt) duck or pork fat
1 onion, peeled and chopped
2 carrots, peeled and chopped
4 garlic cloves, peeled
1 bay leaf
12 black peppercorns

Preheat the oven to 150°C, 300°F, Gas Mark 2.

Melt the fat in a deep roasting tray, then add the vegetables, bay leaf and peppercorns. Add the duck legs in one layer or overlapping. Cover with aluminium foil, or a lid, and cook for 2 hours in the preheated oven. Check occasionally to ensure that the fat is not bubbling. Leave to cool overnight, then place in the refrigerator for 2 days. (The duck will keep in the fat for 10 days.)

To serve, remove the duck legs from the fat. Place, skin side down, in a roasting pan and cook in the oven at 180°C, 350°F, Gas Mark 4 for 15–20 minutes, or until the skin becomes very crisp. Serve hot with some sweet and sour red cabbage.

A silver rod of light hits Lough Gill in County Sligo, giving relief to the layered landscape of Knocknarea and Queen Maeve's tomb.

One of the smallest country houses in Ireland, Coopershill is hidden deep in woodland where tiny forest flowers and creeping plants wrap the feet of lichen-covered beech and chestnut trees. The Arrow River runs through the five-hundred-acre estate, bridged only once on the winding, dappled avenue: this is the sole entrance to and exit from the house. The story goes that layers of sheepskin, bloated and preserved by bogwater, now provide the solution to the regular subsidence of the old stone bridge. The screeching sounds emanating from the wild undergrowth are nothing more sinister than the call of the peacocks that add further charm and character to

ence of the hotel business in several countries and first returned to Sligo to run the restaurant at Knockmuldowney, which he and his wife restored in 1982 and then expanded into a small hotel. The high standard of personal service that he achieved at Knockmuldowney is now applied to Markree. Whether you are a sportsman, or a tourist in search of some of the magnificent scenery that characterizes the area, Markree is an excellent centre for your stay.

Lough Gill – in which lies the island which inspired Yeats's poem *The Lake Isle of Innisfree* – is easily accessible from any of the country houses mentioned above.

But in your haste to see this beautiful and evocative countryside don't pass straight through Sligo town. Stop awhile to visit Hargadon's pub in O'Connell Street: a quick pint – or two if you're lucky – would be in proper order.

My next recommended stop is at Reveries Restaurant at Rosses Point overlooking Sligo Bay. In its tiered conservatory setting it offers a crisply modern contrast to the more traditional dining rooms of most country houses. Damien Brennan and Paula Gilvarry offer a very imaginative and up-to-date menu that often includes venison and pigeon, but does not overlook more modest fare: I was pleasantly surprised to see cockles included on the menu when I ate there. To end your meal, the restaurant prides itself on its comprehensive selection of Irish cheeses.

No drive through County Sligo can ignore the massive, regal Benbulben. Buttressing a stack of spine-backed hills that sprawl like prehistoric monsters under a constantly changing patchwork of turbulent skies, macho Benbulbin stands square-jawed to the sea. What a contrast with the feminine roundness of the view of Knocknarea on the other side of the bay! Its name, however, presents a much harsher image: in Gaelic Knocknarea means 'Hill of Executions', and a huge cairn on its summit is reputed to be the burial place of the legendary and bloodthirsty Queen Maeve. And when you get there it turns out to be a place of rough scree and steep precipices, leading to one of the largest megalithic cemeteries in Europe.

Coopershill. Within, there is more birdlife to take the unwary by surprise: to the uninitiated the backchat of the family's African grey parrot can sometimes sound as though murder is being committed in the kitchen!

Yet another of the great houses of the region is Markree Castle. Situated in the middle of a thousand-acre estate, it has been owned by the Cooper family for over three hundred years; the original house, however, has been altered many times over the years – its impressive facade is attributed to Francis Johnston in 1802. Today perhaps the most striking feature of the house is the nineteenth-century Italian plasterwork. The present owner, Charles Cooper, has had experi-

The run up to Donegal from Sligo along the coast road through Bundoran is straightforward, but at

Grange it is well worth devoting time to a small detour to explore the wonderful seascapes and small beaches at Mullaghmore. I recall with pleasure entering Donegal on a hot, sunny day in April. There was a very warm, southerly breeze and the forecast was for heatwave conditions to continue for a few days – totally out of character for Donegal and certainly for that time of year. Just short of Donegal town is St Ernan's House Hotel, an excellent place to stay whilst touring this part of the country. The sun was just beginning to dip as I crossed the causeway to St Ernan's, idyllically set on its own tidal island amongst many others in a blissfully quiet setting. That day it reminded me of Mykonos.

St Ernan's, named after an early Christian monk known as the 'Man of Iron', is another beautiful Georgian house built by one J. Hamilton, a wealthy young landowner related to the Duke of Wellington and a ward of the Pakenhams of Strokestown in County Roscommon. Without any formal training whatsoever, Brian and Carmel O'Dowd have been running it as a small country house hotel since 1987; Carmel was formerly a teacher and Brian a banker. The house has what they charmingly call 'twelve plus one' airy bedrooms, all elegantly furnished. Brian is developing an extensive walled garden and a series of walks that weave through eight acres of luscious woodland, in late spring carpeted in places with luxuriant wild garlic. The island is surrounded by sandbanks and mudflats that provide a wealth of food at low tide for large numbers of wading birds. At full moon and low tide the eerie call of the curlews will lull you magically to sleep.

Food at St Ernan's seems to complement the house – the portions are generous, yet the dishes are light and exquisitely presented. The kitchen is run by master chef Jim McLaughlin; he started in the business as a lad of fourteen, yet years later his enthusiasm for his art remains undaunted. Jim likes to be ahead of everything, and his wealth of professional experience enables him to operate with the precision of Swiss timing; unlike the atmosphere surrounding some chefs, who seem to work best in an atmosphere close to dementia, often the loudest sound to be heard from Jim's kitchen is a contented whistle.

DONEGAL

Donegal has often been characterized as the land of the potato, tweed and fish. Donegal town is the home of the famous tweed, whose roots are firmly fixed in the local wool trade and resultant cottage weaving industry. This heritage has not been forgotten, and the true Donegal herringbone and 'knop' (flecked) cloth are still woven today.

Even a major tweed mill like that of the Magees started in a small way. The business was set up in the 1860s, the original Magee eventually taking on a partner, Robert Temple, in 1887. At first they sold hand-woven tweeds, having travelled by jaunting car to centres like Ardara or Kilcar to purchase cloth from cottagers who used to spin and weave their own wool. The cottage weavers brought their tweed to market packed in a woven reed basket called a creel, with one length (about seventy yards) packed on each side of a donkey's back. After examination and selection by the hawk-eyed buyers it would be taken back to Donegal for cleaning and shrinking, after which the finished cloth could be sold to discriminating customers around the world.

After the First World War demand rose; as a result much of the casual buying from cottage weavers ceased and Magees took over the weaving themselves. At last it was possible to introduce an element of quality control, but without sacrificing the unique feel and appearance of hand-woven tweed. Today the business remains as healthy as ever: new weaves and designs have been evolved, and new colours are introduced seasonally to match the demands of the world's leading designers and couturiers.

In recent times Magees have expanded into men's tailoring and are now the largest such firm in Ireland. Their retail shop in Donegal must surely be one of the few places on earth where you can select a cloth that has been hand-woven on the premises and where they will make you a suit, a coat or any garment you choose – in fact all the stages, from fleece to finished garment, are controlled under one roof.

Originally, Donegal tweed was woven on a white warp, and interest and colour were added by using speckled yarn in the weft. Looking round at the granite hills of Donegal, with their subtle greys and browns,

Shake hands with
All the neighbours,
And kiss the colleens all.
You're as welcome
As the flowers in May,
Back home to Donegal.
SHAKE HANDS WITH YOUR UNCLE DAN
Johnny Patterson

greens and purples, it is easy to see where the inspiration for these colour combinations came from. There are still cottagers who weave tweed on handlooms in their homes, though of necessity it must be a part-time occupation since they also have to sow crops, cut turf and do a multitude of other jobs on their small farms scattered over the region.

The road westward from Donegal town goes to the great fishing port at Killybegs, where the return of the fishing fleet to the pier right in the middle of the town is heralded by screaming flocks of swooping, thieving seagulls. From here I recommend the coast drive through Kilcar (another major weaving centre) and on to Slieve League, at nearly two thousand feet Donegal's highest cliffs. This is not a climb for the fainthearted or the unfit or those who suffer from vertigo, since narrow ledges above endless drops have to be braved before the spectacular view over five counties and the broad Atlantic can be enjoyed.

The villages of Ardara and Glencolumbkille are within easy reach of here. The former contains an interesting 'folk village' museum of old Irish cottages of various ages, showing the furnishings and way of life of past times. At Ardara, if you are feeling peckish (and if you have scrambled to the top of Slieve League, you will probably be ravenous), the Lobster Pot restaurant with its impressive shop front is a good stopping place. Don't be put off by the late twentieth-century chip shop decor with its essential slot machines and plastic ketchup dispensers. Amongst the predictable hamburgers and chilliburgers you will find mouth-watering fresh salmon salads, seafood chowder, garlic mussels and goujons of monkfish, as well as the standard fried cod and haddock. I opted for that old favourite fried haddock and chips – and was served with the best I have ever had.

North of Donegal town, Letterkenny punctuates a tour of this region with a definite question mark – whether to turn right into the Inishowen Peninsula, or to carry on up to Rathmullan and Fanad. Both are equally rewarding, but my own first choice would be to visit Rathmullan House with its sandy beach on Lough Swilly.

The house comes as the first pleasant surprise a few miles after leaving the quaint village of Ramelton. Built in the late eighteenth century, but considerably enlarged in the nineteenth, Rathmullan passed through marriage to the Batt family – local landlords, bankers and linen brokers. The connection is commemorated by Batts Walk, a pathway which leads along the shoreline to the village.

Since 1962 this gracious house has been owned by Bob and Robin Wheeler. It is surrounded by beautiful award-winning gardens that slope down to the shores of the lake. The trees – weeping elms, beeches and giant chestnuts – contribute to the effect of this serene and delightful setting. At dawn, however, the serenity is shattered by the harsh cawing of a 'murder of the crows', heralding the vermilion sunrise over Lough Swilly.

Inside the house, the extraordinary canopied dining room is divided into three sections, resulting in a pavilion-like, spacious atmosphere yet without any feeling of isolation. The excellent menu includes the best of locally caught fish such as salmon and sea trout, and Donegal lamb and beef. Breakfast, as in so many country houses, is a feast not to be missed; unusually it features carrageen, a traditional seaweed dish.

For swimmers, Rathmullan is doubly blessed. Apart from its temptingly clean, sandy white beach on Lough Swilly, it also has what are called the Egyptian Baths. These in fact comprise a modern, indoor, salt-

Dear Erin, how sweetly thy green bosom rises!
An emerald set in the ring of the sea.
Each blade of thy meadows my faithful heart prizes,
Thou queen of the west! the world's cushla ma chree!
CUSHLA MA CHREE
John Philpot Curran

Peeping into the drawing room at Rathmullan House, County Donegal. A flower-bedecked antique pedestal table is framed in the doorway with its ornately detailed architrave, one of many in the house. Through the drawing room window can be glimpsed one of the great mature trees that are a feature of the award-winning gardens sloping down to Lough Swilly.

water swimming pool, constantly maintained at about 70 degrees Fahrenheit and particularly safe since the maximum depth is just under six feet.

The drive northwards towards Portsalon reveals the almost Aegean splendour of the deserted golden Bally-mastacka beaches, curving gently for some five miles. The pleasant circular tour to Milford and on again towards Downings, the home of the world-famous McNutts tweed mill, is a must. The road meanders through low-profile countryside that skirts the pounding blue Atlantic, and ever new and more exquisite sandy beaches can be discovered round every corner. The route back from Downings takes you through the villages of Portnablagh, Dunfanaghy and Creeslough to Falcarragh, all part of a small Gaelic-speaking area. Not far from Falcarragh is the evocative-sounding Bloody Foreland, named not after a reputation for shipwrecks but after the colour of the setting sun as reflected in its stone. Along this coast giant sand-dunes reach tower-like into the sky and deep into the imagination, recalling the deserts of Africa or Arabia.

The drive back to Letterkenny through Gortahork takes you through turf country, rough and marshy bogland – then suddenly Mount Errigal rises like a perfect cone, an almost identical twin of El Tiede in Tenerife.

Here you can enjoy the solitude and wilderness of Glenveagh National Park, where red deer and falcons are more prolific than man. It is possible to ramble for miles through this mountainous region without coming across another human soul. For nature in a tamer form, visit the gardens at the extraordinary Gothic castle after which the park was named, donated to the Irish nation on the death of its owner, Henry McIlhenny. In the thirties and forties it was the scene of lavish parties that were the toast of international society, and celebrities such as Greta Garbo and Cecil Beaton dined here.

If, instead of the Rathmullan tour, you decide to tour the Inishowen Peninsula, as you leave Letterkenny you cannot help but notice a sudden change in the scenery. For the previous three hundred miles this book has described a circular tour round Ireland from the west Cork–Kerry borders right up to Donegal through continuous rugged coastal, lakeland and mountainous scenery. Now, for the first time, the traveller's eye is met with an extensive area of very flat, well-cultivated and well-worked land. Known as the Lagan valley, it runs along the south-eastern edge and into the heart of Lough Swilly, separating the two peninsulas.

The soil here is very rich and makes a major contribution to Irish agriculture. Large parcels of land have been reclaimed from the sea using Dutch engineering techniques, and the lie of the land instantly reminds one of the polders of Holland. Being so far north it does get its fair share of rain, but the soil is free-draining and is used to grow barley and potatoes as well as grazing sheep and dairy cattle. Typical of all coastal headlands, the earth is enriched constantly with the wind-borne deposits of minerals from the salty sea air. Grazing on this type of grassland gives dairy herds improved milk yields and lamb a special flavour: gastronomes know it as *pré-salé* (saltmarsh) lamb, and it is sought out by discerning continental buyers.

The sun was still blazing away as I made my way up to Fahan, south of Buncrana on the eastern shore of Lough Swilly, to visit Reggie Ryan at the Restaurant St John. Although they were the work of man rather than nature, the surrounding fields were a beautiful sight. The ridges of newly planted potatoes were breaking up the lush, green pasturelands, interspersed every now and again by bursts of cadmium yellow rape, echoed by the equally brilliant 'whins' or gorse that grows across on the other, rougher side of Lough Swilly.

The first time I met carpet-manufacturer-turned-restaurateur Reggie Ryan was on a photographic assignment to Inishowen. He greeted my journalist companion and myself as though we were missionaries: no one, it seemed, ever came up this far to enquire or to spread the word about this most wonderful part of Donegal. Although the area contains no country houses of the type so often praised in this book, Reggie has an expert knowledge of local guest houses and hotels and will do everything in his power to ensure a comfortable stay in north Donegal for his patrons and friends.

The Restaurant St John, which has been open for ten years, is situated right on the shore of Lough Swilly. It stands next to the St Johns yacht club and faces Rathmullan, which is just three miles across the bay. The very successful partnership between Reggie and his chef, Phil McAvee, a former domestic science teacher, has resulted in many awards – and no wonder. They have available at their doorstep some of the best ingredients in Ireland, including the famous Lagan lamb, superior white fish such as brill and monkfish from Greencastle and an abundance of quality shellfish from Malin Head. The freshest of vegetables and herbs are obtained from the garden in front of the house. Consequently Reggie and Phil have decided to keep the food quite simple, letting the superb ingredients speak for themselves. Rack of lamb is extremely popular and complemented by a seasonal gooseberry or apple and mint jelly.

It was at St John that I was introduced to carrageen moss: a type of milk jelly derived from heating seaweed together with milk. After straining and setting,

Carrageen Moss

Carrageen moss, found around the northern and western shores of Ireland, is rich in iodine and potassium. Down through the years it has been used as a health food, and during the Irish famine of 1840–1843 it was the only food available in coastal areas.

SERVES 8–10
25 g (1 oz) carrageen moss
2 l (3¹/₂ pt) milk
finely grated peel of 1 lemon
75 g (3 oz) sugar
fresh fruit to decorate

Trim the moss by pulling off any shells or grit, and steep in cold water for 10–15 minutes until soft and spongy. Drain and rinse under cold water.

Put into a saucepan with the milk, lemon peel and sugar. Simmer for 10–15 minutes until the mixture thickens and coats the back of the spoon.

Strain into wet, individual 7.5 cm (3 in) ramekins or one large 1.75 l (3 pt) mould. Leave in the refrigerator to set – 1 hour for the ramekins, 3–4 hours for the large mould. Turn out when set and decorate with fresh fruit and/or a fruit purée (strawberries, blackcurrants, redcurrants, raspberries etc).

Gooseberry & Mint Jelly

'This is the ideal accompaniment for roast Donegal mountain lamb – one of the most succulent and memorable meals Ireland can produce.' Phil Mcafee

1.8 kg (4 lb) gooseberries, topped and tailed
600 ml (1 pt) water
preserving sugar
1 large bunch of fresh mint, washed and bruised
25 g (1 oz) fresh mint leaves, finely chopped

Put gooseberries and water in the preserving pan, and simmer until the fruit is soft and broken, about 15–20 minutes. Strain the mixture overnight through a jelly bag.

Measure the liquid and for every 600 ml (1 pt) obtained, add 450 g (1 lb) preserving sugar. Stir this over a low heat until the sugar has dissolved. Tie up the bunch of mint, and add to the pan. Boil hard for 5–10 minutes until a set is obtained (use the saucer test, see page 76).

Remove the bunch of mint, and skim the jelly well. Add the chopped mint and stir through the jelly. Leave to cool for about 30 minutes, then pour into small warmed sterilized jars and cover.

*'The mountains were thrown higgledy-piggledy into the distance
where the sea was. The white dusty road wound round the near
flank of the valley and then fell gracefully away to the one-arched
bridge below. Among the few tufted oaks beyond the bridge the
church lurked. A cluster of thatched houses crouched about it. Bird
song had shrivelled and died.'*

EVENING IN IRELAND

Bryan MacMahon

the resulting jelly can be served as a savoury starter (at Rathmullan, if you recall, it makes an appearance at breakfast) or sweetened to make a pudding. Carrageen is quite beneficial to the digestive system and very much a traditional Irish dish.

St John is open in the evenings only, so Reggie suggested that I tour Inishowen and come back later for dinner. By following the signposts – Inishowen One Hundred – marking the hundred-mile scenic route you will discover some of the most unspoilt and remote beauty spots in Ireland. If you have travelled this far north, it is worth making the extra effort to see the best of one of Ireland's most beautiful and spectacular counties.

I went on through Buncrana and then 'climbed' the Mamore Gap, which for the motorist is a very special experience indeed. It is probably the nearest you will get to being launched into space. As straight as a die, the approach road goes up and up and up for eight hundred feet to the cleavage of the Uris and Mamore Hills. But just as one is expecting the rocket booster to render one's trusty vehicle airborne, nothing happens. One is, however, definitely aerial: suddenly, with the car at a standstill, one finds oneself looking down at the most unusual sight – an extensive plateau of small, dyked-off fields adjacent to the wrinkled sea. To the left lie a beautiful deserted beach and small harbour with a little group of cottages dotted around. 'Out of this world and into Leenan', as someone once put it, is an accurate description of this moment.

The descent into Leenan is as tight as a ringlet of hair, so take it easy. The thatched cottages that remain are probably the most traditional on the whole west coast of Ireland. Most of them are spotlessly clean, with that characteristic icing sugar finish and annually replaced golden straw thatch, embellished by vividly contrasting primary-coloured window frames and doors. The roofs, which curve rather than rise to a point, are tied down with hairnets of binding twine on to wooden pegs; this is to protect them from the relentless north-west winds. The whole atmosphere of this little oasis is blissfully quiet, timeless and quite magical. The local community of fishermen and small farmers seems to have turned its back on the wall of mountains and found privileged isolation – content to gaze seaward. From Leenan go on to the tip of Ireland at Malin Head, passing through the town of Carndonagh – the hub of Inishowen. Now, still following the Inishowen One Hundred scenic route, you must take the higher of the two options signposted at the five-finger strand to Knockamanybens.

The west and north-west coasts of Ireland abound in breathtaking mountain scenery, silvery, winding rivers, sheets of wind-ruffled lake and beckoning golden beaches; but here at Knockamanybens there is something that can't be put into words – an aura of 'spirit of place'. You can't touch it; you can't describe it. You can't taste it; you can't smell it. I can't photograph it: spirit of place.

The small fishing port of Malin Head is the most northerly village in Ireland, and home to one of the nicest groups of people I have ever encountered. The pier was originally built in 1884, to receive cargo boats. At this time the local fishermen bravely launched their double-ended druntons – 24-foot clinker-built boats with an auxiliary gaff sail – from the beach into the often mountainous seas that constantly thrash this ragged coastline. By the mid-1950s fishing had died out, though lobsters were still caught. Even then, in the early seventies the local fishermen were complaining that crabs were all they were catching in their lobster pots – and lots of them, too. But a canny fish merchant told them to go back and fish for as many crabs as they could catch: he would purchase

them all. The local fishermen followed his suggestion and discovered a deep trench not far offshore that contained a seemingly endless migration of crabs. At that time there was hardly any commercial value in catching crabs in Ireland, but the fish merchant had the good business sense to convert the disused railway station into a crab processing plant. The gamble paid off: today this factory is thriving and Malin Head has become one of the great crab-fishing centres of Europe.

Not surprisingly, the village boasts the most northerly tearoom in Ireland – a recently converted old cottage with its interior preserved in the traditional style. The fare includes locally caught salmon, crab and lobster, and there is an interesting craft room. Such isolated communities as this often have to bend the rules a little – one local story recalls how a transatlantic liner once stopped offshore here, in the middle of nowhere, to transfer a homecoming lady passenger to a local boat that took her home.

ABOVE Straw as opposed to reed thatching is characteristic of the cottage architecture of County Donegal. There is no guttering on this house – the rain just runs straight off, and the thatch is held in place not with a net but with pegs and twine.

OVERLEAF A charming little lodge with Gothic touches on the shore of Lough Esk in County Donegal. Now sadly lacking the love and attention it must once have enjoyed, none the less it still contrives to look a pretty sight in the evening light of midsummer.

LEITRIM

A pleasant exit from Donegal would be to take the road from Kinlough, skirting the southern shores of Lough Melvin, into Rossinver. Lough Melvin itself is yet another famous trout and salmon lake. We are now in County Leitrim. Here, in this sparsely populated, undeservedly forgotten county, where nature is little interfered with, the landscape is one of unkempt beauty. But do not look for grandeur and great sweeping vistas: this countryside is one of rolling hills; compacted, rushy fields; wild, colourful hedgerows; lakes famous for coarse fishing; and lowland bogs that harbour snipe, teal, woodcock and other wildfowl. These wetlands form gentle boundaries with the neighbouring counties, Sligo and Roscommon, in a most unusual harmony.

This lowly county has become a focus for alternative lifestyles, organic farming methods and cheesemaking. With its mild, damp climate, Leitrim has proved to be a perfect place to grow coniferous trees commercially. Rossinver is the home of Eden Plants – an organic farm run by Dolores Keegan and Rod Alston, which specializes in herbs and salad vegetables. In fifteen years the number of species of herb grown and sold here has risen to over a hundred. The land itself was not particularly rich, but with dedication and careful husbandry Dolores and Rod have created a wonderful standard of gardening that is infinitely pleasing to the eye, especially in midsummer. They have undoubtedly been major catalysts in the renaissance in good-quality produce for the restaurants and country houses of Ireland.

The layered necklaces of wild pink and white dog roses that festoon the summer hedgerows in the environs of Rossinver have given rise to what is known locally as the 'Rose Walk', actually a drive meandering around countless miles of country lanes. These and the neighbouring hedgerows of Sligo and Roscommon are in fact magnificent at any time of the year. In late spring the blackthorn blossom gives the budding green foliage on the crests of the hedges a white dusting reminiscent of the dot effect in a Pointillist painting by Seurat; while at the butt of the hedge and in ditches the dappled light picks out a carpet of primroses. In midsummer elder, honeysuckle, blackberry blossom,

BELOW One of the organic gardener's best friends is the ladybird, seen here earning its living on the courgettes at Eden Plants, Rossinver, County Leitrim. Ladybirds traditionally prey on aphids, a major plant pest.

LEFT The fruits of autumn. Hazelnuts, acorns and horse chestnuts picked wild from the hedgerows in the Lough Key Forest Park.

BELOW Midsummer flowers from the Roscommon–Sligo borders. Some, such as the honeysuckle, foxgloves, woodbine, ox-eye daisies and orchids, are truly wild; the roses started life as garden escapes which have happily colonized the abundant hedges of the area.

OVERLEAF Shooting wigeon, teal and mallard late one midwinter afternoon in the wetlands of Sligo. The old larch boat, built by the late Tommy Conlan, is based on a seventeenth-century design.

foxgloves, wild orchids, yellow flag irises, dog roses, ox-eye daisies and poppies, to name but a few, explode in a riot of colour through these same hedges. In late autumn the rusty reds and browns of the falling foliage expose an abundance of fruits and berries: a rich crop of elder, rowan, rosehips, sloes, blackberries and hazelnuts.

For me, this is a spectacular example of how rural Ireland has retained nature at its best.

These hedgerows know no man-made borders and we have by now almost surreptitiously slipped into County Roscommon. There may be few country houses in these parts to stay in, but Roscommon was once peppered with great estates. The houses at their centre represent some of the finest examples of Ireland's architectural heritage and include work by John Nash and Richard Cassells.

ROSCOMMON

Strokestown House is the last major eighteenth-century stately home to survive in the county. The house itself is the ancestral home of the Pakenham-Mahons and today looks much the same as it did when it was built. Designed by Cassells and strongly influenced by the work of the Italian architect Andrea Palladio, it is built in true Palladian style with a main central block and a curved east and west wing. The original estate covered some thirty thousand acres and was the largest in Ireland after Rockingham. Most of this land was under tenancy, but the main house kept a working farm of nearly two thousand acres. In the days before the Great Famine of the 1840s, and the subsequent mass emigrations, this estate had a direct bearing on the lives of tens of thousands of people.

Luke Dodd, the curator of Strokestown and nephew of the present owner – local businessman Jim Callery – has helped to keep alive this piece of Ireland's heritage. The house remains as it was last lived in by Mrs Hales Pakenham-Mahon until 1981. There is access to extensive memorabilia here documenting the social history of the house and its times, including fading photographs and certificates of former Crufts winners displayed in the tiny dogs' hospital. All the furniture and decorative items purchased through the centuries are still in place here – the family was prosperous enough never to have to sell anything. This policy was made clear even before Jim Callery bought the property in 1978 – before the auctioneer's hammer had fallen he had made a vow to keep Strokestown just as it was: a corner of Irish history preserved in amber.

Admirable though this approach to the past is, for many people it is the landscape rather than the architecture for which they visit Ireland. Further north in Roscommon, nearer to Sligo, Lough Key and its forest park – formerly the vast Rockingham estate – are especially worth a visit. With its wooded shorelines the lake harbours a prolific mayfly hatchery and commands some spectacular views.

In the heyday of these large Irish estates it was quite common to plant wild garlic on the borders of woodland and pasture. In late spring, when the overwintered sheep and cattle were introduced again to the grazing land, the garlic had an excellent medicinal

OPPOSITE George Taylor of Mohill in County Leitrim, a great conservationist and skilful hunter, with his red setter, a brace of wild pheasant and a bag of snipe and woodcock. His 'distressed' Barbour would now be a collector's item.
OVERLEAF Strokestown House, County Roscommon – the main façade showing the typical central block and flanking wings of Palladian architecture. This layout, evolved by the Italian architect Andrea Palladio in the seventeenth century for landowners in the Veneto who wished to combine an imposing residence with a working farm, later found great favour in Ireland. The wings were often elegantly disguised barns or stables, both functional and adding to the apparent grandeur of the house.

LEFT The library at Strokestown: the great Chippendale mahogany bookcase is one of the finest and most valuable in Ireland. Strokestown, though now inhabited only by a curator, is an architectural fly preserved in amber. It still contains all the original furniture, fittings and *objets d'art*, from the servants' quarters via the grand reception rooms to the nursery, that were accumulated by the Pakenham family over two centuries and more.
RIGHT An Irish winter still life: a cock pheasant, woodcock (bottom right) and snipe are displayed on bracken, beech leaves, sphagnum moss and bog grasses.
OVERLEAF Acres of pungently-smelling wild garlic gently push the bluebells aside in the woods of Lough Key Forest Park. Said by some to combine the flavours of garlic and chives, this wild herb, once planted on the great estates as spring feed for livestock, makes a useful and inventive addition to the kitchen.

effect on them. As the estates crumbled, the lush white carpets of wild garlic spread through secluded areas of undisturbed woodland, embroidered every now and they by bluebells and wild strawberries.

To me Lough Key is a very special place, the key to my passion for Ireland, for mayfly fishing and for wild places in general. On one occasion, after two and a half days fruitlessly fishing in monsoon conditions, I attempted to light a fire and make a cup of tea on Orchard Island, one of the many in the lake. Suddenly I was distracted by an interminable screeching din. The torrential rain had temporarily ceased and shafts of sunlight had brought the now steaming water to life. The noise that had sounded like two cob swans fighting over territory was in fact a cob subduing a pen in order to mate. I forgot my boiling kettle. I no longer needed a cup of tea. I pushed the boat out and was suddenly in the centre of one of the miracles of nature. An otter was playing cheekily alongside, mayflies were hatching and trout rising. Closer to the mainland I saw a herd of fallow deer springing through the undergrowth, red squirrels were scurrying from tree to tree and in a flash of electric blue a kingfisher darted along the shoreline. It was a glimpse of heaven.

AND BRIGHT IN THE SUN SHONE THE EMERALD PLAIN

LONGFORD   CAVAN
WESTMEATH   KILDARE
LAOIS   OFFALY

OPPOSITE After a storm on Lough Ree ('The King's Lake') in County Westmeath, dramatic evening sunlight charges a Scots pine with an unexpected amber glow.
ABOVE Rowan and mint jelly is served with pigeon by John Doyle at his restaurant, Doyle's Schoolhouse at Castledermot in County Kildare.

Ireland has such a wealth of good things to offer that visitors often bypass the counties at its heart. 'The midlands' may indeed be a somewhat off-putting name, but to ignore them in one's rush to discover the sophistication of Dublin, the gastronomic paradise of Cork or the savage beauty of the west coast is to deny oneself something of the essence of the land. The region is for the most part green and lush, well watered by streams and rivers and fine lakes, and it breeds some of the finest horses encountered anywhere in the world. There are also mountains to provide distant views and good days out for hillwalkers, and vast boglands where birdwatchers may spend many a silently satisfying hour with their binoculars.

The counties of the central plain and the midlands, except Cavan and Kildare, have two main characteristics in their landscape. The first is the great river which almost divides Ireland into two: all the myriad waterways of the region drain into the Shannon and eventually find their way to the broad Atlantic. This is ideal country for those who like messing about in boats, and there is a large marina at Banagher in Offaly. The second major feature is a vast expanse of flat, commercially harvested bogland that seems to go on forever. Known as the Bog of Allen, it stretches unhindered through the midlands, rolling vast, eerie carpets of peat-brown turf or bog cotton across several county boundaries. The Grand Canal cuts a much-used pleasure link right through this bogland and through several major towns in its hinterland before joining the Shannon itself.

Almost as if someone had suddenly switched on a light, a field of rape glows against a brooding, darkling sky just before a storm near Enfield, County Meath.

192

CAVAN & WESTMEATH

County Cavan in the north of the region, flanked by Monaghan and Leitrim and with the Ulster county of Fermanagh as its northern border, is known as the drumlin county – the county of little hills. As a result it is dotted with little valleys and little – or not so little – lakes. Cavan enjoys an eleven-month tourist season due to its excellent reputation for coarse fishing. Since the late sixties that reputation has been spread through word of mouth by Fred and Bert, Fritz and Hans, Jacques and Pierre and possibly even Giuseppe. In the twelfth month the fish are allowed to rest. To cater for this evolving cosmopolitan economy – no tourist development programmes here – the matriarchs of Cavan have built on 'B & B extensions', opened guest houses and small private hotels, and developed a service industry based on the simple but irreplaceable values of warm hospitality and good service.

Lough Sillan, Lough Oughter, Lough Gowna and the lakes of Killykeen hang like jewels on a necklet of rivers – the Annalee and Erne – draped over the very heart of Cavan. Much of the judicious development of facilities for the coarse fisherman in Cavan, since the pioneering days of the sixties, has benefited from the knowledgeable stewardship and commitment of Hugh Gough. In the old days his knowhow was shared over a pint across the bar in his pub in Cavan town. Today that expertise has been officially recognized and he works for the Central Fisheries Board.

OPPOSITE A catch of bronze bream from the Shannon, caught with bread. At the end of the day's sport the fish are weighed – these specimens weigh about 3–4 lb each – and gently returned to the water.
LEFT Not quite a monster of the deep but nevertheless a 20 lb five- to eight-year-old female pike, lightly hooked on a brilliantly coloured plug bait. After being weighed and photographed, the fish was slipped once more into the darkness of a small cave in County Cavan.
OVERLEAF Two magnificent tench weighing $4\frac{1}{2}$ and $5\frac{3}{4}$ lb respectively, which I caught in a secret lake in County Roscommon. One of the best escapades of my boyhood was to get up at dawn in midsummer and go tench fishing. Tucked away in a dark corner of a lake, I would sit waiting for the sun to rise, in anticipation of the brightly coloured floats sailing away and finally dipping when they were taken by a fish. A magical moment.

South of Cavan, the town of Athlone in Westmeath is, in a sense, the main crossroads of Ireland, from which most people would look outwards to Galway, Sligo, Clare and so on. But let us turn the tables, regard it as a focal point, and see what lies closer at hand.

At Collinstown in this county Sue Farrell makes Gigginstown (pronounce it like an Irish jig) cheese: her farm is hard to find, but fortunately her cheese is widely available in the shops in these parts. At Mullingar, in eastern Westmeath, you can find the Multyfarnham Deer Farm, where Chris Burley manages over a thousand head of fallow deer and sells venison. The lakes around here – Loughs Ennel, Owel and Derryvara – were once renowned for their trout.

OFFALY & LAOIS

Fluttering tufts of bog cotton drying off in the hot air of a raised bog in the Irish midlands.

Returning to Athlone and then going south towards County Offaly you will come to what is perhaps Ireland's greatest ruined monastic settlement: Clonmacnoise, founded in the fifth century. Commanding a low hill overlooking the Shannon, it now includes the remains of a castle and a cathedral, plus a number of churches, towers and Celtic crosses.

Offaly is also the home of Tullamore Dew – Irish liqueur whiskey – one of the great tastes of Ireland. In the town of Tullamore is an excellent pub and restaurant, the Bridge House, where you will find pleasant staff and good food.

The raised bog at Clara is the most important reason for botanists and other conservationists visiting County Offaly. Because of its uniqueness in a European context this area – Clara Bog – has been designated as being of international scientific importance. The origins of the bog have been traced back over ten thousand years. Bog moss and lichens grow in abundance here, as do bog rosemary, deer sedge, bog cotton and cross-leaved heaths. A series of carnivorous plants have colonized several of the hollows and pools in the bog. And a wide range of insects and animals have made this area their home, the hare being the most numerous amongst them. Foxes, red grouse and curlew are also to be found here, as are kestrel, snipe and merlin, and the common lizard finds Clara Bog an agreeable habitat. On the western side there is a woodland containing birch, willow, burberry, brambles and purple moor grass which provides further cover for rare insects.

Birr Castle, still in County Offaly but nearly on the Tipperary border, is situated in elaborate gardens that are open to the public (though the house is private and cannot be visited). The castle, all crocketed and pinnacled in nineteenth-century Gothic taste, also houses a giant telescope; it was installed by a former Earl of Rosse, whose descendants still live there today. Oxmanstown Mall in Birr town is possibly the prettiest Georgian street in Ireland.

The Slieve Bloom Mountains, to the east of Birr, form the border with County Laois. But the most famous landmark in these parts, to my mind, is Morrissey's pub in Abbeyleix.

KILDARE

West of Offaly and Laois, and flanked to the east by Dublin, lies County Kildare. A very well-known Irish sports writer once remarked that, to the Irishman, 'if the cow is his wife, then the horse is his mistress'. The Irishman's weakness for a flutter on the horses is known the world over, and there is no better place to flirt than at the Curragh of Kildare or at Goff's sales ring where serious horses are sold for silly money.

The Curragh is the nerve centre of Irish racing and home of the Irish Derby. In essence, it is a vast open heath with many natural 'gallops' set against a picturesque rolling backdrop, framed by dark, piney woods on a blue and darker blue horizon. Several of Ireland's top trainers have their stables here, including John Oxx, Kevin Prendergast and Dermot Weld, trainer of Go-Go, who in 1990 became the first horse from outside the USA to win the 122-year-old Belmont Stakes. Weld, also a practising veterinary surgeon, trains 120 flat racers and steeplechasers in his yard at the Curragh. He is quick to stress the importance of the horse-racing industry as a job provider, claiming that twenty-five thousand people are either directly or indirectly employed by it and its ancillary services. It is obviously important to the Irish economy, with so many foreign owners coming to Ireland to have their horses trained here – and at up to £180 per horse per week.

But not all this vast workforce's time is spent appraising, training and generally looking after the needs of horses. Still in Kildare, John Doyle's converted schoolhouse restaurant at Castledermot is popular with the horse fraternity and others. 'The John Doyle', a rather eccentric figure, can often be seen wandering around in his blue and white apron, gathering rowanberries from the trees in front of the restaurant to make his own particular version of mint jelly – served with his very good woodpigeon. Doyle's Schoolhouse is a veritable larder of fine, robust country food – pike, rabbit and pigeon regularly feature on its rich and lusty menu. Don't be frightened for the magnificent peacocks everywhere – definitely for decorative purposes only. For those with time to spare, the Schoolhouse provides accommodation in tastefully decorated attic rooms, with airy skylights and antique paraphernalia.

If tomorrow we found ourselves in the charge of a junta of colonels up from the Curragh, how many people would take to the barricades in defence of the Dáil?
THE IRISH TIMES (1971)
John Maurice Kelly

Pigeon Breast with Lime & Peppery Pineapple

Pigeons are shot locally for this dish. The carcasses, boiled up with vegetable trimmings and flavourings, make a very good and gamey stock.

SERVES 4

8 pigeon breasts

25 g (1 oz) butter

1 tbsp vegetable oil

salt and freshly ground pepper

tomato and watercress to
   garnish

SAUCE

150 ml (5 fl oz) white wine
   vinegar

165 g (5$^1/_2$ oz) granulated sugar

juice of 4 limes (save the peel)

1 l (1$^3/_4$ pt) pigeon stock

PINEAPPLE GARNISH

1 small pineapple

6$^1/_2$ tbsp white wine
   vinegar

3$^1/_4$ tbsp red wine vinegar

2 tbsp whole black
   peppercorns

6 tbsp granulated sugar

CANDIED ZEST GARNISH

zest of 4 limes

zest of 4 lemons

2 tbsp granulated sugar

2 tbsp water

Make the sauce first. Place the vinegar and sugar in a small saucepan, and heat to melt the sugar. Boil until the mixture begins to caramelize. Add the lime juice and cook for 10 minutes, then add the pigeon stock. Cook slowly, uncovered, for at least an hour to reduce (you need about 300 ml/10 fl oz). Season with salt and pepper as needed, and reserve.

For the pineapple garnish, remove the pineapple skin. Cut the pineapple in quarters lengthwise. Remove the central core, but save any juice that comes from the fruit. Cut into large chunks. Place both vinegars, peppercorns and sugar in a saucepan and simmer for 30 minutes. Add the pineapple and any juices, and continue cooking for 20 minutes. Remove from the heat and set aside.

Cut the lime and orange zest into very thin strips. Make a sugar syrup by bringing the sugar and water to the boil without stirring. Cook the lime and orange strips in the syrup for about 30 minutes until soft and candied. Set aside. (These keep well in a jar in the refrigerator.)

Heat the butter and oil in a frying pan and cook the pigeon breasts over low heat for 3–5 minutes, depending on taste (but they should be rare).

To serve, spoon some sauce on to each plate. Slice the pigeon breasts and place on top of the sauce. Spoon a little sauce over the meat, then sprinkle the candied zest over. Place some of the pineapple on each plate and decorate (if desired) with a tomato cut like a flower on some fresh watercress leaves.

Walnut & Almond Gâteau

These ingredients make for a very light cake mix, but John Doyle
suggests that it is even lighter if up to three more egg whites are included.
You could also add fresh fruit to the cream for the filling.

MAKES 2 × 20 CM (8 IN) CAKES
350 g (12 oz) caster sugar
7 eggs, 6 of them separated
100 g (4 oz) shelled walnuts,
    finely chopped
100 g (4 oz) ground almonds
1 tsp vanilla extract
75 g (3 oz) cornflour
300 ml (10 fl oz) whipping

cream, whipped and
sweetened with 1–2 tbsp
caster sugar

COFFEE CUSTARD
300 ml (10 fl oz) milk
1 tbsp caster sugar
2 egg yolks
a few drops of coffee essence

Preheat the oven to 220°C, 425°F, Gas Mark 7, and butter and flour two 20 cm (8 in) round cake tins.

Mix together the sugar, the whole egg and the 6 egg yolks. Beat well so that a smooth paste is obtained. Add the walnuts, almonds, vanilla and cornflour and stir together well. Beat the 6 egg whites until stiff, then gently incorporate with the other ingredients. Pour into the cake tins.

Bake in the preheated oven for 35 minutes. Remove from the oven and cool in the tin. Remove when cold, and cut into three layers horizontally.

While the cake is baking, make the custard. Heat the milk with the sugar to dissolve, then bring to the boil. Beat the yolks in a bowl, then pour the hot milk on to the yolks, stirring continuously. Mix well and return to the pan. Stir over gentle heat until the mixture thickens and coats the back of your wooden spoon. Pour into a cold bowl, and add the coffee essence. Leave to cool.

Spread two of the layers with whipped cream. Place the layers on top of each other and coat the top one with the coffee-flavoured custard.

Not a care in the world – the nicest possible way to go missing, to forget, for a while at least, about 'the way the world wags'.

The midlands are rightly famous for another fast-run sport – greyhound racing. Visitors who enjoy a night at the dogs will be pleased to learn that there are some very good tracks at Newbridge, Mullingar and Longford. The flat land of these parts is favoured by greyhound trainers 'in the know'. When hot weather hardens the walks, or heavy rain makes the going heavy on the farmland, the dogs are switched to the softer, lighter bogland tracks where their delicate toes can develop to race fitness without fear of a sprain.

Tony Murphy, who trains, breeds and vets greyhounds in Monasterevin, told me that, apart from the essential good breeding, a dog must be trained to perfection to be any good at all. This includes combing and massaging the animal to the sound of music (preferably a radio) for twenty minutes each day. This relaxes the dog and gets it used to changing or unpredictable sounds – like those at a racetrack. Tony will also flash a torch every now and again in front of his dogs' faces. Greyhounds – good greyhounds, that is – need good nerves and must react single-mindedly to the running hare.

Much sport, then, but no grandeur in the midlands; nor any great country houses to stay in. But hospitality will be assured wherever you go. Perhaps for the very reason that it has had less contact with tourism than some other parts of Ireland, this is a region frozen in time – a must to stop and savour.

We have halted on our journey at the crossroads of Ireland, or, more correctly, staring out over the vastness of the Bog of Allen in the middle of nowhere, wondering which way to go. My only advice to you now is that commonly given by wise old folk as they lean on their bicycles on some remote country road, every day of the week in Ireland. 'If I was you, I wouldn't start from here at all.'

He lived the good life
And he cast a lovely lime
FISHING AND THINKING
Arthur Aston

IRISH TOURIST BOARD OFFICES

Ireland
Bord Failte, Baggot Street Bridge, Dublin 2.
Tel 01 765871 Telex 93755 Fax 01 764764
for general postal enquiries
Bord Failte, PO Box 273, Dublin 8
Northern Ireland
53 Castle Street, Belfast BT1 1GH
Tel 0232 327888 Telex 74560 Fax 0232
249237
Foyle Street, Derry Tel 0504 369501
England
150 New Bond Street, London W1Y 0AQ
Tel 071 493 3201 Telex 266410 Fax 071 493
9065
France
9 Boulevard de la Madeleine, 750001, Paris
Tel 1 42 61 84 26 Telex 210601 Minitel 3616
IRLANDE
West Germany
Untermainanlage 7, 6000 Frankfurt/Main 1
Tel 069 23 64 92 Telex 414628 Fax 069 23 46
26 Btx 22081
Netherlands
Leidsestraat 32, 1017 PB Amsterdam
Tel 020 22 31 01 Telex 11648
Belgium
postal enquiries only
c/o Dept Infopost, Chaussée D'Alsemberg
860, 1180 Bruxelles
United States of America
757 Third Avenue, New York, NY 10017 Tel
212 418 0800 Telex 422234 Fax 212 308 1485
Canada
10 King Street East, Toronto M5C 1C3 Tel
416 364 1301 Telex 06 22084 Fax 416 363
6783
Australia
MLC Centre, 38th Level, Martin Place,
Sydney, NSW 2000 Tel 02 232 7177 Telex
AA 22917 Fax 02 959 3478

While every care has been taken to ensure
accuracy in compiling this section, the
Publishers regret they cannot accept
responsibility for any errors or omissions.
   Telephone numbers given in this directory
are for calling within Ireland. If calling from
outside the Republic, omit the initial 0 from
the number given, and precede the number
with the code for Ireland. (From UK 010 353,
from USA 011 353, from Australia 00 11 353)
   In addition to the hotels given below,
accommodation is available in guesthouses,
farmhouses and self-catering cottages. Contact
your nearest Irish Tourist Board for their
Hotels and Guesthouses and **Farm
Holidays in Ireland** booklets. Rent an Irish
Cottage Ltd, Shannon Airport House,
Shannon, Co Clare, is one of many self-
catering cottage companies.
   In the information which follows, the
material is given chapter by chapter, and
where possible county by county in the order
in which they appear in the book. In Chapter
1, however, the city of Dublin appears first, as
does Cork in Chapter 3. Sometimes the region
is treated as a whole. Addresses, telephone
numbers, brief facts and suggestions are given
for hotels, restaurants, places of interest
including historical buildings, gardens,
museums, archaeological sites and wildlife
reserves; and sports such as angling, sailing
and watersports, golf, horse riding, cycling
and walking.

The information is necessarily brief, and the
Bord Failte (Irish Tourist Board) or your
tourist office will be able to help with further
details. The Irish Tourist Board publishes
many fact-filled and extremely helpful leaflets,
a number of which are referred to here.

HOTELS AND RESTAURANTS

Hotels, restaurants, and pubs are listed
alphabetically county by county within the
area covered by each chapter. The hotels and
restaurants and some pubs mentioned in the
book are listed here with addresses, telephone
numbers, numbers of bedrooms (with bath
unless stated), seating capacity for restaurants,
opening times and credit card facilities. All the
hotels in the book are noted for their food, and
meals are often available to non-residents,
though advance booking is always advised.
Some places not mentioned in the book have
also been included as they are convenient and
can be recommended. Some establishments
are off the beaten track, so details of how to
find them are sometimes included. Major
credit cards mentioned are AM – Access/
Mastercard, DC – Diners Club, Visa –
Barclaycard/Visa, Amex – American Express.

PLACES OF INTEREST

This covers important historical buildings,
such as those run by the Historic Houses,
Castles and Gardens Association, including the
great Irish houses of the 18th century, and also
castles and cathedrals. Gardens open to the
public are listed, some museums and the main
archaeological sites whether neolithic remains
or evidence of early Christian or monastic
settlements. Further information on nature
reserves and national parks can be obtained
from:
The Wildlife Service, Leeson Lane, Dublin 2
or
The Irish Peatland Conservation Council,
3 Lower Mount Street, Dublin 2
   Some birdwatching sites are listed and
further information on the unique
birdwatching possibilities is available from:
The Irish Wildbird Conservancy, Ruttledge
House, 8 Longford Place, Monkstown, Co
Dublin

SPORT

Details of several sporting possibilities are
given with addresses and telephone numbers
of national bodies and other centres.

ANGLING

Angling is one of the main reasons many
people come to Ireland. For further details on
deep-sea or shore fishing contact the Irish
Federation of Sea Anglers, 67 Windsor Drive,
Monkstown, Co Dublin, Tel 01 806873, or
consult the Bord Failte leaflet.
   The season for salmon and sea trout opens
on 1 January, though many rivers do not open
this early, and ends on 30 September, though
sea trout can be fished later than this date.
Licences are required for these fish and can be
obtained from:
The Central Fisheries Board, Balnagowan
House, Mobhi Boreen, Glasnevin, Dublin 9
Tel 01 379206
or any of the regional fisheries (details in each
region), or most tackle shops. Permits must
also be obtained from the owner of the fishery.

Some fisheries are available for rent for the
season. Apply to:
**Department of Tourism, Fisheries and
Forestry**, Fisheries Administration, Leeson
Lane, Dublin 2 Tel 01 615666
   Salmon and sea trout fishing on Lough
Conn, Lough Corrib and Lough Currane is
free. Licences are not necessary for brown and
rainbow trout but permits are required by
some fisheries. The Bord Failte leaflet on game
fishing gives lists of the fisheries and local
accommodation centres. There are no licence
requirements for coarse or pike fishing, and
the season is open, but there are some
regulations about rods. See the Bord Failte
leaflet on coarse fishing. It also gives a list of
bait stockists.

SAILING AND WATERSPORTS

With such a varied coastline and with the
increasing numbers of marinas on the south
and south-west coast, all types of sailing are
popular. Details on aspects of yachting and
windsurfing from:
Irish Yachting Association, 3 Park Road,
Dun Laoghaire, Co Dublin Tel 01 800239
   Irish waters are ideal for learning to sail, and
details of sailing schools in relevant regions are
given. More information from:
The Irish Association for Sail Training,
Confederation House, Kildare Street, Dublin 2
Tel 01 779801
Waterskiing takes place on inland water and
round the coast. For details of competitions
and waterski clubs contact:
Irish Waterski Association, Mount Salus,
Knockaree, Dalkey, Co Dublin Tel 01 855205
Canoeing is extremely popular in Ireland,
with so many quiet waterways to explore, and
several fast-flowing rivers. Sea canoeing too is
a growing sport. For further details, and
information about courses and competitions,
contact:
Irish Canoe Union, 4–5 Eustace Street,
Dublin 2 Tel 01 719690
   Canoe hire information from:
Irish Canoe Hire, 25 Adelaide Street, Dun
Laoghaire, Co Dublin Tel 01 800251/844288
Cruising the inland waterways, whether on
canals or navigable rivers and loughs, is a
peaceful and fascinating way of seeing the
country. Addresses are given for companies
hiring narrow boats or cruisers as well as
details of shorter pleasure cruises.

GOLF

Visitors are welcome at Irish golf courses.
Addresses are given for the courses generally
considered the best, but Bord Failte will
provide a list of all the courses in the country.
A day's green fee costs on average IR£8 but
this will vary. Many holiday operators offer
all-in golfing holidays visiting several courses.

HORSES

Riding stables in each region are listed, and
most of these will offer facilities ranging from
children's lessons to trekking and trail rides.
Hotels offering riding holidays are listed, and
some riding establishments with
accommodation. Many hunts welcome
visitors who are very experienced riders. They
should arrange with the hunt secretary or
master in advance.

CYCLING

This is increasingly popular in Ireland. The roads are uncrowded and it is a perfect way to see the countryside. The Raleigh Rent-a-Bike and the Bike Store renting scheme operate throughout the country. Local addresses from:
Raleigh Rent-a-Bike, Raleigh Ireland Ltd, Raleigh House, Kylemore Road, Dublin 10 Tel 01 261333 Fax 01 261770
The Bike Store, 58 Gardiner Street, Dublin 1. Tel 01 725399/725931 Fax 01 364763

Bord Failte has several leaflets with suggested routes for cyclists throughout the country. Some of the long-distance tours are mentioned here. There are some holiday companies specializing in cycling holidays.

WALKING

COSPOIR, the national sports council, is creating a network of waymarked trails throughout the country, intending eventually to have a route right round Ireland. Many of these trails are complete, with direction posts, stiles and footbridges. The paths use old drove roads, farm tracks or footpaths, and take you past some of the country's monuments or through its most stunning countryside. Leaflets for these long-distance routes are available from the Tourist Board offices. Further information is available from: COSPOIR, Long Distance Walking Routes Committee, Hawkins House, Dublin 2.

Shorter marked walks or nature trails are available in all the Forest Parks throughout the country and the three national parks. These are mentioned in the relevant chapters. There are addresses of companies offering walking holidays in Ireland.

For information about climbing in Ireland contact:

The Federation of Mountaineering Clubs of Ireland, 20 Leopardstown Gardens, Blackrock, Co Dublin Tel 01 881266

TRADITIONAL MUSIC

Traditional music is thriving throughout the country and is not hard for visitors to find, whether in pubs or in sessions put on specially for visitors in hotels. There is a three-day national festival, the All Ireland Fleadh, every year on the last weekend in August, held in a different town each year. There are also regular performances by branches of Comhaltas Ceoltoiri Eireann throughout the country. This is the central organization for the promotion of traditional music, song and dance. Contact:
Comhaltas Ceoltoiri Eireann, Culturlann na hEireann, Belgrave Square, Monkstown, Co Dublin Tel 01 800295

MONAGHAN LOUTH MEATH DUBLIN WICKLOW CARLOW KILKENNY WEXFORD WATERFORD

MAIN BORD FAILTE OFFICES

Baggot Street Bridge Dublin 4 Tel 01 765871
14 Upper O'Connell Street Dublin 1
   Tel 01 747733 Telex 32462 Fax 01 786275
Dublin Airport Tel 01 376387 01 375533
   Telex 32491
St Michaels' Wharf Dun Laoghaire
   Tel 01 806984/5/6 Fax 01 802641
Monaghan Town (June–Aug) Co Monaghan
   Tel 047 81122
Market Square Dundalk Co Louth
   Tel 042 35484 Fax 042 38070
Newgrange (May–Sept) Co Meath
   Tel 041 24274
Wicklow Town (June–Sept) Co Wicklow
   Tel 0404 67904
Carlow (July–Aug) Co Carlow Tel 0503 31554
Shee Alms House Rose Inn Street Kilkenny
   Co Kilkenny Tel 056 21755
Crescent Quay (Feb–Dec) Wexford Co
   Wexford Tel 053 23111
41 The Quay (Feb–Dec) Waterford Co
   Waterford Tel 051 75823 Fax 051 77388

CALENDAR OF EVENTS

February
Castlecomer Folk Festival, Co Kilkenny
Feb–Mar Dublin Film Festival
March
Arklow Music Festival, Co Wicklow
Kilkenny Irish Week, Kilkenny
St Patrick's Day Parade, Dublin, and
   throughout the country
Feis Ceoil Music Festival, Dublin
Easter
Irish Grand National, Fairyhouse, Co Meath

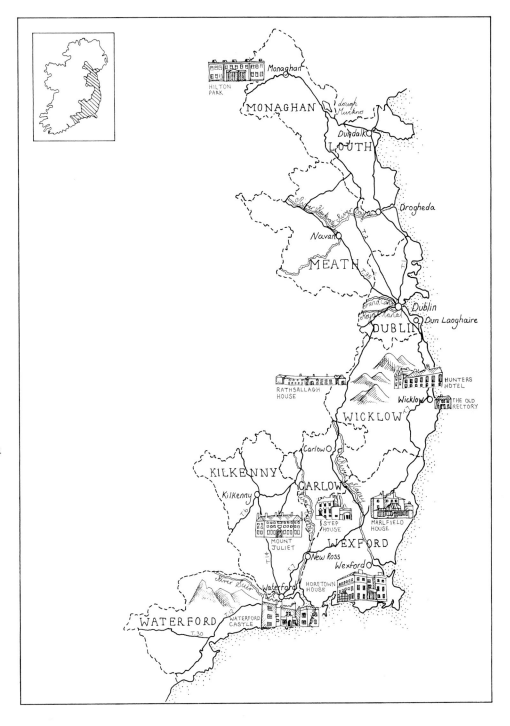

April
Jazz Festival, Howth, Co Dublin
International Opera Season, Dublin
May
Farney Angling Festival, Carrickmacross, Co
 Monaghan
Spring Show and Industries Fair, Dublin
Great Leprechaun Hunt, Carlingford, Co
 Louth
June
Garden Festival, Co Wicklow
Dublin Traditional Music Festival
Monaghan International Band Festival
Dun Laoghaire Summer Festival, Co
 Dublin
Festival of Irish Music in Great Country
 Houses at Russborough House
July
Strawberry Fair, Enniscorthy, Co Wexford
Clones Agricultural Show, Clones, Co
 Monaghan
Kilmore Quay Seafood Festival, Co
 Wexford
Clogherhead Prawn Festival, Clogherhead,
 Co Louth
Acorn Festival, Newbliss, Co Monaghan
August
Castleblayney Festival, Co Monaghan
Kilkenny Arts Week
Royal Dublin Horse Show
September
Waterford International Festival of Light
 Opera
Irish Autumn Fair, Dublin
Carlingford Folk Festival, Co Louth
Dublin Theatre Festival
Monaghan County Arts Festival
October
Wexford Opera Festival, Theatre Royal,
 Wexford
November
Dublin Indoor International Horse Show

HOTELS AND RESTAURANTS

CITY OF DUBLIN

Hotel Conrad
Earlsfort Terrace, Dublin 2. Tel 01 765555
Telex 91872 Fax 01 765424 Open all year. All
major credit cards. 190 rooms. Heart of
Dublin, just off St Stephen's Green
Jurys Hotel and Towers
Pembroke Road, Ballsbridge, Dublin 4. Tel 01
605000 Telex 93723 Fax 01 605540 Open all
year. All major credit cards. 390 rooms.
5 minutes from city centre
Longfields Hotel
10 Fitzwilliam Street Lower, Dublin 2. Tel 010
353 1761367 Fax: 010 353 1761542 Open all
year except Christmas Day and St. Stephen's
Day (26 Dec). All major credit cards.
Shelbourne Hotel
St Stephen's Green, Dublin 2. Tel 01 766471
Telex 93653 Fax 01 616006 Open all year. All
major credit cards. 165 rooms. City centre
Westbury Hotel
Grafton Street, Dublin 2. Tel 01 791122 Telex
91091 Fax 01 797078 Open all year. All major
credit cards. 200 rooms. City centre
Aisling Restaurant
Shelbourne Hotel, St Stephen's Green, Dublin
2. Tel 01 766471 Open 1230–1430, 1830–2230
Mon-Sat, 1230–1430, 1830–2200 Sun. All
major credit cards. Seats 65. In Shelbourne
Hotel
Cafe Klara
35 Dawson Street, Dublin 2. Tel 01 778611/
778313 Open 1230–2330. Closed Christmas
Day and New Year's Day. Credit cards AM,
Visa. Seats 140

Capers
4 Nassau Street, Dublin 2. Tel 01 684626
Open in the evening.
Le Coq Hardi
35 Pembroke Road, Ballsbridge, Dublin 4. Tel
01 684130 Open 1200–1500, 1900–2300.
Closed Sat lunch, Sun, public holidays. All
major credit cards. Seats 20
The Embassy Garden Restaurant
Jurys Hotel, Dublin 4. Tel 01 605000 Open
0700–1000, 1230–1415, 1815–2245. All major
credit cards. Seats 80. In Jurys Hotel
The Grey Door
23 Upper Pembroke Street, Dublin 2. Tel 01
763286/766890 Open 1230–1430, 1830–2300.
Closed Sun, public holidays. All major credit
cards. Seats 30
Kish Restaurant
Jurys Hotel, Dublin 4. Tel 01 605000 Open
1830–2245. Closed Sun. All major credit
cards. Seats 50. In Jurys Hotel
Locks
1 Windsor Terrace, Portobello, Dublin 8. Tel
01 543391/538352 Open 1230–1400,
1915–2300. Closed Sat lunch, Sun, public
holidays. All major credit cards. Seats 48
Lord Edward
23 Christchurch Place, Dublin 8. Tel 01
542420 Open 1230–1430, 1800–2245. Closed
Sat lunch, Sun, Mon. All major credit cards.
Seats 40
Old Dublin
91 Francis Street, Dublin 8. Tel 01 542028/
542346 Open 1200–1400, 1930–2230. Closed
Sat lunch, Sun, public holidays. All major
credit cards. Seats 65
Patrick Guilbaud Restaurant
46 James Place Dublin 2 Tel 01 764192/601799
Open 1230–1400, 1930–2215 Closed Sat
lunch, Sun, public holidays Seats 50 All major
credit cards
Ryan's Pub and Restaurant
28 Parkgate Street Dublin 8 Tel 719352/776097
Open 1230–1430, 1900–2200 Closed Mon
evening, Sat lunch, Sun, Good Friday,
Christmas Seats 32
The Soup Bowl
2 Molesworth Place Dublin 2 Tel 01 618918
Open 1230–1530, 1830–2330 All major credit
cards Seats 35

CAFES AND LUNCHTIME

Bewleys
Grafton Street Dublin 2 Tel 01 776761
Open 0730–2000 Closed Sun
Fitzers in the National Gallery
Mitchell's in Kildare Street
Pasta Fresca in Chatham Street Tel 01 792402

PUBS

The Bailey 2 Duke Street
The Brazen Head Bridge Street
Ryan's 28 Parkgate Street
Cavanagh's De Courcy Square, Glasnevin

Co MONAGHAN

Hilton Park
Clones, Co Monaghan. Tel 047 56007 Fax
047 56003 Closed Oct–Mar. Credit cards
Visa, AM. 5 rooms (2 with bath). 5km (3m)
out of Clones on L46 to Ballyhaise
Nuremore Hotel
Carrickmacross, Co Monaghan. Tel 042
61438 Fax 042 61853 Open all year.
Restaurant open 1300–1430, 1800–2145. All
major credit cards. 51 rooms. Seats 80

Co MEATH

Ardboyne Hotel
Dublin Road, Navan. Tel 046 23119 Fax 046
22355 Open all year. Restaurant open

1230–1500, 1700–2200. All major credit cards.
27 rooms. Seats 100
Alix Gardner's Cookery School,
Kensington Hall, Grove Park, Rathmines,
Dublin 4. Tel 01 960045
Alix Gardner provides a range of cookery
courses from 3-month Cordon Bleu to shorter
specialized courses including traditional Irish
cooking. She also runs Gourmet Tours
throughout Ireland, visiting restaurants,
meeting chefs and learning about Irish
cookery. For more details contact the above
address
Beauparc
Slane, Co Meath. Tel 041 24207 Telex 43784
Fax 041 24401 Open all year. All major credit
cards. 8 rooms. Across the river from Slane
Castle

Co DUBLIN

(See beginning of list for hotels, restaurants
and pubs in Dublin City)
King Sitric
East Pier, Howth, Co Dublin. Tel 01 325235/
326729 Open 1230–1430, 1830–2300. Closed
Sun, public holidays. All major credit cards.
Seats 60
The Old Schoolhouse
Coolbanagher, Swords, Co Dublin. Tel 01
402846 Open 1230–1430, 1900–2230. Closed
Sat lunch, Sun, public holidays. All major
credit cards. Seats 80
The Park Restaurant
26 Main Street, Blackrock, Co Dublin. Tel 01
886177 Open 1230–1415, 1930–2145. Closed
Sat lunch, Sun, Mon, Tues after public
holidays. All major credit cards. Seats 50

Co WICKLOW

Hunter's Hotel
Rathnew, Co Wicklow. Tel 0404 40106 Open
all year. Restaurant open 1300–1500,
1930–2100. All major credit cards. 18 rooms.
Turn off N11 on Dublin side of Rathnew, just
before village
The Old Rectory
Wicklow Town, Co Wicklow. Tel 0404
67048 Closed Nov–Easter. All major credit
cards. 5 rooms. Turn off N11 on Dublin side
of Wicklow Town
Rathsallagh House
Dunlavin, Co Wicklow. Tel 045 53112 Fax
045 53343 Closed Christmas–New Year.
Credit cards Visa, AM, DC. 10 rooms. 3k
(2m) outside Dunlavin
Tinakilly House Hotel
Rathnew, Co Wicklow. Tel 0404 69274/
67227 Fax 0404 67806 Open 1230–1430,
1930–2130. All major credit cards. Seats 60.
14 rooms
Tree of Idleness
The Seafront, Bray, Co Wicklow. Tel 01
863498/828183 Open 1930–2300, 1930–2200
Sun. Closed Mon, Good Friday, end
Aug–mid Sept, Christmas. Credit cards Visa,
AM, DC. Seats 60

Co CARLOW

The Step House
Borris, Co Carlow. Tel 0503 73401 Fax 0503
73395 Open 1900–2230 (Bistro 1130–0030).
Closed Sun, Mon, Feb. Credit cards Visa,
AM, Amex. Seats 30. 6 rooms

Co KILKENNY

Club House Hotel
Patrick Street, Kilkenny Town. Tel 056 21994
Fax 055 27398 Open all year. All major credit
cards. 23 rooms (18 with bath)
Hotel Kilkenny
College Road, Kilkenny Town. Tel 056

62000 Fax 056 65984 Open all year. Credit cards Visa, AM, Amex. 60 rooms
Mount Juliet
Thomastown, Co Kilkenny. Tel 056 24455 Telex 80355 Fax 056 24522 Open all year. All major credit cards. 32 rooms
Newpark Hotel
Castlecomer Road, Kilkenny Town. Tel 056 22122 Telex 80080 Fax 056 61111 Open all year. Restaurant open 1230–1430, 1830–2200. All major credit cards. 60 rooms. Seats 65

PUBS
Kyteler's Inn
St Kieran Street, Kilkenny Town. Tel 056 21064

Co WEXFORD
Horetown House
Foulksmills, Co. Wexford. Tel 051 63633/63706 Fax 051 63633 Closed mid-Jan–mid-Mar. No credit cards. 12 rooms without bath
Marlfield House
Gorey, Co Wexford. Tel 055 21124 Telex 80757 Fax 055 21572 Closed 2 weeks Jan. Restaurant open 1300–1430, 1930–2130. All major credit cards. 19 rooms. Seats 90
Talbot Hotel
Trinity Street, Wexford Town. Tel 053 22566 Telex 80658 Fax 053 23377 Open all year. All major credit cards. 103 rooms

PUBS
Farmers Kitchen
Wexford Town (3km/2m out of town on the Rosslare road)

Co WATERFORD
Jurys Ardree Hotel
Ferrybank, Waterford City. Tel 051 32111 Telex 80684 Fax 051 32863 Closed Christmas. All major credit cards. 100 rooms
The Tower Hotel
The Mall, Waterford City. Tel 051 75801 Telex 80699 Fax 051 70129 Open all year. All major credit cards. 80 rooms
Waterford Castle
The Island, Ballinakill, Co Waterford. Tel 051 78203 Telex 80332 Fax 051 79316 Open all year. All major credit cards. 31 rooms
Katy Riley's Kitchen
Tramore Road, Waterford City. Tel 051 75608

HISTORIC BUILDINGS
CITY OF DUBLIN

Christchurh Cathedral, Lord Edward Street. Open May–Sept, Mon–Sat 0930–1700, Oct–April, Tues–Sat 0930–1245, 1400–1700, Sat 0930–1245
St Michans' Church, Church Street Open Mon–Fri 1000–1245, 1400–1645, Sat 1000–1245
St Patrick's Cathedral, Patrick Street Open Mon–Fri 0900–1800, Sat 0900–1600
The Bank of Ireland, Butt Bridge
Dublin Castle, Lord Edward Street Open Mon–Fri 1000–1215, 1400–1700. Sat, Sun 1400–1700
Four Courts, Inns Quay Open Mon–Fri 0930–1700
General Post Office, O'Connell Street
Leinster House, Kildare St Open when Parliament not sitting, Tues–Sat 1000–1700, Sun 1400–1700
Marsh's Library, Patrick Street Open Mon, Wed–Fri 1400–1600, Sat 1030–1230
Powerscourt Town House, South William Street Open daily except Sundays and public

holidays Tel 01 7944144
Royal Hospital, Kilmainham, Open Sat and public holidays 1400–1700, Sun 1200–1700, July–Aug Tues–Sun 1200–1700 Tel 01 718666
Trinity College and Library, College Green Open Mon–Fri 0930–1645, Sat 0930–1245

MUSEUMS
CITY OF DUBLIN

National Gallery, Merrion Square. Open Mon–Fri 1000–1700, (–2100 Thurs), Sat 1000–1300, Sun 1400–1700
National Museum of Irish Antiquities, Kildare Street. Open Tues–Sat 1000–1700, Sun 1400–1700
Chester Beatty Library and Art Gallery, Shrewsbury Road. Open Tues–Fri 1000–1700, Sat 1400–1700
Douglas Hyde Gallery, Trinity College (Nassau Street). Open Mon–Sat 1100–1700
Guinness Museum and Visitors' Centre, James's Street. Open Mon–Fri 1000–1500
Irish Whiskey Corner, Bow Street Tel 01 725566
Irish Life Viking Adventure, St Audoen's, High Street. Open 0900–1600 Tel 01 720288

OUTSIDE DUBLIN

Castle Leslie, Glaslough, Co Monaghan. Open June–Aug 1400–1800
Slane Castle, Co Meath Open Mar–Oct Sun 1400–1800 Tel 041 24207
Newbridge House, Donabate, Co Dublin Open April–Oct Mon–Fri 1000–1700, Sun 1400–1800 Tel 01 436534/5
Malahide Castle, Co Dublin Open April–Oct Mon–Fri 1000–1245, 1400–1700, Sat 1100–1800, Sun and public holidays 1400–1800. Nov–Mar Sat, Sun and public holidays 1400–1700 Tel 01 452655/452371
James Joyce Tower, Sandycove, Co Dublin Open April–Oct Mon–Sat 1000–1300, 1400–1700, Sun 1430–1700
Killruddery House and Gardens, Bray, Co Wicklow Open May, June, Sept 1300–1700 Tel 01 863405
Russborough, Blessington, Co Wicklow Open Easter–Oct, Sun and public holidays, daily June–Aug 1430–1730 Tel 045 65239
Rothe House, Co Kilkenny Open April–Oct Mon–Sat 1030–1230, 1400–1700, Sun 1500–1700; Nov–Mar Sat, Sun 1500–1700 Tel 056 22893
Monaghan County Museum St Mary's Hill, Monaghan Town Tel 047 82928
Enniscorthy Museum, Castle Street, Co Wexford
Waterford Crystal Factory, Waterford Tel 051 73311
Agricultural Museum, Johnstown Castle Murrintown, Co Wexford Open Mon–Fri 0900–1700, Sat, Sun, May–Oct 1400–1700
Irish National Heritage Park, Ferrycarrig, Co Wexford Open summer 0900–1900, winter 1000–1600

GARDENS
CITY OF DUBLIN

National Botanic Gardens, Glasnevin, Dublin 9 Open Mon–Sat 0900–1800, Sun 1100–1630 Tel 01 377596/374388
45 Sandford Road, Ranelagh, Dublin 6 Visits by written appointment

Butterstream, Trim, Co Meath Visits by written appointment
Howth Castle Gardens, Howth, Co Dublin Open daily 0800–sunset Tel 01 322624
Beech Park, Clonsilla, Co Dublin Open Mar–Oct 0900–1700 Tel 01 867676

Fernhill Gardens, Sandyford, Co Dublin Open at any time by appointment Tel 01 956000
Powerscourt, Enniskerry, Co Wicklow Open Mar–Oct 0900–1730 Tel 01 867676
Killruddery, Bray, Co Wicklow Open May, June, Sept, daily 1300–1700
Mount Usher Gardens, Ashford, Co Wicklow Open Mar–Oct Mon–Sat 1030–1800, Sun 1100–1800 Tel 0404 40116/40205
Altamont Gardens, Tullow, Co Carlow Open Sun Easter–Oct 1400–1800 Tel 0503 57128
John F. Kennedy Arboretum, New Ross, Co Wexford Open all year Tel 051 88171
Johnstown Castle Demesne, Murrintown, Co Wexford Open all year daily 0900–1730 Tel 053 42888
Kilmokea, Campile, Co Wexford Open by arrangement Tel 051 88109
Lismore Castle Gardens, Lismore, Co Waterford Open Sun–Fri, 1345–1645 Tel 058 54424
Mount Congreve, Co Waterford Open by appointment only Tel 051 84115

ARCHAEOLOGICAL AND CHRISTIAN SITES
Brugh Na Boinne, Co Meath: Dowth, Knowth and **Newgrange**: Interpretive Centre Open June–Sept 1000–1900, Mar–May 1000–1300, 1400–1700
Kells, Co Meath
Tara, Co Meath
Mellifont Abbey, Drogheda, Co Louth
Monasterboice, Drogheda, Co Louth
Glendalough, Co Wicklow
Ardmore, Co Waterford
Jerpoint Abbey, Co Kilkenny
Duiske Abbey, Graiguenamanagh, Co Kilkenny

NATURE RESERVES
Glendalough/Glenealy, Co Wicklow Two adjoining reserves, the first a glacial valley with sessile oaks and conifer plantations, the second heathland and blanket bog
Glen of the Downs, Co Wicklow Sessile oaks typical of Co Wicklow
Sally Gap, Co Wicklow Mountain blanket bog south of Dublin
The Raven Nature Reserve, Co Wexford Dunes and sandbanks with several rare plants and many birds, especially species of tern

BIRDWATCHING
Carlingford Lough, Co Louth Flocks of scaup in winter
Dundalk Bay, Co Louth Huge numbers of oystercatchers in autumn. Bar-tailed godwits, golden plover, knot and dunlin in winter
North Bull Island, Co Dublin National nature reserve. Winter feeding grounds for Brent geese, ducks including red-breasted merganser, goldeneye, pintail and shoveler. Short-eared owls on saltmarshes. Interprative centre
Wicklow Mountains Peregrine, merlin, hen harrier and ring ouzel in the uplands
Wexford Harbour and Wexford Slobs In winter the world's highest numbers of white-fronted geese, sometimes Canada, barnacle and snow geese. Many species, some rare, of duck
Lady's Island, Co Wexford National nature reserve. Breeding terns, wintering swans and ducks
Saltee Islands, Co Wexford Nesting seabirds in summer – guillemots, puffins, gannets, cormorants, kittiwakes and auks

Hook Head, Co Wexford Spring and autumn migrants can include firecrest, woodchat, shrike and icterine warbler
Tramore and Dungarvan Bays, Co Waterford Saltmarshes at Tramore attract Brent geese, wigeon and grey plover. Waders as well at Dungarvan

ANGLING

Local information from:
The Manager, Eastern Region Fisheries Board, Balnagowan House, Mobhi Boreen, Glasnevin, Dublin 9, Tel 01 379206/379209

SEA FISHING

Deep sea fishing with boats available from Dungarvan and Ardmore
Shore fishing from Clogher Head, off Dalkey Island, from Dun Laoghaire to Killiney and Bray. Also from:
Greystones, Wicklow, Arklow, Gorey, Courtown, Wexford Harbour, Rosslare Harbour, Kilmore Quay, Arthurstown, Fethard, Duncannon, Ballyhack, Passage East, Dunmore East, Tramore, Dungarvan, Ardmore

GAME FISHING

Salmon on R Boyne, R Blackwater, R Nore, R Slaney, R Suir
Brown trout on R Barrow, R Greese, R Nore, R Suir
Brown trout and rainbow trout fisheries in Lough Creevy, Lough Emy and White Lake
Clonanav Farmhouse River Suir Angling School gives instruction in casting and fishing. Ballymacarberry, via Clonmel, Co Waterford Tel 052 36141
Blackwater Lodge Hotel gives trout and salmon fishing tuition. Upper Ballyduff, Co Waterford Tel 058 60235

COARSE FISHING

Pike: Lough Muckno, R Barrow at Carlow and Graiguenamanagh
Bream, rudd, tench, roach etc in Grand Canal, R Barrow, R Blackwater, Lough Muckno, Lough Moynalty, Ballyhoe Lake

WATERSPORTS

SAILING

The best sailing in the region is on the south coast, based at Dunmore East, but plenty takes place along the east coast. Dun Laoghaire Harbour is an important centre of Ireland's yachting, home of the Royal St George and the Royal Irish Yacht Clubs.
Other yacht clubs in the region include: Skerries Yacht Club, Howth Yacht Club, Malahide Yacht Club, The National Yacht Club, Dun Laoghaire Motor Yacht Club, Wicklow Yacht Club and Waterford Harbour Yacht Club.
Sailing tuition available at:
Dun Laoghaire Sailing School, 115 Lower Georges Street, Dun Laoghaire, Co Dublin Tel 01 806654
Dolphin Offshore Sailing Group, Chamco House, Bray Road, Shankill, Co Dublin Tel 01 823688/953739
Fingall Sailing School, Upper Strand Road, Broadmeadow Estuary, Malahide, Co Dublin Tel 01 451979 Fax 01 452920

WINDSURFING

Dunmore East provides the best windsurfing in the country. Contact Waterford Harbour Sailing Club

Tuition and hire also available at:
Wind and Wavesurfing School, 16A The Crescent, Monkstown, Co Dublin Tel 01 844177
Fingall Sailing School, Malahide (for address see Sailing)

WATERSKIING

Best places are Lough Muckno, Sandycove (Dun Laoghaire), Waterford and Wexford coasts, and on the Lacken Reservoir, Co Wicklow.
Muckno Waterski Club, Lough Muckno, Co Monaghan. Contact: David Boyd Tel 042 40115
Waterford Waterski Club, River Suir, Grannagh, Waterford. Contact: Michael Daniels Tel 051 55138/78359
Wexford Waterski Club, Wexford Harbour Boat Club, River Slaney. Contact: Thomas McGuiness Tel 053 22374

SURFING

East Coast Surf Club Contact Kevin Cavey, 15 Glen Avenue, The Park, Cabinteely, Dublin 18 Tel 01 695022 (work)
South Coast Surf Club Contact Margaret O'Brien-Moran, 7 Marine Terrace, Tramore, Co Waterford Tel 051 86582
Best beaches at Bray, Brittas Bay, Magheramore, Jack's Hole, Courtown (with strong southerly winds). Bigger waves on the south coast at Tramore Strand, Annestown, Bunmahon Bay.

CANOEING

Sea Canoeing at Tramore, Co Waterford, and Saltee Islands, Co Wexford
Canoe Surfing at Tramore
Canoeing Touring on the rivers Liffey, Barrow (some rapids), Nore, Boyne, Slaney (white water conditions in upper reaches when high), Suir and Blackwater.
Canoe equipment shops at
All Weather Marine, Grand Canal Quay, Dublin 2 Tel 01 713655
Marine Sales, Tubbermore Road, Dalkey, Co Dublin
Canoe courses available at
Tiglin Adventure Centre, Ashford, Co Wicklow Tel 0404 40169

BEACHES

Sandy beaches at Greenore, Laytown, Bettystown, Dollymount Strand, Bull Island, Brittas Bay, Arklow, Courtown, Curracloe, Rosslare, Kilmore Quay, Hook Head, Dunmore East, Tramore, Annestown, Bunmahon, Dungarvan, Ardmore

CRUISING

Grand Canal and R Barrow south of Athy down to New Ross
Boats for cruising from the Grand Canal to the R Barrow can be hired from:
Celtic Canal Cruisers Ltd, Tullamore, Co Offaly Tel 0506 21861
Cruising Restaurant: contact Dick Fletcher,
Galley Cruising Restaurant, Bridge Quay, New Ross, Co Wexford Tel 051 21723
River trips on the R Barrow and R Nore from New Ross to Inistioge, and on the Suir to Waterford.

GOLF

County Louth Golf Club, Baltray, Drogheda, Co Louth Tel 041 22329/22444
Headfort Golf Club, Kells, Co Meath Tel 046 40146/40639
The Royal Dublin Golf Club, North Bull Island, Dollymount, Dublin 3 Tel 01 336346

Portmarnock Golf Club (generally considered one of the world's finest links), Portmarnock, Co Dublin Tel 01 323082/323183
Woodbrook Golf Club, Bray, Co Wicklow Tel 01 824799/822532
Carlow Golf Club, Deerpark, Carlow, Co Carlow Tel 0503 31695/42599
Kilkenny Golf Club, Glendine, Kilkenny, Co Kilkenny Tel 056 22125
Rosslare Golf Club, Rosslare Strand, Co Wexford Tel 053 32203
Courtown Golf Club, Kiltennel, Gorey, Co Wexford Tel 055 21533
Tramore Golf Club, Tramore, Co Waterford Tel 051 86170

HORSE RIDING

Riding stables:
Greystones Equestrian Centre (residential), Castle Leslie, Glasslough, Co Monaghan Tel 047 88100 Telex 43657 DPLH EI attn G Bellew
Bellingham Stables, Castlebellingham, Co Louth Tel 042 72175
Ashton Equestrian Centre, Ashton Manor, Castleknock, Dublin 15 Tel 01 387611/383236
Bel-Air Hotel Riding School, Ashford, Co Wicklow Tel 0404 40109
Brennanstown Riding School Ltd, Hollybrook, Kilmacanogue, Bray, Co Wicklow Tel 01 863778
Broomfield Riding School, Broomfield, Tinahely, Co Wicklow Tel 0402 8117
Broom Lodge Stables, Broom Lodge, Nun's Cross, Ashford, Co Wicklow Tel 0404 40404
Inchanappa House Hotel, Ashford, Co Wicklow Tel 0404 40230
Kilmullen Stables, Kilmullen Lane, Newtownmountkennedy, Co Wicklow Tel 01 819906
Carrigbeg Stables, Bagenalstown, Co Carlow Tel 0503 21962
Rathvinden Equestrian Centre, Leighlinbridge, Co Carlow Tel 0503 21740
Thomastown Equitation Centre, Thomastown, Co Kilkenny Tel 056 24112
Horetown Equestrian Centre (residential), Horetown House, Foulksmills, Co Wexford Tel 051 63786/63633 Telex 80658 Fax 051 63763
Boro Hill Equestrian Centre Ltd, Clonroche, Enniscorthy, Co Wexford Tel 054 34102
The Mill Riding Centre, The Mill, Rathnure, Enniscorthy, Co Wexford Tel 054 55112
Kilotteran Equitation Centre, Kilotteran, Nr Waterford, Co Waterford Tel 051 84158
Melody's Riding Stables organize trail rides with accommodation overnight in farmhouses or hotels. The Comeragh Mini Trails: Ballymacarberry, Nr Clonmel, Co Waterford Tel 052 36147
The Wicklow Trail is a 6-day accompanied ride through the Wicklow Mountains with accommodation in manor houses. Contact: Ms Grainne Sugars, The Wicklow Trail, Calliaghstown Riding School, Calliaghstown, Rathcoole, Co Dublin Tel 01 589236

HUNTING

The main hunts in the region which welcome visitors are:
The Louth Hunt Tel 041 53348
Ballymacad Hunt (Co Meath) Tel 049 41573
The Meath Hunt Tel 0405 57014
Tara Harriers (Co Meath) Tel 046 21474
Fingal Harriers (Co Dublin) Tel 01 491467
Bray Harriers (Co Wicklow) Tel 01 694403

Shillelagh and District Hunt (Co Wicklow)
    Tel 01 972266
Wicklow Hunt   Tel 0402 32485
Kilkenny Hunt   Tel 056 26143
North Kilkenny Hunt   Tel 056 33209
Island Hunt (Co Wexford)   Tel 054 77125
Wexford Hunt   Tel 051 21225
Waterford Hunt   Tel 051 84142
West Waterford Hunt   Tel 058 54110

HORSE-DRAWN CARAVANS

Contact: Dieter Clissman Horse-drawn
Caravans, Carrigmore Farm, Wicklow, Co
Wicklow   Tel 0404 8188

HORSE RACING

At Leopardstown, Co Dublin

CYCLING

The suggested long cycling routes in the
region are **The Land of Gods and Heroes**,
which takes you along the River Boyne, and
past many of the ancient monuments of the
area; **The Garden of Ireland**, through the
Wicklow Mountains; **The Sunny South-east
Corner**, a gentle ride along the Wicklow
coast; **The Rivers of Mount Leinster**,
following the valleys of the Barrow and the
Slaney, and **Cliffs, Coves and Mountains**
which traces the Waterford coast and then
inland round the Knockmealdown Mountains
to follow the River Suir back to the coast.
Cycling holidays arranged by:
Easy Riders Cycling Holidays, 8 Tetrarch
Grove, Clonee, Co Meath   Tel 01 255484

The Bike Store, 58 Lower Gardiner Street,
Dublin 1   Tel 01 725399   Telex 33527
Mrs Mary Byrne, Ballyknockan House,
Glenealy, Nr Ashford, Co Wicklow   Tel 0404
44627
Gold Coast Holidays, Clonea Strand Hotel,
Dungarvan, Co Waterford   Tel 058 42249/
42416   Telex 80283

WALKING

The official marked walking trails in the area
are:
The Tain Trail (30 km) Circular route from
Carlingford to Omeath, then to the ridge of
Carlingford Mountains (430 km). Then it
descends through forest to Ravensdale, the Big
River Valley and back along the Golyin path.
The Grand Canal Towpath You can walk
along the towpath from Celbridge near
Dublin, west to Edenderry in Co Kildare, or
from Celbridge to Robertstown.
The Barrow Towpath Along the Barrow
Line Canal and the River Barrow, from
Rathangan through Athy and Carlow Town
to Graiguenamanagh, where you can connect
with the South Leinster Way
South Leinster Way (94 km) From Kildavin
in Co Carlow, through forest tracks over the
edge of Mount Leinster, along the River
Barrow Navigation, through
Graiguenamanagh and Inistioge, along the
River Nore, and finally across wide lonely
uplands and down into Carrick-on-Suir, Co
Kilkenny, where the path joins the first stage
of the Munster Way.

The Munster Way follows the River Suir,
through Clonmel into the Nore Valley and
along the northern edges of the
Knockmealdown Mountains. This part of the
trail ends at the Vee, a deep gap in the hills.
The Wicklow Way (132 km) from Marlay
Park in Co Dublin, climbs from the Dublin
lowlands through the Dublin Mountains to the
Wicklow Mountains. After Aghavannagh the
way takes you through softer country past
interesting antiquities until it reaches Clonegal
(Co Carlow).
   Other walks include the **Boyne Towpath**
(33 km) from Navan to Drogheda passing
Newgrange and the site of the Battle of the
Boyne; **The Dublin Trail** (41 km) which
follows the northern edge of the Wicklow
Mountains; the **Wexford Coast Trail** (12 km)
which takes you round Carnsore Point from
Rosslare; and **Avondale Forest Park**, Co
Wicklow.
Walking holidays in the area can be arranged
by:
Andrews Travel Consultants Ltd (ATC),
10 Meadow Vale, Blackrock, Co Dublin   Tel
01 984646/893390   Telex 33296   Fax 01
8985239
USIT Ltd, 19–21 Aston Quay, Dublin 1   Tel
01 778117/798833   Telex 93714   Fax 01 778843
Nick Becker, Knockreagh House,
Knockrath, Rathdrum, Co Wicklow   Tel 0404
4646
Heritage Rambles, Lismore Travel, 47 The
Quay, Waterford, Co Waterford   Tel 051
72126

TIPPERARY
CORK KERRY

MAIN BORD FAILTE OFFICES

The Castle (July–Aug), Cahir, Co Tipperary
    Tel 052 41453
Town Hall (April–Sept), Cashel, Co
    Tipperary   Tel 062 61333
Clonmel (July–Aug), Co Tipperary   Tel 052
    22960
James Street, Tipperary   Tel 062 51457
Tourist House, Grand Parade, Cork   Tel 021
    273251   Fax 021 273504
Town Hall, Skibbereen, Co Cork   Tel 028
    21766
Main Street (July–Aug), Youghal, Co Cork
    Tel 024 92390
Town Hall, Main Street, Killarney, Co Kerry
    Tel 064 31633   Fax 064 34506
Aras Siamsa, Godfrey Place, Tralee, Co
    Kerry   Tel 066 21288

CALENDAR OF EVENTS

February–April
Yacht racing at Kinsale, Co Cork
March
West Cork Drama Festival, Clonakilty, Co
    Cork
April
Killarney Easter Folk Festival, Co Kerry
Ballydehob Easter Races, Co Cork

May
Cork International Choral and Folk Dance Festival
Pan Celtic International Festival, Killarney, Co Kerry
Bantry Mussel Festival, Co Cork
Raft Race and Aquatic Weekend, Kinsale, Co Cork
Kinsale Yacht Club Fun Week, Co Cork
Listowel Writers Week, Listowel, Co Kerry
June
Kenmare Walking Festival, Kenmare, Co Kerry
Charleville Cheese Festival, Co Cork
Kinsale Arts Week, Co Cork
Durrus Community Carnival, Durrus, Bantry, Co Cork
Windsurfing racing, Oysterhaven, Co Cork
July
Walter Raleigh Potato Festival, Youghal, Co Cork
Schull Festival, Co Cork
Festival of West Cork, Clonakilty, Co Cork
Castletownsend Regatta, Co Cork
International Folk Dance Festival, Cobh, Co Cork
Cahirmee Horse Fair, Cahirmee, Co Cork
Mallow Folk Festival, Co Cork
Castletownsend Festival of Music, Co Cork
Skibbereen Agricultural Show, Co Cork
Festival of the Bard, Lisavaird, Co Cork
Welcome Home Week and Maid of the Isle Festival, Skibbereen, Co Cork
August
Annual Puck Fair, Killorglin, Co Kerry
Kinsale Regatta and Festival, Co Cork
Calves Week Regatta, Schull, Co Cork
Festival of the Carberrys, Leap and Glandore, Co Cork
Castletownbere Festival of the Sea, Co Cork
Rosscarbery Carnival and Regatta, Co Cork
Baltimore Regatta, Co Cork
Crookhaven Regatta, Co Cork
Cobh People's Regatta, Co Cork
Cahir Castle Norman Festival, Co Tipperary
Glandore Regatta, Co Cork
Rose of Tralee International Festival, Co Kerry
Busking Festival, Clonakilty, Co Cork
September–October
Film Festival, Cork
October
Kinsale Gourmet Festival, Co Cork
Guinness Jazz Festival, Cork
Feile Cleire, Clear Island Arts Festival

HOTELS AND RESTAURANTS

Co TIPPERARY

Clonmel Arms
Sarsfield Street, Clonmel, Co Tipperary. Tel 052 21233 Telex 80263 Fax 052 21526 Open all year. All major credit cards. 34 rooms (26 with bath)
Dundrum House
Dundrum, Cashel, Co Tipperary. Tel 062 71116 Telex 70255 Fax 062 71366 Open all year. Restaurant open 1900–2130, Sun 1230–1430, 1900–2130. All major credit cards. 55 rooms. Seats 65

CORK CITY

HOTELS

Arbutus Lodge Hotel
Montenotte, Cork. Tel 021 501237 Telex 75079 Fax 021 502893 Open all year. All major credit cards. 20 rooms

Fitzpatrick Silver Springs
Tivoli, Cork. Tel 021 507533 Telex 76111 Fax 021 507641 Open all year. All major credit cards. 110 rooms
Jurys Hotel
Western Road, Cork. Tel 021 276622 Telex 76073 Fax 021 274477 Open all year. Glandore Restaurant open 0730–2300. All major credit cards. 185 rooms. Seats 100. 5 minutes' walk from city centre

RESTAURANTS

Clifford's Restaurant
23 Washington Street West, Cork. Tel 021 275333 Open 1230–1415, 1900–2230. Closed Sun, Mon, Sat lunch. All major credit cards. Seats 34
Flemings
Silver Grange House, Tivoli, Cork. Tel 021 821621/821178 Open 1230–1400, 1900–2300. All major credit cards. Seats 52
Oyster Tavern
Market Lane, off Patrick Street, Cork. Tel 021 272716 Fax 021 275768 Open 1230–1430, 1900–2300. Closed Sun. All major credit cards. Seats 104
Crawford Gallery
Emmet Place, Cork. Tel 021 274415

PUBS

Mutton Lane Inn, off Patrick Street, Cork
Jury Rooms, off Washington Street, Cork
Cork's at **Jurys Hotel**

Co CORK

Acton's Hotel
Pier Road, Kinsale, Co Cork. Tel 021 772135 Telex 75443 Fax 021 77231 Open all year. All major credit cards. 57 rooms. Overlooking Kinsale Harbour
Assolas House
Kanturk, Co Cork. Tel 029 50015 Fax 029 50795 Closed Nov–mid-Mar. Restaurant open 1900–2030. All major credit cards. 9 rooms. Seats 25. Turn right off the N72 Mallow–Killarney road, to Kanturk
Ballylickey Manor House
Ballylickey, near Bantry, Co Cork. Tel 027 50071 Fax 027 50124 Closed Nov–Mar. Credit cards Amex, Visa. 11 rooms. On main N71 road between Bantry and Glengariff
Ballymaloe Country House and Restaurant
Shanagarry, Midleton, Co Cork. Tel 021 652531 Telex 75028 Fax 021 652021 Closed at Christmas. Restaurant open 1300–1430, 1900–2400. All major credit cards. 30 rooms. Seats 90. On the L35, 3.5 km (2 m) after Cloyne going towards Ballycotton
Ballymaloe Cookery School, Shanagarry, Co Cork. Tel 021 645785
Run by Tim and Darina Allen, the school offers 12-week certificate courses starting in June and September, as well as a variety of shorter speciality courses throughout the year
Bantry House
Bantry, Co Cork. Tel 027 50047 Open all year. 10 rooms (6 with bath). On the outskirts of Bantry
Christy's Hotel
Blarney, Co Cork. Tel 021 385011 Telex 75589 Fax 021 381111 Open all year. All major credit cards. 25 rooms. In village of Blarney
Longueville House
Mallow, Co Cork. Tel 022 47156 Fax 022 47459 Closed 20 Dec–Feb. Restaurant open 1300–1400, 1900–2100. All major credit cards. 16 rooms. Seats 50. 6 km (4 m) from Mallow on N72 to Killarney

Sea View House Hotel
Ballylickey, Nr Bantry, Co Cork. Tel 027 50073/50462 Closed Nov–Mar. Restaurant open 1330–1430, 1900–2130. All major credit cards. 13 rooms. Seats 40. On Bantry–Glengarriff road

RESTAURANTS

Aherne's Seafood Bar
163 North Main Street, Youghal, Co Cork. Tel 024 92424 Open 1230–1415, 1830–2130. Closed Mon (except July–Aug), Sun, Good Friday, Christmas. All major credit cards. Seats 40
An Sugan
Wolfe Tone Street, Clonakilty, Co Cork. Tel 023 33498 Open 1230–1430, 1800–2200. Bar food 1100–2230. Closed Good Friday, Christmas Day. Credit cards AM, Visa. Seats 48
Bistro Seafood Winebar
Guardwell, Kinsale, Co Cork. Tel 021 774193/772470 Open 1830–2300 Mon–Sat, 1300–2300 Sun. Closed lunch Mon–Sat. Credit cards AM, Visa. Seats 55
Blair's Cove House Restaurant
Blair's Cove, Durrus, Co Cork. Tel 027 61127 Open 1930–2130 Tues–Sat, 1300–1400 Sun. Closed Mon, Nov–Feb. All major credit cards. Seats 70
Blue Haven Hotel
Pearse Street, Kinsale, Co Cork. Tel 021 72209 Open 1030–2330. Closed Christmas Day. All major credit cards. Seats 70
Cottage Loft
6 Main Street, Kinsale, Co Cork. Tel 021 772803 Open 1900–2230. Closed Mon in winter. Credit cards AM, Visa. Seats 50
Dunworley Cottage Reastaurant
Butlerstown, Bandon, Co Cork. Tel 023 40314 Open 1830–2200 Wed–Sat, 1300–2030 Sun. Closed Mon, Tues. All major credit cards. Seats 30
Finins
75 Main Street, Midleton, Co Cork. Tel 021 631878/632382 Open 1200–1500, 1900–2200. Closed Sun, Christmas Day. All major credit cards. Seats 40
Man Friday
Scilly, Kinsale, Co Cork. Tel 021 772260 Open 1900–2230. Closed Sun, last 2 weeks Jan. Credit cards AM, Visa. Seats 60
Skippers
Lower O'Connell Street, Kinsale, Co Cork. Tel 021 774043 Open 1300–1430, 1900–2230. All major credit cards.
The Vintage Restaurant
Main Street, Kinsale, Co Cork. Tel 021 772502 Open 1900–2230. Closed mid-Jan–Feb, Sun. All major credit cards. Seats 50

Co KERRY

Ballyseede Castle Hotel
Ballyseede, Tralee, Co Kerry. Tel 066 25799 Telex 73050 Open all year. Credit cards AM, Visa, Amex. 10 rooms. On main Tralee–Killarney road
Doyle's Seafood Bar and Townhouse
John Street, Dingle, Co Kerry. Tel 066 51174 Fax 066 51816 Closed Nov–Mar. Restaurant open 1230–1415, 1800–2100. All major credit cards. 8 rooms. Seats 40. In centre of Dingle
Park Hotel Kenmare
Kenmare, Co Kerry. Tel 064 41200 Telex 73905 PARK EI Fax 064 41402 Closed Jan–Mar. Restaurant open 1300–1400, 1900–2100. All major credit cards. 48 rooms. Seats 100. Beside Kenmare golf club

HISTORIC BUILDINGS

Damer House, Roscrea, Co Tipperary Open Easter–Nov, weekdays 1000–1700, Sat, Sun 1400–1700 Tel 0505 21850

Holycross Abbey, Cashel, Co Tipperary

Bantry House, Bantry, Co Cork Open all year except Christmas Day 0900–1800 Tel 027 54007

Blarney Castle and Rock Close, Blarney, Co Cork Open all year except Christmas Eve and Christmas Day, Mon–Sat, May 0900–1900, June–July 0900–2030, Aug–Sept 0900–1930, Oct–April 0900–sundown. Sun, summer 0900–1730, winter 0900–sundown Tel 021 385252

Blarney Castle House and Gardens, Blarney, Co Cork Open June–mid-Sept, Mon–Sat 1200–1800 Tel 021 385252

Dunkathel, Glanmire, Co Cork Open May–Oct Tel 021 821014

Fota House, Carrigtuohill, Co Cork Open Mar–Oct, Mon–Sat 1100–1800, throughout year Sun and public holidays 1400–1800 Tel 021 812555

Riverstown House, Glanmire, Co Cork Open May–Aug, Thurs–Sat 1400–1800 Tel 021 821205

Charles Fort, Kinsale, Co Cork Open June–mid-Sept 1000–1830, April–June, mid-Sept–Oct, Tues–Sat 1000–1700, Sun 1400–1700, Nov–Mar Mon–Fri 0800–1630

Muckross House Killarney, Co Kerry Open all year Mar–June, Sept–Oct 0900–1800, July–Aug 0900–1900, rest of year 1100–1700 Tel 064 31440

GARDENS

Annes Grove Gardens, Castletownroche, Co Cork Open Easter–Sept Mon–Sat 1000–1700, Sun 1300–1800 Tel 022 26145

Bantry House Garden, Bantry, Co Cork Open all year 0900–1800, May–Sept 0900–2000 Tel 027 50047

Creagh Gardens, Skibbereen, Co Cork Open April–Sept 1000–1800 Tel 028 21267

Ilnacullin, Garinish Island, Glengarriff, Co Cork Open May–Oct. Groups by appointment Tel 027 63040 or 01 613111

Fota Estate, Carrigtuohill, Co Cork Open April–Oct Mon–Sat 1000–1800, Sun 1100–1800 Tel 021 276871

Timoleague Castle Gardens, Timoleague, Bandon, Co Cork Open Easter, May–Sept, 1200–1800 Tel 023 46116

Dunloe Castle Gardens, Beaufort, Killarney, Co Kerry Open May–Sept. Groups by appointment Tel 064 31900/44111

Derreen Gardens, Lauragh, Co Kerry Open April–Sept 1100–1800 Tel 064 83103

MUSEUMS

Nenagh Heritage Centre, Nenagh, Co Tipperary Open May–Oct Mon–Fri 1030–1700, Sat, Sun 1430–1900 Tel 067 32633

Fethard Folk Farm and Transport Museum, Co Tipperary Open May–Sept Mon–Sat 1000–1800, Sun 1330–1600 Tel 052 31516

Cork Public Museum, Fitzgerald Park, Cork Open Mon–Fri 1100–1300, 1415–1700 (1800 June–Aug) Tel 021 20679

Triskel Arts Centre, Tobin Street, South Main Street, Cork Tel 021 272022

Crawford Municipal Art Gallery, Emmet Place, Cork Open Mon–Fri 1000–1700, Sat 0900–1300 Tel 021 273377

Ballyferriter Museum, Dingle, Co Kerry

ARCHAEOLOGICAL AND CHRISTIAN SITES

Rock of Cashel, Co Tipperary

Athassel Priory, Golden, Co Tipperary

Gallarus Oratory, Dingle, Co Kerry

Skellig Michael, Co Kerry

Staigue Fort, Sneem, Co Kerry

NATURE RESERVES

Killarney National Park, Co Kerry A huge area (10,000 hectares) south of Killarney which contains the largest area of natural woodland left in Ireland, lakes, mountains, all set against the backdrop of Ireland's highest mountain range, Macgillycuddy's Reeks. The mild moist climate produces thick growth of mosses and ferns, and allows the existence of plants otherwise only known in Europe. Most famous of these is the arbutus or strawberry tree. Red deer live in higher areas and are the only remaining native red deer in Ireland. Visitors' Centre at Muckross House, where details of the nature trails within the park are available

Derrynane National Historic Park, Co Kerry Sand dunes by the shore of Derrynane Bay. Marsh and woodland habitats. The rare Kerry lily grows on Abbey Island, accessible on foot across the sands

The Gearagh, Macroom, Co Cork An ancient forest on the River Lee. Rare species of plants and large numbers of wildfowl

Gougane Barra, Co Cork A small lake which is the source of the River Lee. On an island reached by a causeway stood the cell of St Finbar, the 6th-century patron saint of Cork. A church stands in its place. Forest park nature trails and a car trail

BIRDWATCHING

Ballycotton, Co Cork Spoonbills, egrets and avocets on the marshes

Old Head of Kinsale Great and sooty shearwaters and skuas in spring and autumn

Cape Clear Island Ornithological observatory

Dursey Island, Bull Rock, Co Cork In summer breeding gannets

The Skelligs, Co Kerry Huge seabird colonies – 20,000 pairs of gannets on Little Skellig (Irish Wildbird Conservancy, no landing). Puffins and shearwaters on Great Skellig

Puffin Island, Co Kerry Puffins and Manx shearwaters. Permit required to visit this Irish Wildbird Conservancy Reserve

Akeragh Lough, Co Kerry Lagoon near Ballyheigue attracting autumnal visitors from North America – rare dowitchers and pectoral sandpipers

ANGLING

Local information from:
Manager, Southern Regional Fisheries Board, Anglesea Street, Clonmel, Co Tipperary Tel 052 23971/23624
Manager, South-Western Regional Fisheries Board, 1 Nevilles Terrace, Massey Town, Macroom, Co Cork Tel 026 41221/41222

SEA FISHING

Deep-sea fishing with boats available off: Ballycotton, Cobh, Crosshaven, Midleton, Passage West, Kinsale, Courtmacsherry, Clonakilty, Leap, Baltimore, Waterville, Valentia Island, Dingle, Tralee, Fenit

Sea angling Charters from Carbery Self-skippered Charter Boats or Courtmacsherry Sea Angling Centre Tel 023 46427

Shore fishing from Youghal, Ballycotton, Courtmacsherry, Ballinskelligs Bay, Inner Dingle Bay, Dingle Peninsula (Dunquin, Ballyferriter, Ballydavid, Castlegregory), Tralee Bay (Fenit), Ballyheigue, Ballybunion

GAME FISHING

Salmon on R Blackwater at Ballyduff, Fermoy; R Suir at Ballymacarberry and Clonmel; Lough Acoose, Lough Currane, Lough Leane

Trout on R Suir and its tributaries at Dundrum, Cashel, Golden, Bansha, Tipperary, Aherlow, Cahir, Clonmel and Ballymacarberry; R Nenagh; Lough Derg at Dromineer and Puckane; Lough Leane

Sea trout at Waterville, Co Kerry

COARSE FISHING

Pike on Lough Derg, R Lee and its reservoirs at Ballingeary, Inchigeelagh, and Macroom. Further coarse fishing on Lough Derg, R Blackwater, especially roach and dace.

WATERSPORTS

SAILING

The south-western waters are the most popular sailing area of the whole Irish coast, whether for ocean sailing, cruising or racing. There are numerous harbours and many marinas all round the coast.

The main centres are Cork Harbour – Crosshaven, Kinsale–and the many anchorages of west Cork round to Mizen Head.

This region also has the inland sea of Lough Derg, where much sailing and other watersports take place, with Dromineer the main centre.

Yacht clubs in the region include:
East Ferry Marina, Cobh; Royal Cork Yacht Club, Crosshaven; Kinsale Yacht Club; Baltimore Sailing Club; Schull Sailing Club; Bantry Sailing Club; Tralee Sailing Club; Lough Derg Yachting Club, Dromineer.

Yacht charters available from:

Yachting International Ireland, 44 Kilbane, Castletroy, Co Limerick Tel 061 333206 Fax 061 46650 (Based at Trident Hotel, Kinsale, Co Cork)

Kilmacsimon Boatyard Ltd, Kilmacsimon Quay, Bandon, Co Cork Tel 021 775134

Rossbrin Yacht Charters, Rossbrin Cove, Schull, Co Cork Tel 028 37165

Skellig Yacht Charter Holidays, Skellig, Monkstown, Co Cork Tel 021 841428/271971

Atlantic Yacht Charters, Ballylickey, Bantry, Co Cork Tel 027 50352

Shannon Sailing Ltd, Callista, Dromineer, Nenagh, Co Tipperary Tel 067 24295 Telex 31645

Sailing tuition from:

Glenans Irish Sailing Club, 28 Merrion Square, Dublin 2 Tel 01 611481 Telex 30519 (Sailing waters: west and south-west coast)

Baltimore Sailing School, The Pier, Baltimore, Co Cork Tel 028 20141

International Sailing Centre, 5 East Beach, Cobh, Co Cork Tel 021 811237

Knights Water Sports Centre Dromineer, Nenagh, Co Tipperary Tel 067 24295

TRADITIONAL SAILING

Cruises available on traditional Galway hookers with skippers and crews along the Kerry and Cork coast. Contact: Teach Dearg Restaurant, Scarteenakillen, Ballydehob, Co Cork Tel 028 37282

WINDSURFING

All round the coast (Schull is an international centre), and on Lough Derg hire and instruction available at:

Oysterhaven Boardsailing Centre, Oysterhaven, Kinsale, Co Cork Tel 021 770738 Fax 021 770776
International Sailing Centre, 5 East Beach, Cobh, Co Cork Tel 021 811237
Schull Watersports Centre, The Pier, Schull, Co Cork Tel 028 28554
Derrynane Sea Sports, Bunavalla, Caherdaniel, Co Kerry Tel 0667 5266

WATERSKIING

Boats and hire available at many sailing centres. For freshwater ski sites contact:
Carrigadrohid Waterski Club, Caum Cross, Macroom, Co Cork Tel 021 277707 (Aidan Fitzpatrick)
Cork Power Boat and Waterski Club, Farran Forest National Park, Farran, Co Cork Tel 021 292411 (Sean Kennedy)

SURFING

Best beaches on the south coast are Garrettstown, Courtmacsherry, Inchadoney, Ownahincha and Barleycove. The other area good for surfing is the north coast of the Dingle Peninsula between Slea Head and Ballybunion, especially at Brandon Bay, Banna Strand and Ballyheigue.

CANOEING

Canoe surfing at Garrettstown, Co Cork and Waterville, Co Kerry.
Canoeing on the Fermoy stretch of the R Blackwater, but watch the anglers! The R Lee from the Inniscarra Cemetery to Cork County Hall.

BEACHES

Sandy beaches all round the coast in tiny coves. Good beaches west of Youghal in Ballycotton Bay, Ownahincha, Schull, Crookhaven, Barleycove, Ballinskelligs Bay, Rossbeigh Strand, Inch, Brandon Bay, Tralee Bay and Banna Strand.

GOLF

Clonmel Golf Club, Lyrenearle, Clonmel, Co Tipperary Tel 052 21138
Cork Golf Club, Little Island, Co Cork Tel 021 353451
Douglas Golf Club, Douglas, Co Cork Tel 021 895297
Mallow Golf Club, Ballyellis, Mallow, Co Cork Tel 022 21145
Monkstown Golf Club, Parkgarriffee, Monkstown, Co Cork Tel 021 841376
Muskerry Golf Club, Carrigrohane, Co Cork Tel 021 385297
Youghal Golf Club, Knockaverry, Youghal, Co Cork Tel 024 92787
Ballybunion Golf Club, Ballybunion, Co Kerry Tel 068 27146
Killarney Golf and Fishing Club, Killarney, Co Kerry Tel 064 31242
Tralee Golf Club, Barrow, Ardfert, Tralee, Co Kerry Tel 066 36379
Waterville Golf Club, Waterville, Co Kerry Tel 0667 4133/4102

HORSE RIDING

Hotels offering riding holidays:
Ardnavaha House Hotel, Ballinascarthy, West Cork Tel 023 49135 Fax 023 49136
Arbutus Lodge Hotel, Montenotte, Cork Tel 021 501237 Fax 021 502893 (hunting holidays only)

RIDING STABLES

Ashroe Riding School, Ashroe, Nr Newport, Co Tipperary Tel 061 378271
Ballycormac House and Stables, Aglish, Borrisokane, Co Tipperary Tel 067 21129
Blarney Riding Centre, The Paddock, Killowen, Blarney, Co Cork Tel 021 385854
Clonmeen Lodge Riding School (Accommodation available), Banteer, Co Cork Tel 029 56090
Foleys Riding and Trekking Centre, Killowen, Newmarket, Co Cork Tel 029 60048
Hitchmough Riding School, Highland Lodge, Monkstown, Co Cork Tel 021 371267
O'Regan's Riding Centre, Minister's Cross, Crookstown, Co Cork Tel 021 336387
Pinegrove Riding School, Pinegrove, Whites Cross, Co Cork Tel 021 303857
Raleigh Riding Centre, Raleigh House, Macroom, Co Cork Tel 026 41018
Skevanish Riding Centre, Skevanish, Innishannon, Co Cork Tel 021 775476
West Cork Horse Trekking Centre Co Ltd, Rooska, Bantry, Co Cork Tel 027 50221
Glenbeigh Riding Stables, Glenbeigh, Co Kerry Tel 066 68143

TRAIL RIDES

The Lough Derg Gourmet Ride A trail ride following the shore of Lough Derg, with forest trails, hills and mountains as well as gourmet food and accommodation for seven nights. Contact: Mrs Rosetta-Ann Paxman, Ballycormac House, Aglish, Borrisokane, Co Tipperary Tel 067 21129
Dingle Peninsula Trail Contact: William J O'Connor, El Rancho Farmhouse, Ballyard, Tralee, Co Kerry Tel 066 21840
Killarney Reeks Trail Contact: Donal O'Sullivan, Killarney Riding Stables, Ballydowney, Killarney, Co Kerry Tel 064 31686 Fax 064 34119

HUNTING

The main hunts which welcome visitors in this region are:
Co Tipperary
The Golden Vale Hunt Tel 0502 41276
North Tipperary Hunt Tel 067 32033
Ormond Hunt Tel 067 21105
Scarteen Hunt (The Black and Tans) Tel 062 51248
Tipperary Hunt Tel 052 56156
Co Cork
Duhallow Hunt Tel 022 29350
United Hunt Tel 021 505965/277399
West Carberry Hunt, Eldon Hotel, Skibbereen, Co Cork
Muskerry Hunt Tel 021 771472

HORSE-DRAWN CARAVANS

Contact David Slattery
Slattery's Horse-Drawn Caravans, 1 Russell Street, Tralee, Co Kerry Tel 066 26277 Fax 066 25981

CYCLING

The south-west of Ireland is perfect cycling terrain. There are numerous and varied routes throughout the region. The recommended long-distance routes take in the main attractions of the area.
Slates, Stars and Silvermines: this ride skirts the east coast of Lough Derg and passes old slate quarries, Birr Castle and the Silvermines. **The Land of Edmund Spenser** is a ride through Tipperary along the valley of the River Blackwater, and through the Galtee

and Kilworth mountains. **The Lakes and Rivers of West Cork:** this ride takes in Cork and Kinsale and follows the valleys of the Lee and the Bandon, crossing the Shehy mountains at the Deer's Pass. **The Coast of West Cork:** harbours, coves and inlets from Glengarriff round the peninsula to Kenmare. **The Ring of Kerry:** this famous circular route travels beside the sea, through the Killarney National Park, up hills and through valleys. **The Mountains of Dingle:** a mainly lowland ride round the Dingle Peninsula, rising to 500 m to cross the Conor Pass.
Cycling holidays arranged by:
Travel Ireland, 76 Grand Parade, Cork. Tel 021 275911
Sile Bean Ui Ghormain, Glaise Bheag, Baile na nGall, Dingle, Co Kerry. Tel 066 55162
Michael O'Halloran Fossa Leisure Holidays Ltd, Fossa, Killarney, Co Kerry. Tel 064 31497
The Brandon Hotel, Tralee, Co Kerry. Tel 066 23333 Telex 73130 Fax 066 25019

WALKING

The two completed walking trails are the **Kerry Way** and the **Dingle Way**:
The Kerry Way (200 km) goes through wonderful scenery round the Iveragh Peninsula. There are no very high climbs on this walk, but marvellous views are available across to the mountains of Macgillycuddy's Reeks. The route can be joined at several places from the main road, affording shorter walks for those who do not want to attempt the full circuit.
The Dingle Way (Sli Chorcha Dhuibhne) (153 km) encircles the Dingle Peninsula with splendid views across Dingle Bay to the south, and following the coast on the north of the peninsula.
As yet uncompleted walks are the 80-km **Beara Way** which takes the walker from Kenmare round past Gougane Barra to Glengarriff and along the length of the Beara Peninsula to Cod's Head.
The Great Southern Trail will stretch from Rathkeale in Co Limerick south-west to Tralee to join up with the Dingle Way.
The projected extension of the **Munster Way** from Fermoy to Kenmare will link all these walks with the eastern network.
Also shorter walks in forest parks at Gougane Barra, and Doneraile near Mallow; the woody coastline of Glengarriff Harbour, on paths along the cliffs of Mizen Head or the Knockmealdown mountains.
Hill walking in MacGillycuddy's Reeks – Carrantoohill is the highest point, and the popular route is via Hag's Glen and Devil's Ladder, but it is essential to have experience in hill walking, and only to approach it in assured clear weather.
Walking holidays can be arranged by:
Ballinacourty House, Glen of Aherlow, Co Tipperary Tel 062 56230
Clonmel Arms Hotel, Clonmel, Co Tipperary Tel 052 21233
Brian Hensey, Irish Mountain Holidays, Monafodda, Roscrea, Co Tipperary Tel 0509 31150
Travel Ireland, 76 Grand Parade, Cork Tel 021 275911 Telex 75363
Walking the Best of Kerry, Country Walking Holidays, Curragraigue, Blennerville PO, Dingle Peninsula, Co Kerry Tel 066 24467
Killarney Valley Holidays, 43 High Street, Killarney, Co Kerry Tel 064 33144

CLARE LIMERICK GALWAY

MAIN BORD FAILTE OFFICES

The Granary, Michael Street, Limerick City, Co Limerick Tel 061 317552 Telex 70604 Fax 061 315634

Adare (June–Aug), Co Limerick Tel 061 86255

Clare Road, Ennis, Co Clare Tel 065 28366

Shannon Airport, Co Clare Tel 061 61664/61565/61604

Cliffs of Moher (Mar–Aug), Co Clare Tel 065 81171

Victoria Palace, Nr Eyre Square, Galway City, Co Galway Tel 091 63081 Telex 50170 Fax 091 65201

Clifden (June–Aug), Co Galway Tel 095 21163

Ballinasloe (July–Aug), Co Galway Tel 0905 42131

CALENDAR OF EVENTS

March
Irish Week, Ennis, Co Clare
Clare Drama Festival, Co Clare
International Marching Band Competition, Limerick
Limerick Church Music International Choral Festival

April
Brass Band Festival, Ennis, Co Clare

May
Fleadh Nua, Ennis, Co Clare

May–September
Burren Painting Course, Lisdoonvarna, Co Clare

June
Ennis Arts Festival, Co Clare
Abbeyfeale Folk Festival, Co Limerick
Waterskiing Championships, Co Clare
Angling Festival, Fanore, Co Clare

July
Salthill Harp Festival, Co Galway
Portumna Street Festival, Co Galway
Quilty Lobster Festival, Co Clare
Galway Races

August
Galway Arts Festival
Connemara Pony Show, Clifden, Co Galway
Cruinniu na mBad Galway Hooker Festival, Kinvara, Co Galway

September
Clarinbridge Oyster Festival, Co Galway
International Oyster Festival, Galway

October
Ballinasloe Great October Fair, Co Galway
International Gort Festival of Traditional Irish Music, Co Galway

HOTELS AND RESTAURANTS

Co CLARE

Dromoland Castle
Newmarket on Fergus, Shannon, Co Clare. Tel 061 71144 Telex 70654 Fax 061 36335 Open all year. All major credit cards. 73 rooms. Outside Newmarket on Fergus on the N18 Limerick–Ennis road.

Fitzpatrick Shamrock Hotel
Bunratty, Co Clare. Tel 061 361177 Telex 72114 Fax 061 61252 Open all year. Restaurant open 1230–1430, 1900–2130. All major credit cards. 100 rooms. Seats 100. In the grounds of Bunratty Castle on the N18 Limerick–Ennis road

Claire's Restaurant
Ballyvaughan, Co Clare. Tel 065 77029 Open

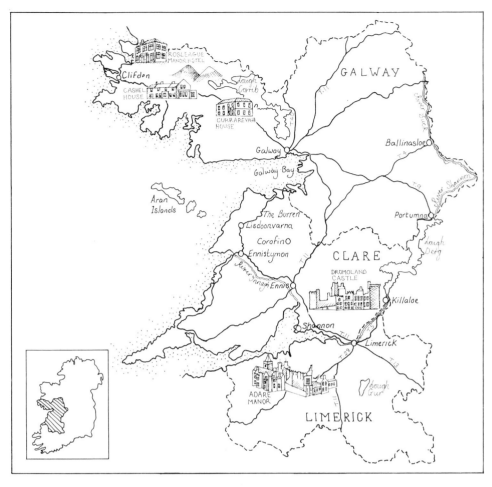

1830–2200. Closed Sun–Thurs, Oct–Easter Mon in Sept. All major credit cards. In Manus Walsh Craft Shop, Ballyvaughan, on the N67 Kilcolgan–Lisdoonvarna road

Durty Nelly's
Bunratty, Co Clare. Tel 061 364861. Includes these two:

Oyster Restaurant
Open 1030–2230. Closed Sun, Good Friday, Christmas Day. Seats 55. **Loft Restaurant** Open 1030–2230 Mon–Sat, 1200–2230 Sun. Closed Good Friday, Christmas Day. Seat 65. Credit cards AM, Amex, DC. All next to Bunratty Castle

MacCloskey's
Bunratty House Mews, Bunratty, Co Clare. Tel 061 364082 Open 1900–2200. Closed Sun, Mon, 20 Dec–end Jan. All major credit cards. Seats 55. Behind Bunratty Castle

PUBS

Gus O'Connor's Doolin, Co Clare

Co LIMERICK

Adare Manor
Adare, Co Limerick. Tel 061 86566 Telex 70733 Fax 061 86124 Open all year. All major credit cards. 64 rooms. In Adare village, on the N22 Limerick–Killarney road

Dunraven Arms Hotel
Adare, Co Limerick. Tel 061 86209 Telex 70202 Fax 061 86541 Open all year. All major credit cards. 45 rooms

Greenhills Hotel
Ennis Road, Limerick City. Tel 061 53033 Telex 70246 Fax 061 53307 Closed Christmas Day. All major credit cards. 55 rooms

Jurys Hotel
Ennis Road, Limerick. Tel 061 55266 Telex 70766 Fax 061 326400 Open all year. All major credit cards. 96 rooms

The Mustard Seed
Adare, Co Limerick. Tel 061 86451 Open 1900–2200. Closed Sun, Mon, 22 Dec–end Jan. Credit cards AM, DC, Visa. Seats 45

PUBS

Matt The Thresher Birdhill (on the Limerick–Tipperary border)

Co GALWAY

Ardilaun House Hotel
Taylor's Hill, Galway. Tel 091 21433 Telex 50013 Fax 091 21546 Closed Christmas. Restaurant open 1300–1430, 1900–2230. All major credit cards. 91 rooms. Seats 150. Between Galway City and Salthill

Cashel House Hotel
Cashel, Co Galway. Tel 095 31001 Telex 50812 Fax 095 31077 Closed Nov–mid-Feb. Restaurant open 1930–2030. Credit cards AM, Amex, Visa. 29 rooms. N59 Galway–Clifden, turn left at Recess

Currarevagh House
Oughterard, Connemara, Co Galway. Tel 091 82312 Closed Nov–Mar. No credit cards. 15 rooms. N59 Galway–Oughterard. Turn right in village square and follow lakeshore road for 6 km (4 m)

Inagh Valey Inn
Recess, Co. Galway. Tel: 010 353 95 34608 Open all year. No credit cards

Great Southern Hotel
Eyre Square, Galway City. Tel 091 64041 Telex 50164 Fax 091 66704 Open all year. Restaurant open 1830–2200. All major credit cards. 120 rooms. Seats 100. Eyre Square in centre of Galway City

Rosleague Manor Hotel
Letterfrack, Connemara, Co Galway. Tel 095 41101 Fax 095 41168 Closed Nov–Mar. Restaurant open 2000–2130. Credit cards AM,

AE, Visa. 15 rooms. On N59 11 km (7m) NE of Clifden just before Letterfrack
Sweeney's Oughterard House Hotel
Oughterard, Connemara. Tel 091 82207 Fax 091 82161 Restaurant open 1930–2100. Closed 6 days at Christmas. All major credit cards. 20 rooms. On N59, west of Oughterard
Drimcong House Restaurant
Moycullen, Co Galway. Tel 091 85115/85585 Open 1900–2230. Closed Sun, Mon, Jan, Feb. All major credit cards. Seats 50. On N59 13 km (8 m) NW of Galway
The Drimcong Food and Wine Experience
Gerry Galvin gives several four-day (Tues–Fri) demonstration cookery courses for 10–12 people in November and December each year. For further details contact: Gerry Galvin at Drimcong House Tel 091 85115/85585
Moran's Oyster Cottage
The Weir, Kilcolgan, Co Galway. Tel 091 96113/96083 Open 1030–2330 Mon–Sat. 1200–1400, 1600–2300 Sun. Closed Good Friday, Christmas Day. Credit cards Amex, Visa. Seats 100. Kilcolgan is at junction of N67 and N18. Watch for signposts to restaurant
O'Grady's Seafood Restaurant
Clifden, Connemara, Co Galway. Tel 095 21450 Open 1230–1500, 1800–2200. Closed Christmas, mid-Jan–mid-Mar. Credit cards AM, DC, Visa. Seats 60. In Market Street, Clifden (N59)
The Zetland House Hotel
Cashel, Connemara, Co Galway. Tel 010 353 9531111 Fax 010 353 9531117 Proprietors: John and Mona Prendergast. Open 1st April–31st October; open for woodcock and snipe in season. Credit cards: Access, Visa, Amex, DC

PUBS

Paddy Burke's Clarinbridge, Co Galway
King's Head High Street, Galway City
McDonagh's Oranmore, Co Galway

HISTORIC BUILDINGS

Bunratty Castle, Bunratty, Co Clare
Open all year 0930–1730 Tel 061 361511
Open for medieval banquets
Cratloe Woods, Cratloe, Co Clare
Open June–Sept, Mon–Fri 1000–1700, Sat, Sun 1100–1700, Oct–May, Mon–Fri 1000–1700, closed weekends
Knappogue Castle, Quin, Co Clare
Open May–Sept 0930–1730 Tel 061 361511
Open for medieval banquets
Castle Matrix, Rathkeale, Co Limerick Open Mar–Oct, Mon 1400–1800. Other times by arrangement Tel 0502 26110
Glin Castle, Glin, Co Limerick Open May 1000–1200, 1400–1600. Other times by arrangement Tel 068 34173
Dunguaire Castle, Kinvara, Co Galway
Open May–Sept Tel 091 37108 Open for medieval banquets
Kylemore Abbey, Connemara, Co Galway
Open Feb–Nov 1000–1800 Tel 095 41146
Thoor Ballylee, Gort, Co Galway Open May–Sept 1000–1800 Tel 091 31436/63081 (off season)
Aughnanure Castle, Oughterard, Co Galway Open June–Sept 1000–1800.

ARCHAEOLOGICAL AND CHRISTIAN SITES

Ennis Friary, Ennis, Co Clare
Killinaboy Tau Cross, Corofin, Co Clare
Quin Abbey, Co Clare
Cong Abbey, Co Galway
Dun Aengus, Inishmore, Aran Islands
Clonfert Cathedral, Banagher, Co Galway

Kilmacduagh Monastery, Gort, Co Galway
Ross Errilly, Headford, Co Galway
St Macdara's Island, Co Galway

MUSEUMS

Clare Heritage Centre, Corofin, Co Clare
Open Mar–Oct 1000–1800 Tel 065 27955
Bunratty Folk Park, Bunratty, Co Clare
Open 0930–1900 Tel 061 361511
Craiggaunowen Project, Quin, Co Clare
Open May–Sept 1000–1800 Tel 061 361511
Lough Gur Interpretive Centre, Lough Gur, Co Limerick Open May–Sept Tel 061 361511
Museum Arainn, Kilronan, Inishmore, Aran Islands

NATURE RESERVES

The Burren, Co Clare. Bare limestone hills containing unique mixture of flowers, ranging from Arctic species to Mediterranean and even tropical, all growing together. Over 22 types of orchid. Best time to visit mid-May. Not only botanical interest but also archaeological monuments, ring forts, castles and tombs. Potholes and caves for serious speleologists. Aillwee Cave near Ballyvaughan has guided tours. Aillwee Cave Visitor Centre open Mar–Sept Sat 1000–1700, Sun 1400–1700, Oct–Mar Sat, Sun 1000–1500. Burren Display Centre at Kilfenora, tel 065 88030, gives audiovisual explanation of the geology and geography of the area. Open Mar–Oct 0930–1700 (1900 in July and Aug)
The Cliffs of Moher, Co Clare. Sheer cliffs rising 230 m (700 ft) from the Atlantic. Walks along the cliff. Many seabirds congregate here. Visitor Centre open Mar–Oct 1000–1800
Dromore, Co Clare. 10 km (6 m) north of Ennis, woodland and wetland area giving refuge to the pine marten
Ballinstaig Woodland, Coole, Nr Gort, Co Clare. Created by Lady Gregory, a variety of forest and dwarf woodland
Connemara National Park, Co Galway. 2000 hectares (5000 acres) of rugged scenery including quartzite peaks and peat bogs. Flora includes heathers, alpines and blanket bog plants. Red deer have been introduced, and the Connemara ponies run wild. Visitor Centre at Letterfrack, tel 095 41054, open daily April–Sept 1000–1830. Guided walks, nature trails, bogland conservation work, audio visual information, picnic areas
Roundstone Bog, Co Galway. Spectacular blanket bog between Roundstone and Clifden

BIRDWATCHING

Cliffs of Moher Puffins, guillemots, razorbills, choughs and ravens in summer
Shannon Estuary Huge numbers of duck and waders on mudflats in winter. Best area is Fergus estuary on north shore, for black-tailed godwits in spring and dunlin in winter
River Shannon between Portumna and Lanesborough. Meadows, flooded in winter, attract numerous waders, ducks and geese
Rahasane Turlough Nr Craughwell, Co Galway. Ducks and swans on wetlands in winter
Lough Corrib Co Galway. Gatherings of coot and pochard in autumn
Rostaff Lake Co Galway. Irish Wildbird Conservancy hide to view winter duck and white-fronted geese
Roundstone Bog Co Galway. Feeding area for Greenland white-fronted geese, merlin and golden plover
Portumna Forest Park has birdwatching hides as well as nature trails and forest walks

MUSIC

Teach Ceoil: Traditional music in Corofin, Co Clare, and in Adare, Co Limerick. Contact: Tel 061 317522 or local tourist offices

ANGLING

Local information from:
Manager, Shannon Regional Fisheries Board, Thomond Weir, Co Limerick Tel 061 55171
Manager, Western Regional Fisheries Board, The Weir Lodge, Earl's Island, Co Galway Tel 091 63118/63119/63110

SEA FISHING

Deep-sea fishing, with boats available, off Inishbofin Island, Cleggan, Clifden, Doonbeg, Roundstone, Ballyvaughan, Liscannor. **Sea angling** charters from Clare Coast Charter, Ballyvaughan Tel 065 77014
Shore fishing from Inishbofin, Renvyle, Cleggan, Clifden, Rossaveal, Inverin, Spiddal, Fanore, Ballyvaughan, Lisdoonvarna, Liscannor, Doonbeg

GAME FISHING

Salmon all over Connemara, especially in R Owenmore, R Bundorragh, R Erriff, R Owenglin, Lough Conn, Lough Corrib, Lough Inagh, and the Kylemore Loughs.
Brown trout in Lough Corrib, Lough Mask, Lough Inchiquin and the Clare lakes, Scarriff, Mountshannon, Whitegate, Portumna and Lough Derg. Sea trout at Clifden, Ballynahinch, Renvyle and Cashel.
Ballynahinch Castle Hotel has salmon fishing seminars: Ballinfad, Co Galway Tel 095 31006
Lakeland Country Home School of Casting teaches trout angling: Portacarrow, Oughterard, Co Galway Tel 091 82121

COARSE FISHING

Pike, rudd, tench, roach in Lough Derg, Lough Corrib, the Clare lakes and R Shannon.

WATERSPORTS

SAILING

Yachts can be chartered from:
Connemara Yacht Charters, Drinagh Harbour, Errislannan, Clifden, Co Galway Tel 095 21332
Yachting International Ireland, 44 Kilbane, Castleroy, Limerick, Co Limerick Tel 061 333206 Fax 061 46650
Sailing instruction available from:
Galway Sailing Centre, 8 Father Griffin Road, Galway City Tel 091 63522
Sailing on Lough Derg. Numerous yacht charter companies at bases like Killaloe and Scarriff.

WINDSURFING

For the experienced windsurfer the Atlantic beaches are challenging, and wave jumping is possible in some places. Calmer waters on Lough Derg.
To hire equipment for all watersports by the hour, day or week, with optional instruction, contact:
Shannonside Activity Centre, Killaloe, Co Clare Tel 061 76622/45396 Telex 70056 Fax 061 48182
Galway Sailing Centre, address as above. Based at Renville Harbour, Oranmore

WATERSKIING

To be found on the south of Lough Derg.
O'Brien's Bridge Waterski Club, O'Brien's Bridge, Co Clare Tel 061 310263/87278

SURFING

West Coast Surf Club. Contact Noel Walsh: Ballyvara, Doolin, Co Clare Tel 065 74337 (home)
Best beaches at Doughmore, Spanish Point, Silver Strand, Lahinch, Cornish Point, Moy Bay, Fanore Strand. Surfboards can be hired at the lifeguard hut on Lahinch Strand.

CANOEING

Sea canoeing on the Galway coast, and on the Clare coast at Lahinch.
Sea canoeing courses at:
Little Killary Adventure Centre, Salruck, Renvyle, Co Galway Tel 095 43411
Canoe surfing at Doonbeg, Co Clare
Canoeing on Connemara lakes and R Shannon

BEACHES

Sandy safe beaches on Co Clare's south coast, at Kilkee, Lahinch, Mannin Bay, Aran Islands, Spiddal. Many sandy coves north of Galway round to Ballina.

CRUISING

River Shannon and Lough Derg.
NB Lough Derg should be treated as an inland sea. Weather conditions should be respected and crossings should be made in the company of another vessel.
Cruises and hire from:
Derg Line, Killaloe, Co Clare Tel 061 76364 Telex 70120 Fax 061 76205
Emerald Star Line (based at Portumna), 47 Dawson Street, Dublin 2 Tel 01 6798166/ 6798162 93494 Portumna Tel: 0509 41120
Shannon Castle Line (based at Williamstown Harbour Tel 0619 27042), Dolphin Works, Ringsend, Dublin 4 Tel 01 600964 Fax 01 689091

Pleasure cruises from Killaloe.
Short cruises or hotel accommodation on luxury barges:
Shannon River Floatels, Killaloe, Co Clare Tel 061 76364/76688 Telex 70120 Fax 061 76205
Chartered self-catering holidays from Killaloe. Contact Michael Bugler:
Shannon Barge Cruisers, Ogonnelloe, Tuamgraney, Co Clare Tel 0619 23044

GOLF

Lahinch Golf Club, Co Clare Tel 065 81002 (one of Ireland's finest links)
Shannon Golf Club (alongside the airport runways), Co Clare Tel 061 61020
Connemara Golf Club, Ballyconneely, Clifden, Co Galway Tel 095 21153
Galway Golf Club, Blackrock, Salthill, Co Galway Tel 091 22169

HORSE RIDING

RIDING STABLES

Clonmore Riding Centre, Quilty, Co Clare Tel 065 87020
Clarina Riding Centre, Clarina, Co Limerick Tel 061 301189/29726
Aille Cross Equestrian Centre, Loughrea, Co Galway Tel 091 41216
Errislannan Manor Riding Centre, Clifden, Co Galway Tel 095 21134
Hazelwood House and Stables, Creganna, Oranmore, Co Galway Tel 091 94275
Rathcannon Equestrian Centre, Rathcannon, Kilmallock, Co Limerick Tel 063 90557
Cashel House Hotel has its own riding centre. Tel 095 31001

TRAIL RIDES

For the Connemara Trails, contact: William Leahy, The Connemara Trail, Aille Cross, Loughrea, Co Galway Tel 091 41216

HUNTING

The main hunts which welcome visitors are:
The County Clare Hunt (Ennis) Tel 065 21472
The County Limerick Hunt Tel 063 90575
Stonehall Harrier Hunt Club Tel 061 393286
The East Galway Hunt Tel 0905 85767
The North Galway Hunt Tel 093 24843
The Blazers Tel 091 26211

WALKING

The official marked walking trails are:
The Burren Way which takes you from Ballyvaughan across the fascinating landscape of the Burren. Further details from COSPOIR
The Aran Islands Trails on Inis Mor, Inis Meain and Inis Oirr are designed to show the communities living on these islands
The Western Way when finished will go from Oughterard through the mountains to Clew Bay.
Connemara National Park contains self-guided trails and guided walks Between May and December, guided walks in the Burren area every day except Sunday. Contact Colin Bunce, Tel 065 21885
Walking holidays can be arranged by:
Walk Ireland, 20 Fergus Lawn, Tulla Road, Ennis, Co Clare Tel 065 20885
Connemara Gateway Hotel, Oughterard, Co Galway Tel 091 82328
Limerick Travel Ltd, Bedford Row, Limerick Tel 061 43844
Renvyle House Hotel, Renvyle, Connemara, Co Galway Tel 095 43511/43444

MAYO SLIGO DONEGAL LEITRIM ROSCOMMON

MAIN BORD FAILTE OFFICES

The Mall, Westport, Co Mayo Tel 098 25711 Fax 098 26709
Knock Airport, Co Mayo Tel 094 67247
Aras Reddan, Temple Street, Sligo, Co Sligo Tel 071 61201 Fax 071 60360
The Quay, Donegal Town, Co Donegal Tel 073 21148
Derry Road, Letterkenny, Co Donegal Tel 074 21160 Fax 074 25180
Bridge Street (June–Sept), Carrick-on-Shannon, Co Leitrim Tel 078 20170
The Old Jail (June–Aug), Roscommon, Co Roscommon Tel 0903 6356

CALENDAR OF EVENTS

March
Western Drama Festival, Tubbercurry, Co Sligo
St Patrick's Week Festival, Kiltimagh, Co Mayo
June
Glencolumbkille Traditional Music Festival, Co Donegal
Lough Conn and Cullen Angling Festival, Lough Conn, Co Mayo

Surfing Championships, Rossnowlagh, Co Donegal
Glencolumbkille Seafood Festival, Co Donegal
Castlebar International Four Days Walks, Co Mayo
Ardara Weavers' Fair, Co Donegal
July
An Tostal, Festival of Irish Music, Dance and Singing, Drumshanbo, Co Leitrim
Curragh Race, Lough Glaisdobharchu, Co Donegal
Mary from Dungloe Festival, Dungloe, Co Donegal
Isle of Lough Key Festival, Boyle, Co Roscommon
Castlerea International Rose Festival, Co Roscommon
Pilgrimage to Croagh Patrick, Co Mayo
August
Ballyshannon Folk and Traditional Music Festival, Co Donegal
O'Carolan Folk, Harp, and Traditional Irish Music Festival, Keadue, Co Roscommon
Yeats Summer School, Sligo
Sea Angling Festivals, Killala Bay, Co Mayo
September
Sligo Arts Festival, Sligo

HOTELS AND RESTAURANTS

Co MAYO

Ashford Castle
Cong, Co Mayo. Tel 092 46003 Telex 53749 Fax 092 46260 Closed at Christmas. Restaurant open 1300–1430, 1900–2130. All major credit cards. 83 rooms. Seats 180
Breaffy House Hotel
Castlebar, Co Mayo. Tel 094 22033 Telex 53790 Open all year. Restaurant open 1300–1430, 1900–2100. All major credit cards. 40 rooms. Seats 100
Delphi Lodge
Leenane, Co Galway (Lodge itself in Co Mayo). Tel 095 42213/42245 Fax 095 42212 Open all year. No credit cards. 7 rooms.
Enniscoe House
Castlehill, Crossmolina, Ballina, Co Mayo. Tel 096 31112 Telex c/o 40855 Closed Nov, Dec, Mar. Credit cards, AM, Visa, Amex. 6 rooms.
Mount Falcon Castle
Ballina, Co Mayo. Tel 096 21172 Telex 40899 Closed Christmas–Feb. All major credit cards. 10 rooms (8 with bath).
Newport House
Newport, Co Mayo. Tel 098 41222 Telex 53740 Fax 098 41613 Open mid-Mar–Sept. All major credit cards. 19 rooms.

Co SLIGO

Coopershill
Riverstown, Co Sligo. Tel 071 65108 Telex 40301 (Attn Coopershill) Fax 071 65466. Open mid-Mar–Oct. All major credit cards. 6 rooms.
Cromleach Lodge Country House
Lough Arrow, Castlebaldwin, via Boyle, Co Sligo. Tel 071 65155 Closed Christmas. Restaurant open 1800–2100. Credit cards, AM, Visa, Amex. 13 rooms. Seats 40.
Markree Castle and Knockmuldowney Restaurant
Collooney, Co Sligo. Tel 071 67800 Fax 071 67840 Open all year. Restaurant open 1300–1430, 1930–2130. All major credit cards. 14 rooms. Seats 75.
Sligo Park Hotel
Pearse Road, Sligo. Tel 071 60291 Telex 40397 Fax 071 69556 Open all year. Restaurant open 1230–1415, 1830–2115, Sat,

Sun 1300–1415, 1900–2100. All major credit cards. 60 rooms. Seats 90.
Temple House
Ballymote, Co Sligo. Tel 071 83329 Open April–20 Dec. Credit cards Visa, Amex. 5 rooms (3 with bath).

RESTAURANT

Reveries
Rosses Point, Co Sligo. Tel 071 77371 Open Tues–Sat from 1930. Closed 2 weeks Nov, Christmas. Credit cards AM, Visa.

PUBS

Hargadon's Pub, O'Connell Street, Sligo

Co DONEGAL

Bruckless House
Bruckless, Co Donegal. Tel 073 37071 Fax 073 37266 Open April–Sept. No credit cards. 5 rooms (2 with bath).
Hyland Central Hotel
The Diamond, Donegal Town, Co Donegal. Tel 073 21027 Telex 40522 Fax 073 22295 Closed Christmas. Credit cards AM, Visa, Amex. 75 rooms.
Mount Errigal Hotel
Ballyraine, Letterkenny, Co Donegal. Tel 074 22700 Telex 91880 Open all year. All major credit cards. 56 rooms.
Rathmullan House
Rathmullan, Co Donegal. Tel 074 58188 Fax 074 58200 Closed Jan, Feb. Restaurant open 1900–2045. All major credit cards. Take Ramelton road from Letterkenny. Turn right in Ramelton for Rathmullan.
St Ernan's House Hotel
St Ernan's Island, Donegal. Tel 073 21065 Fax 073 22098 Closed Nov–Mar. Credit cards AM, Visa. 11 rooms. 3 km (2 m) south of Donegal.
Woodhill House
Ardara, Co Donegal. Tel 075 41112 Open all year. All major credit cards. 5 rooms without bath.

RESTAURANTS

Harvey's Point Restaurant
Harvey's Point, Lough Eske, Donegal Town. Tel 073 22208 Open 1230–1430, 1900–2200. Closed Jan–Mar. All major credit cards.
Restaurant St John
Fahan, Co Donegal. Tel 077 60289 Open 1800–2200. Closed Mon, Good Friday, Christmas. All major credit cards. Seats 44.

HISTORIC BUILDINGS

Westport House, Westport, Co Mayo Open June–Aug, Mon–Fri 1130–1800, Sat, Sun 1400–1800; May and Sept daily 1400–1700
Lissadell House, Drumcliffe, Co Sligo Open May–Sept, Mon–Sat 1400–1715 Tel 071 63150
Doe Castle, Creeslough, Co Donegal Open daily thoughout the year
Donegal Castle, Donegal Open all year
Boyle Abbey, Boyle, Co Roscommon Open June–Sept 1000–1800, rest of year key with caretaker
Clonalis House, Castlerea, Co Roscommon Open May–June, Sat–Sun 1400–1800; June–Sept, Mon–Sat 1100–1730, Sun 1400–1730
Strokestown Park House, Strokestown, Co Roscommon Open June–Sept, Tues–Sun 1200–1700 Tel 078 33013

GARDENS

Glenveagh Castle Gardens, Churchill, Co Donegal Open Easter–October 1030–1830 Tel 074 37088/37090

ARCHAEOLOGICAL AND CHRISTIAN SITES

Ballintubber Abbey, Castlebar, Co Mayo
Creevykeel, Cliffony, Co Sligo
Carrowmore, Co Sligo
Glencolumbkille, Killybegs, Co Donegal
Grianan of Aileach, Co Donegal

NATURE RESERVES

Glenveagh National Park, Co Donegal A rugged stretch of wild land including Mount Errigal and Slieve Snaght, with the Poisoned Glen in the south-west. Lough Veagh is in the centre of the park, its castle gardens growing rare tender plants. Red deer roam the slopes and birds include merlin, peregrine, pipits and stonechats. Visitor Centre has audiovisual displays and there are nature trails and guided nature walks
Owenboy, Co Mayo A blanket bog containing rare mosses
Knockmoyle/Sheskin, Co Mayo Lowland bog managed by the Wildlife Service
Owenduff, Co Mayo Largest stretch of undisturbed peatland in the country
Ceide Fields, Co Mayo Extraordinary area of spectacular cliffs and boglands. Ceide Fields Centre at Ballycastle has audio-visual material

BIRDWATCHING

Clare Island, Co Mayo Colonies of seabirds, also choughs, corncrakes, corn buntings
Downpatrick Head, Co Mayo Fulmars nest on sheer cliffs
Lissadell, Co Sligo Greenland barnacle geese winter in the national nature reserve
Sheskinmore Lough, Co Donegal Breeding waders in summer, barnacle and white-fronted geese in winter.
Horn Head, Co Donegal Breeding razorbills
Lough Swilly, Co Donegal Whooper swans in late autumn, white-fronted geese and waders in winter

ANGLING

Local information from:
Northwestern Regional Fisheries Board, Ardnarce House, Abbey Street, Ballina, Co Mayo. Tel 096 22623/22788
The Manager
Northern Regional Fisheries Board, Station Road, Ballyshannon, Co Donegal. Tel 072 51435

SEA FISHING

Deep-sea fishing with boats available off Achill Island (shark), Westport, Belmullet, Killala, Killybegs, Rathmullan
Diving centres off Clew Bay (Clare Island), Blacksod Bay
Shore fishing from Belmullet and Killybegs

GAME FISHING

Salmon R Bundorragha, R Erriff (Delphi Lodge) R Bundrowes, R Moy at Ballina, Crossmolina, Foxford, Killala, Inniscrone, Pontoon (Mount Falcon Castle), R Blackoak (Newport House Hotel), Lough Beltra, Lough Conn, Lough Melvin
Sea trout at Delphi, Newport, Burrishoole, Sligo, Drumcliffe, Cliffoney, Bunduff, Dungloe, Burtonport, Creeslough and Kilmacrennan, Lough Glencar, Lough Beagh
Trout on R Moy, R Gweestion and Lough Arrow, Lough Key, Lough Bilberry, Lough Carra, Lough Conn, Lough Mask, Lough Melvin, Lough O'Flynn. There is a School of Casting, Salmon and Trout Fishing at:
Pontoon Bridge Hotel, Pontoon, Co Mayo. Tel 096 56120

Mount Falcon Castle holds weekly salmon angling seminars throughout the season: Ballina, Co Mayo
Cromleach Lodge Hotel holds casting and angling seminars during May: Castlebaldwin, Lough Arrow, Co Sligo

COARSE FISHING

Pike on Lough Allen, Lough Key, Lough Temple House (Temple House Hotel), Lough Cloonacleigha, Upper Shannon river system. Upper Shannon for all coarse fishing. Angling holiday cruises are available from:
Shannon Barge Line, Main Street, Carrick-on-Shannon, Co Leitrim   Tel 078 20520   Fax 078 20112

WATERSPORTS

SAILING

Sailing all round the coast, especially off Mayo.
Mayo Sailing Club, Westport.

WINDSURFING

Clew Bay, Co Mayo, provides ideal conditions for windsurfing.
Hire and instruction available from:
Glenans Irish Sailing Club, Collanmore Island, Clew Bay, Co Mayo   Tel 098 26046

WATERSKIING

Donegal Bay, especially off Rossnowlagh, and Clew Bay, round Clare Island.

SURFING

This coastline has some of the best surfing beaches in Europe. Excellent conditions all the year with waves averaging 1-3.5 metres. Best beaches include: Achill Island, Inniscrone, Easkey, Aughris Bay, Strandhill, Bundoran, Tullan Strand, Rossnowlagh, Ards, Bloody Foreland, Loughros Beg Bay, Rosbeg and the north coast of Donegal from Bloody Foreland to Rosapenna.
   Surfboards from the lifeguard's hut at Strandhill, Co Sligo, at Bundoran, Co Donegal, and from the Rossnowlagh Surf Club. Further information from:
Stevie Burns
County Sligo Surf Club, 8 Hillcrest Park, Strandhill, Co Sligo   Tel 071 68334 (home)
Roci Allan
Rossnowlagh Surf Club, Tigh-na-Mara, Rossnowlagh, Co Donegal   Tel 072 51261 (home)   073 21053 (work)

CANOEING

Canoe surfing is excellent at Easkey, Co Sligo (only for the very experienced). Also at Rossnowlagh and Tullaghan, Co Donegal
Canoeing on the upper reaches of the Shannon. Sea kayaking along the Mayo coast. Contact Little Killary Adventure Centre, Salruck, Renvyle, Co Galway.   Tel 095 43411

BEACHES

South side of Clew Bay, Achill Island, Blacksod Bay, Killala Bay, Enniscrone, Rossnowlagh, Loughros Beg Bay, Rosbeg, Gweebarra Bay, Falcarragh, Sheep Haven.

CRUISING

The River Shannon is navigable from Lough Key and Drumshanbo (via the Leitrim Canal). Cruises and hire from:
Emerald Star Line, 37 Dawson Street, Dublin 2   Tel 01 718870   Telex 93494

Based at Carrick-on-Shannon   Tel 078 20234
Carrick Craft, PO Box 14, Reading RG3 6TA, England   Tel 0734 422975
Based at Carrick-on-Shannon   Tel 078 20236
Pleasure cruises on the Shannon from Lough Key Forest Park. Longer luxury cruises by barge, contact:
Weaver Boats Ltd, Carrick-on-Shannon, Co Leitrim   Tel 078 20204   Telex 31593.
Short cruises on Lough Gill, with a commentary on Yeats' poetry
Lough Gill Cruises, Sligo Town   Tel 071 62540

GOLF

Westport Golf Club, Carrowholly, Westport, Co Mayo   Tel 098 25113
Enniscrone Golf Club, Enniscrone, Co Sligo   Tel 096 36297
County Sligo Golf Club, Rosses Point, Co Sligo   Tel 071 77134
Bundoran Golf Club, Bundoran, Co Donegal   Tel 072 41360
Donegal Golf Club, Murvagh, Co Donegal   Tel 073 21262
North West Golf Club, Lisfannon, Fahan, Lifford, Co Donegal   Tel 074 61027
Rosapenna Golf Club, Rosapenna, Co Donegal   Tel 074 55301

HORSE RIDING

RIDING STABLES

Ashford Riding Centre, Cong, Co Mayo   Tel 092 46024
Claremorris School of Equitation, Lisduff, Claremorris, Co Mayo   Tel 094 71684/71998
Drumindoo Stud and Equitation Centre, Castlebar Road, Westport, Co Mayo   Tel 098 25616
Horse Holiday Farm Ltd, Grange, Co Sligo   Tel 071 66152
The Manor, Ballygawley, Co Sligo   Tel 071 67426
The Old Rectory Stables, Drumcliffe, Co Sligo   Tel 071 63221
Ashleigh Riding School, Rossylongan, Donegal Town, Co Donegal   Tel 073 21097
Lenamore Stables, Muff, Lifford, Co Donegal   Tel 077 84022
Stracomer Riding School, Bundoran, Co Donegal   Tel 072 41685/41787

TRAIL RIDES

Horse Holiday Farm Trails provides trail rides with farmhouse accommodation. Armada Coast and Mountain Trail is a week-long trail with experienced guide along sandy beaches and mountain scenery. Contact: Tilman Anhoid
Horse Holiday Farm Ltd, Grange, Co Sligo   Tel 071 66152   Fax 071 66400
Drumcliffe Beach and Mountain Trail Daily trails covering mountains, beaches and islands. Accommodation at the Old Rectory. Mrs Eileen Blighe, The Old Rectory Stables, Drumcliffe, Co Sligo   Tel 071 63221
Donegal Trail Six-day trail ride through Donegal countryside with expert guide. Small groups and top-grade accommodation. Contact: Terry Fergus-Browne, Stracomer Riding School, Bundoran, Co Donegal   Tel 072 41685   Telex 40675   Fax 072 41002

HUNTING

Co Sligo Harriers, Tel 071 68369
Salmon & Woodcock   Tel 094 56690

CYCLING

There are planned long-distance cycling routes in each of the three large counties of this region. The **Mountains of Mayo** route encircles the northern part of the county, past bogs in the west, cliff scenery in the north, across the Ox Mountains to the edge of Lough Conn and through Glen Nephin. **The Yeats Country** ride through Sligo and Leitrim provides mountain, beach, lake and numerous scenes evoking Yeats' poetry.
   The Hills of Donegal is a ride along some of the finest coastal scenery in Ireland then through the National Park of Glenveagh, with a diversion to Malin Head.
   In August and September there are conducted mountain bike tours round Lough Allen every Monday. Contact: Annette Arnold   Tel 078 41464.
Cycling holidays can be arranged by:
Ballina West of Ireland Cycling Club, c/o American Guesthouse, Ballina, Co Mayo   Tel 096 21350
Tourist Office, The Mall, Westport, Co Mayo   Tel 098 25711   Fax 098 26709
Wild Rose Tours, Kilmacowen, Ballysodare, Co Sligo   Tel 071 67560
Arnolds Hotel, Dunfanaghy, Co Donegal   Tel 074 36208/36142
Forgotten Ireland, Aughagrania, Drumshanbo, Co Leitrim   Tel 078 41464

WALKING

There are few completed long-distance walking routes in the region, but the **Western Way** from Leenane to Killala and Ballina is proposed. There are some marked circular routes round Westport; details available locally.
The Ulster Way in Donegal (Sli Ulaidh) goes from Falcarragh on the north coast across the Donegal Highlands to connect with the Ulster Way of Northern Ireland. There are routes planned to connect this and the Cavan Way.
   Forest walks and nature trails in Ards Forest Park, Lough Key Forest Park. Hill walking on Mount Errigal, Slieve League.

Walking holidays can be arranged by:
Tourist Office, The Mall, Westport, Co Mayo   Tel 098 25711   Fax 098 26709
Donegal Walking Tours, Carrickbreeny, Ballintra, Co Donegal   Tel 073 34192

PILGRIMAGES

The three major places of pilgrimage in Ireland today are situated in this region.
Knock Shrine, Claremorris, Co Mayo. Enquiries to the Rev parish priest, Knock Shrine   Tel 094 88100 or
Knock Shrine Bureau, 29 South Anne Street, Dublin 2   Tel 01 775965
Croagh Patrick, Co Mayo: On the last Sunday in July, pilgrims walk up the mountain, some barefoot
Lough Derg, Station Island, Co Donegal. 3-day retreats June–mid-Aug. The Rev Prior, Lough Derg, Pettigo, Co Donegal

MUSIC

Teach Ceoil Traditional music evenings on Tuesdays and Thursdays in July and August at Ballyliffen, Co Donegal. Contact: Clement Sweeney   Tel 077 76124

CAVAN LONGFORD WESTMEATH KILDARE LAOIS OFFALY

MAIN BORD FAILTE OFFICES

Town Hall (June–Sept), Cavan, Co Cavan
  Tel 049 31942
Main Street (June–Aug), Longford, Co
  Longford Tel 043 46566
Dublin Road, Mullingar, Co Westmeath Tel
  044 48761 Fax 044 40413
Portlaoise (June–Aug), Co Laois Tel 0502
  21178
Birr, Co Offaly Tel 0905 20206

CALENDAR OF EVENTS

February
Cavan International Song Contest, Cavan
Punchestown Bloodstock Sales, Co Kildare
March
3-day Steeplechasing Festival at Punchestown,
  Co Kildare
April
Bailieboro Gala Angling Festival, Co Cavan
May
1000 Guineas at the Curragh
June
Shannon Harbour Canal Boat Rally, Co
  Offaly
Open Coarse Fishing Championships,
  Killeshandra, Co Cavan
Festival of Music in Great Irish Houses,
  Castletown House, Celbridge, Co Kildare
Irish Derby at the Curragh
July
Athlone International Angling Festival, Co
  Westmeath
Edenderry Festival, Co Offaly
Celbridge Summer Festival, Co Kildare
Festival of the Erne, Belturbet, Co Cavan
August
Cavan Lakes and Vales Festival, Co Cavan
Granard Harp Festival, Co Longford
September
Irish St Leger at the Curragh
October
Cootehill Arts Festival, Co Cavan

HOTELS AND RESTAURANTS

Co LONGFORD

PUBS

The Market Bar
Longford Town

Co KILDARE

Moyglare Manor
Maynooth, Co Kildare. Tel 01 286351/286469
Fax 01 285405 Open all year except 3 days at
Christmas. All major credit cards. 17 rooms.
No children under 12
Doyle's Schoolhouse Restaurant
Castledermot, Co Kildare. Tel 0503 44282
Fax 0503 43653 Open 1830–2230 Tues–Sat in
summer, 1930–2200 in winter. Sunday lunch.
All major credit cards. On main
Waterford–Dublin road (N9)

Co LAOIS

PUBS

Morrissey's
Abbeyleix, Co Laois

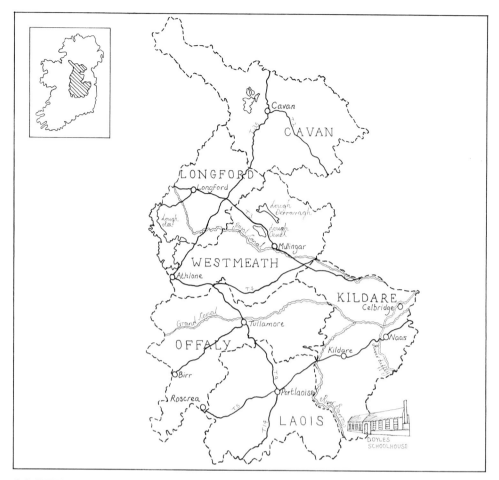

CO OFFALY

Bridge House
Bridge Street, Tullamore, Co Offaly. Tel 0506
21704 Open 1230–1435, 1730–2200. Closed
Good Friday, Christmas Day. Credit cards
AM, Visa, Amex. Seats 75

HISTORIC BUILDINGS

Bellamont Forest, Cootehill, Co Cavan
Open Mon–Fri 1430–1700. Sat by
appointment Tel 049 32227
Carrigglass Manor, Co Longford Open
June–Sept, Mon, Tues, Fri 1200–1700, Sun
1400–1800
Tullynally Castle and Gardens,
Castlepollard, Co Westmeath Open July–Aug
1430–1700 (other times by prior arrangement)
Tel 044 61159/61425
Castletown House, Celbridge, Co Kildare
Open all year. Mon–Fri 1000–1700, Sat
(April–Oct) 1100–1800, Sun and public
holidays 1400–1800 Tel 01 288252
Emo Court and Gardens, Emo, Co Laois
House open Mar–Oct, Mon 1400–1800,
gardens all year 1030–1700 Tel 0502 26110

GARDENS

Japanese Gardens, Tully, Co Kildare Open
Easter–Oct, Mon–Fri 1030–1700, Sat
1030–1730, Sun 1400–1730 Tel 045
21251/21617
Abbeyleix Gardens, Co Laois Open
Easter–Sept 1400–1700
Birr Castle, Demesne, Birr, Co Offaly Open
daily 0900–1300, 1400–1800 (dusk if earlier)
Tel 0509 20056

ARCHAEOLOGICAL AND CHRISTIAN SITES

Fore Abbey, Castlepollard, Co Westmeath
Multyfarnham Friary, Co Westmeath
Clonmacnoise, Co Offaly

MUSEUM

Irish Mist Exhibition Centre, O'Connell
Street, Tullamore, Co Offaly Tel 0506 21586.
Exhibition on the making of this liqueur with
a free sample. Open 0930–1300, 1400–1700

NATURE RESERVES AND BIRDWATCHING

Slieve Bloom Mountains, Co Laois and Co
Offaly Ireland's largest nature reserve.
Stretches of mountain blanket bog and conifer
forests
Pollardstown Fen, Co Kildare North of the
Curragh, an important spring-fed fen. Major
breeding ground for several species including
grebes, peewit and snipe. Information and
birdwatching facilities from the Peatland
Interpretive Centre, Lullymore, Co Kildare
Ardkill Bog, Co Kildare A raised bog with a
variety of bog plants and mosses. Guide
available from Mr Cecil Potterton, Ardkill
Farm, Carbury, Co Kildare
Clara Bog, Co Offaly A large raised bog with
a range of vegetation
Mongan Bog, Co Offaly Pools and
hummocks in a raised midland bog. Just east
of Clonmacnoise it includes a section of the
Shannon callows, rich in flowers and breeding
birds

ANGLING

Above all this is the best region in the country
for coarse fishing.
**The National Coarse Fishing Federation of
Ireland:** Hon Sec: Brendan Coulter, Blaithin,
Dublin Road, Cavan Tel 049 32367
Pike, bream, rudd, tench, roach, perch and
dace are plentiful throughout the lakeland
areas of Cavan and Longford; bases with
accommodation are at Killeshandra,
Bailieborough, Ballybay and Belturbet for the

Upper Erne and Lough Oughter, Finea, Granard, Mount Nugent, Mullingar and Edgeworthstown for Lough Kinale, Lough Derravaragh and the River Inny. Bases at Athlone, Shannonbridge, Banagher and Birr in Co Offaly are good for fishing in Lough Ree and the mid-Shannon system. The Royal Canal, the Grand Canal and the River Barrow also offer plenty of angling.

Trout can be caught in the rivers Little Brosa, Clodia and Silver, with centres at Banagher, Birr and Tullamore, and in the River Liffey upstream of Straffan in Co Kildare, at Naas, Prosperous and Kill. Loughs supplying trout are Lough Ennell, Lough Owel, Lough Glore, and Lough Mount Dalton, and rainbow trout can be found in Lough White and Lough Pallas.

WATERSPORTS

On many of the loughs, especially Lough Ree and Lough Owel.

CANOEING

On the River Shannon, the Grand Canal at Robertstown, the River Barrow from Portarlington to Athy and the Liffey through Co Kildare. The Liffey Descent – the Irish International Marathon Canoe Racing Championship – occurs annually when canoeists challenge the rapids and high water of the Liffey after water has been released from the Poulaphouca Reservoir in September.
Canoe equipment from:
Kemacraft, 21 The Grove, Celbridge, Co Kildare Tel 01 271771

CRUISING

On the Shannon north of Lough Ree which, like Lough Derg, should be treated as an inland sea. Several canals and rivers, islands and smaller lakes are accessible from the lough.
The Grand Canal The Barrow line of the canal starts near Robertstown and joins the River Barrow at Athy. The main canal continues to Shannon Harbour.
Cruises and hire available from:
Athlone Cruisers Ltd, Jolly Mariner, Athlone, Co Westmeath Tel 0902 72892 Telex 24221
Carrick Craft (based Banagher Tel 0902 51187), PO Box 14, Reading RG3 6TA, England Tel 0734 422975

SGS Marine Ltd, Ballykeeran, Athlone, Co Westmeath Tel 0902 85163 Telex 53185
Lowtown Cruisers Ltd, The Boatyard, Robertstown, Naas, Co Kildare Tel 045 60427 Fax 045 60372
Silver Line Cruisers Ltd, Banagher, Co Offaly Tel 0902 51112 Telex 60836
Celtic Canal Cruisers, Tullamore, Co Offaly Tel 0506 21861 Telex 60825 Fax 0506 51994

GOLF

Mullingar Golf Club, Belvedere, Mullingar, Co Westmeath Tel 044 48366
Tullamore Golf Club, Brookfield, Tullamore, Co Offaly Tel 0506 21439

HORSE RIDING
RIDING STABLES

Cavan Equestrian Centre, Shalom Stables, Latt, Co Cavan Tel 049 32017
Redhills Equestrian Centre, Redhills, Co Cavan Tel 047 55042
Donacomper Riding School, Donacomper, Celbridge, Co Kildare Tel 01 288221
Greenhills Riding School, Greenhills, Kill, Co Kildare Tel 045 77370
Kilkea Dressage Centre, Kilkea Lodge, Castledermot, Co Kildare Tel 0503 45112
The Old Mill Riding School, The Old Mill, Kill, Co Kildare Tel 045 77053
Buckley's Riding Establishment, Annagharvey, Tullamore, Co Offaly Tel 0506 43507

HORSERACING

The Curragh for all five Irish classics
Punchestown for steeplechasing
Goff's Bloodstock Sales Ltd, Kildare Paddocks, Kill, Co Kildare Tel 045 77211 Telex 60723 Fax 045 77119
The Irish National Stud and Horse Museum, Tully, Co Kildare Tel 045 21617/21377/21301 Telex 60706 Fax 045 22129

HUNTING

Hunts which welcome visitors include:
Streamstown Harriers, Co Westmeath Tel 044 26128
Westmeath Hunt, Co Westmeath Tel 044 23244
Kildare Hunt, Co Kildare Tel 045 79098
Ward Union Hunt, Co Kildare Tel 049 256524

CYCLING

There is one suggested long-distance route, **The Lakes and Little Hills**, which illustrates the typical characteristics of this region – the drumlins, lakes, forests and bogs. A winding route, it strays into Co Monaghan and Co Leitrim but for the most part is in Cavan and Longford. The second route, further south, is called **The Land of Fionn MacCumhaill**, and crosses the Bog of Allen, the Curragh, climbs the steep sides of the Hill of Allen, and goes through the valleys of the Slieve Bloom mountains. Cycling holidays available from:
Cootehill Tourist Association, Riverside House, Cootehill, Co Cavan Tel 049 52150

WALKING

Long-distance way-marked routes include:
The Cavan Way, a 25-km (15-mile) walk from Blacklion in the north. It passes through limestone country to Shannon Pot, supposedly the source of the Shannon, before travelling along quiet paths to the river itself at Dowra. An extension of this walk will take you along the borders of Lough Allen to Drumshanbo
The Kildare Way is mostly a towpath walk from Celbridge to Robertstown, along the Grand Canal. There are several diversions and extensions, along the Grand Canal, down the River Barrow or north to the Royal Canal, or up the Mount Mellick branch to join the Slieve Bloom Way
The Slieve Bloom Way is a circular route 50 km (30 m) long but with many car parking areas so short walks along it can also be taken. The mountains are split by deep valleys, with many waterfalls and rocky outcrops to provide dramatic scenery
The Fore Valley in Westmeath is good walking country. Forest parks at Killykean, near Cavan Town, and Dun-a-Ri, Kingscourt, Co Cavan, Lough Key Forest Park.
Walking holidays can be arranged by:
Mr and Mrs T. O'Dwyer, Pinegrove, Blacklion, Co Cavan Tel 072 53061
Cootehill Tourist Association, Riverside House, Cootehill, Co Cavan Tel 049 52150
Frank and Rosemarie Kennan, Roundwood House, Mountrath, Co Laois Tel 0502 32120
SGS Marine Ltd, Ballykeeran, Athlone, Co Westmeath Tel 0902 85163

BIBLIOGRAPHY

Traditional Irish Recipes John Murphy (Appletree)
A Taste of Ireland Theodora FitzGibbon (Pan)
The Ballymaloe Cookbook Myrtle Allen (Gill and Macmillan)
Simply Delicious 1 & 2 Darina Allen (Gill and Macmillan)
Poultry and Game Ian McAndrew (Hamlyn/Amazon)
A Feast of Fish Ian McAndrew (Macdonald/Orbis)
Splendid Food from Irish Country Houses Gillian Berwick (O'Brien Press)
Guide to Restaurants in Ireland Consumers' Association of Ireland (O'Brien Press)
Where to Eat in Ireland (Kingsclere Publications)
Dining in Ireland (Bord Failte)

The Houses of Ireland Brian de Breffny and Rosemary Ffolliott (Thames and Hudson)
Churches and Abbeys of Ireland Brian de Breffny and George Mott (Thames and Hudson)
Guide to the National Monuments of Ireland Peter Harbison (Gill and Macmillan)
Concise History of Irish Art Bruce Arnold (Thames and Hudson)
Concise History of Ireland M. and C. Cruise O'Brien (Thames and Hudson)
A Singular Country J.P. Donleavy (Ryan)
Bellamy's Ireland – The Wild Boglands David Bellamy (Country House)
A Green Guide for Ireland John Gormley (Wolfhound Press)
Birds in Ireland Clive Hutchinson (T and AD Poyser)
Book of the Irish Countryside Frank Mitchell (Blackstaff Press)

Irish Nature Companion (Appletree Press)
Nature in its Place: the Habitats of Ireland Stephen Mills (Bodley Head)
The Irish Countryside ed Desmond Gillmore (Wolfhound Press)
In an Irish Garden Sybil Connolly and Helen Dillon (Weidenfeld and Nicolson)
The Gardens of Ireland Michael George and Patrick Bowe (Hutchinson)
Irish Heritage Series Easons, Dublin): Irish wild flowers, Irish trees, the Burren, Mount Usher and Birr
The Ancestor Trail in Ireland Donal F. Begley (Genealogical Office)
Handbook of Irish Genealogy How to trace your ancestry and relatives in Ireland (Heraldic Artists Ltd)
Ireland (photos) W. A. Poucher (Constable)
Ireland Your Only Place Jan Morris and Paul Wakefield (Aurum Press)

General Index

$\mathcal{R}$ecipe Index

AUTHOR'S ACKNOWLEDGMENTS

There is one person above all others to whom I must give a very special thanks, for without him this book would not have been possible. That is to Eddie Shanahan, my agent, who is also unquestionably the driving force behind the Irish fashion industry. Taking this project on board became a complete turnabout for a man who normally runs Elaine's Model Management (a very professional Dublin model agency) and who directs most of Ireland's major fashion shows. For months, with great discipline, he kept me to a rigid programme, showing no mercy. We spent hours and hours working nearly every night and sometimes weekends putting the text and photos together until we finally had a book. So thank you, Eddie, and thank you Yvonne McFarlane, my publisher, for your faith in me and in this book.

Elaine Doody and Susan Howick at Elaine's Model Management also deserve a special mention, as does Jane Forster for her elegant book design.

I would also like to thank collectively all the restaurateurs, chefs, organic growers and breeders, fishermen, cheesemakers and proprietors of country houses and hotels who facilitated me throughout the book; and in particular the following list of friends who have shown considerable interest and given help throughout the whole project: Anne Harris of *The Sunday Independent*, Deirdre MacQuillan; Michael Reynolds of Sawer's of Chatham Street, Dublin; Paddy O'Toole at CineElectric; all at the Colour Lab; Paul and Kieran Cullan; Tony Murphy; George Taylor; 'Red' John Coleman; Ken Whelan of the Salmon Research Station; Pete Walsh at Lough Key Boats; Robert Gillespie; Kate Lane; Monica Murphy at The Cheese Board; Harvey Sambrook and Marie-Pierre Moine, who together gave me the inspiration for the book.

And finally, thanks to Betty Bunn, for putting up with me.